cal issues. This work has significant implica-
tions for the study of virtue ethics, and it
firmly establishes courage as an important virtue deserving utmost consideration in moral
philosophy.

Douglas N. Walton is Professor of Philosophy
at the University of Winnipeg, Manitoba,
Canada. He has published widely in the fields
of theory of argument and informal fallacies;
biomedical ethics; and theory of action. In
1985 he was the winner of the *American Philosophical Quarterly* Prize Essay Competition:
Are Circular Arguments Necessarily Vicious?

COURAGE

COURAGE

A Philosophical Investigation

Douglas N. Walton

107023

UNIVERSITY OF CALIFORNIA PRESS

Berkeley • Los Angeles • London

University of California Press
Berkeley and Los Angeles, California

University of California Press, Ltd.
London, England

Copyright © 1986 by The Regents of the University of California

Library of Congress Cataloging in Publication Data

Walton, Douglas N.
   Courage, a philosophical investigation.

   Bibliography: p.
   Includes index.
   1. Courage.   I. Title.
BJ1533.C8W26   1985   179'.6   85–1149
ISBN 0-520-05443-1 (alk. paper)
Printed in the United States of America

1 2 3 4 5 6 7 8 9

For Karen
I believe in your star,
We are one body, one heart, one soul,
everywhere and always.

. . . both art and virtue are always concerned with
    what is harder; for even the good is better
    when it is harder.

—Aristotle, *Ethica Nicomachea*

That a man has a restful and peaceful life in God
    is good.

That a man endures a painful life in patience is
    better.

But that a man has his rest in the midst of a
    painful life, that is the best of all.

—Meister Eckhart, *Theologia*

Contents

Acknowledgments

MANY INDIVIDUALS HAVE contributed directly or indirectly to the thoughts and arguments expressed in this book. I would especially like to thank Krister Segerberg, my generous and gracious host at the University of Auckland during a study/research leave there in 1982–83. His conversations, written works, and lectures have strongly influenced, and I think much improved, my work on the nature of actions. During the presentation of papers on actions, courageous acts, and practical reasoning at the University of Auckland, several persons particularly influenced my thinking by especially insightful questions, objections, or comments. These include John Bishop, Jan Crosthwaite, Robert Nola, Fred Koon, Christine Swanton, and Martin Tweedale. Some of my arguments on actions and practical reasoning have also been shaped by the writings and conversations of Dagfinn Føllesdal, Dick Epstein, and Robert Audi. Thanks to Max Cresswell for a helpful discussion at Waikanae in March 1983, and to John Wilde for help with some essential library detective work in finding sources. Although I have never met G. H. von Wright, the work of this study is built so much on the foundation laid by his work that I feel it appropriate to humbly acknowledge my indebtedness.

I would like to thank Sarah Shorten for showing me her unpublished manuscript "Aristotle on Courage" and Stephen Davis for sending a copy of his unpublished paper "Act Utilitarianism and Supererogation." My research has been supported by the Social Sciences and Humanities Research Council of Canada through a Leave Fellowship during 1982–83. The University of Winnipeg has also contributed through the grant of a year's research/study leave and research support during 1982–83. Conversations with Vic Shimizu helped me to improve the first chapter in the second draft of the manuscript. Many improvements are a result of the helpful criticisms and suggestions of William Dray, John Wilde, David Heyd, and Fred Berger.

John R. Miles has been a source of supportive guidance, encouragement, and comments beyond an editor's duty. I would like to thank my wife, Karen Walton, who inspires me to keep at my work and at the same time sees to it that I don't get completely lost in it, becoming an inadequate human being and academic zombie. Finally, my thanks to Amy Merrett, whose precise typing has made rereading the various manuscript drafts such an easy and pleasant job.

For kindly sending reports and materials on citations that describe acts of courage, I am grateful to the Carnegie Hero Fund Commission, the Honours Secretariat of the Office of the Governor General of Canada, the Royal Humane Society, and the American Humane Association. These agencies have been most helpful in responding to my queries.

I would like to thank Dave Schultz for preparing the index.

CHAPTER 1

Courage as a
Topic of Inquiry

WHAT IS COURAGE? If confronted by this awkward and somewhat pretentious question, most of us would probably search for an example, some act of courage we have found stirring or notable in some way. Looking for an example is one step toward the truth; it is a necessary and valuable step, but by itself will not provide a satisfactory answer to the question. For there are different kinds of examples of acts we consider to be courageous, and, as Socrates would have said, we need to know what general principle is common to these examples to really find out what courage is.

One example might be characterized by absence of emotion. If courage is the absence of fear, then the dispassionately cool act is thought to be the epitome of courage. But then one might have in mind the bold act of resolute aggression against terrible odds as the hallmark of courage. In this view, courage is the presence of strong emotion and determination of will.

Perhaps the kind of example one might have in mind is that of a bold attack in the face of an overwhelming threat. On September 30, 1971, two young people were attacked by a grizzly bear while hiking in Balu Pass, British Columbia. Malcom Aspeslet tried to protect his companion, but the bear thrust him aside and began to maul her. Aspeslet then leaped on the bear, stabbing at its throat with his hunting knife. They rolled together in the unequal struggle, and the young man sustained deep lacerations to his head and face. For his "persistence in the face of so grave a threat" to save his companion's life, Aspeslet was awarded the Star of Courage (Honors Secretariat 1983).

Certainly this act was courageous, remarkably so. And it was surely characterized by a bold act of resolute aggression against terrible odds. Yet other acts of courage seem more to involve an act of quick, cool

1

thinking in a desperate and dangerous situation. When Friedrich Gaggioli saw a bank robber in a taxi take aim at a police officer trying to open the car door, he grabbed a construction warning flasher and threw it through the window of the taxi. Hit on the arm, the criminal dropped his gun and was subdued by the police officer. For his prompt and courageous act in the danger of gunfire, Gaggioli was awarded the Medal of Bravery (*Investiture Bravery Decorations* 1983). In this case there was certainly "resolute aggression," but what especially characterizes this kind of courage is the quick thinking and judgment that saved a desperate situation.

This is not to immediately rule out the hypothesis that there could be different kinds of courage. However, the view that I will ultimately argue for in this book is that the basic concept of courage is most like what the British call "muddling through"—keeping one's head and doing a creditable job of deliberately acting sensibly and appropriately despite dangerous, painful, or very adverse circumstances. Without wanting to give the game away too early, it may be well to offer an example of an action that, to me, epitomizes courage.

Keeping one's head and using ingenuity to go through a procedure in formidably difficult and dangerous circumstances is certainly a paradigm of courage, especially where the purpose of the procedure is to save life. The following case strikingly illustrates the use of practical reasoning in acting courageously in a difficult, dangerous situation. Staff Sergeant Henry Erwin was the radio operator in a B-29 bomber leading an attack on Koriyama, Japan. It was his job to drop so-called phosphoresce (phosphorous) bombs to mark the target. While the plane was under attack from fighters and flak, one of the phosphoresce bombs launched by Erwin shot back inside the body of the plane, hitting him in the face. The burning bomb completely obliterated his nose and blinded him. The plane became filled with smoke, blacking out the vision of the crew and pilot.

> Sergeant Erwin realized that the aircraft and crew would be lost if the burning bomb remained in the plane. Without regard for his own safety, he picked it up and, feeling his way, instinctively, crawled around the gun turret and headed for the copilot's window. He found the navigator's table obstructing his passage. Grasping the burning bomb between his forearm and body, he unleashed the spring lock and raised the table. Struggling through the narrow passage he stumbled forward into the smoke-filled pilot's compartment. Groping with his burning hands, he

located the window and threw the bomb out. Completely aflame, he fell back onto the floor. The smoke cleared, the pilot, at 300 feet, pulled the plane out of its dive. (*COVA* 1973:549)[1]

For this gallant and heroic act to save the lives of his crew mates, Erwin was awarded the Congressional Medal of Honor. Most of us, if plunged into such circumstances, would no doubt be stunned into agonized inaction. Yet Erwin, blinded and painfully burned, some-how made himself pick up a burning phosphoresce bomb and, hold-ing it, crawl through a series of obstacles to where he reasoned there would be an open window. That a man could maintain his presence of mind and force himself to coolly pursue this terrible course of action, in the midst of what must have been enormous suffering, is a remarkable thing.

In this case, all three characteristics are present: (1) careful presence of mind and deliberate action, (2) difficult, dangerous, and painful circumstances, and (3) a morally worthy intention, in this case im-plemented in an altruistic act to save the lives of others, at the agent's personal risk and suffering. I will argue that these qualities mark the essence of courage, not just in this case but in every case of truly courageous action.

1.1 The Meaning of Courage

Most of us probably have a fairly firm idea that we know what we mean when we judge that an act was courageous. Indeed, our feelings about courage run so deep and strong that the story of a truly cou-rageous act can be uplifting and stimulating. But do we really know what courage is?

We know that courage is often a heroic quality. We think of a scientist, resolutely engaged in a lonely and difficult struggle to com-bat a disease or an important problem in research. We think of a fireman, lying injured and exhausted on a stretcher after valiantly struggling to save lives in a burning building. We think of the Resis-tance heroes and heroines who went to their deaths under torture, never revealing information to their Gestapo interrogators.

But many less conspicuous examples of courageous actions occur in everyday life. The child who confronts a catastrophic illness with unusual dignity and determination is courageous. The construction worker who does his job without complaint even though he knows his work is dangerous is courageous, and we could not accomplish anything without his kind of courage. We know these kinds of actions are courageous, but just what it is that makes them courageous is difficult to put into words. The *Concise Oxford Dictionary*[2] defines courage as "bravery or boldness." As a definition, this account is either uninformative or wrong. That 'courage' is the same as, or very close to, 'bravery' is true but uninformative (circular) until we know what bravery is. But to say that courage is the same as boldness is wrong, for many bold actions can be simply foolish or thoughtlessly, even viciously, aggressive. Most of us would rightly hesitate to allow that such actions must always be called courageous.

The *Merriam-Webster Dictionary*[3] is more helpful: it defines courage (bravery, valor) as "ability to conquer fear or despair." But immediately certain doubts occur. The vicious rapist who overcomes his fear of the police to commit his criminal acts is one we hesitate to call truly courageous. There is also the problem that general abilities may not be manifested on particular occasions: a man or woman who has the ability to conquer fear in most situations may fail in some; another person who generally lacks the ability to conquer fear may act with surprising courage. A good example is provided by the sailor in C. S. Forester's *The Ship*. Ordinary Seaman Triggs had a routinely tedious job in the bowels of a light cruiser during the Second World War. He was an impulsive and not very intelligent man who was always getting into trouble and depended on the other men in the ship to keep him from straying from doing his duty. He was not able to control his emotions, and the crew and officers knew that he was not very dependable if left to his own resources. When on shore leave, he would always get drunk and get into some sort of trouble. He was not an intelligent or thoughtful man, nor did he have outstanding abilities. Despite all this, one day he accomplished an incredibly courageous act.

The ship had come under fire and was severely damaged. The lower chambers were on fire, and many crew members were trapped below. They could only be saved by opening a door controlled by metal wheels, which were red-hot. One of the sailors—Mr. Burney, a very reliable and conscientious man—kept trying to turn the wheels, but as the flesh of his hands burned through he became unable to hold onto them. As Triggs made his way along the deck he heard

Burney's cries, and then saw him, illuminated by flames from the burning oil, bowed over his charred hands.

Although Triggs was not acute mentally, discipline had left a certain mark on him. On shore, he characteristically forgot orders and, muddled by drink, overstayed his leave. It was easy for him to forget orders, but he could function in his gun crew because he would always obey a command as soon as it was conveyed over the loudspeaker.

> Here amid the smoke and flame of the alleyway Triggs, oddly enough, was thinking about nothing except the business at hand. He saw Burney try to turn the wheels and fail, and without hesitation he took up the task. The pain in his hands was frightful, but Triggs was able to ignore it. He flung his weight on the wheels and they moved; again and again they moved, turning steadily. (C. S. Forester, *The Ship* [Toronto: S. J. Reginald Saunders, 1943], p. 217)

Triggs managed to open the door, thereby flooding the magazine and saving the men below. When he was through, the charred bones were visible where the flesh of his palms had been burned away.

I think that Triggs's action, as described in the story, should be considered highly courageous. Given his character, however, it is not clear that we can correctly say he had the "ability to conquer fear or despair." Indeed, the point of this part of Forester's story seems to be that this man had no such ability or disposition. On this particular occasion, he inexplicably stepped forward and did his duty. But the job he happened to do was so terrible that even a capable and normally brave seaman could not bring himself to carry it out. The nice thing about the story is that it shows that people without extraordinary abilities or special self-control can, on a particular occasion, perform an extraordinarily courageous act. It is as though there is a chance for the grace of valor in the humblest and most ordinary person, regardless of his normal "abilities."

The dictionary, then, has not been very helpful. What source of authority can we turn to for a better understanding of the nature of courage?

One cue is that courage is a term of moral commendation. To say that an act is courageous is to imply that the act was good or noble, that it was undertaken for a worthwhile end. At the same time, however, there is danger of moral prejudice and propaganda. What one describes as "courageous" in defense of one's own interests or national affiliation may be described by an enemy as "fanatical." Moreover, it is easy to fall prey to using models of heroic courage as a propagandistic device to further political ends.[4] Hero worship is a notorious tool in the hands of a demagogue, as has been demonstrated, for example, by Adolf Hitler in Nazi Germany. Any evaluation of an act as courageous is strongly tinged with moral overtones and judgments, open to revision.

It appears, then, that no abstract semantics is going to provide *the* meaning of courage. It might seem at first that we could assemble a number of examples of acts of courage, and then come up with some formula, like "ability to conquer fear," that might describe how the concept of courage is used. But, as we will see, there are exceptions to such formulas (counterexamples). And as we reject some of these actions as "courageous" in order to preserve our favorite formula, a normative element in the enterprise becomes apparent. If a courageous act is, by definition, a noble or good action, then our own normative standards must be built into any proposed formula or definition. It seems, then, that understanding courage is a problem for ethics, a matter of defending or criticizing moral values.

If courage is the overcoming of fear, then the problem of understanding courage as a human quality also involves psychology, for fear is a real emotion. Another possibility, however, is that courage should be defined objectively, as persisting in the face of danger or severe difficulty, rather than subjectively, as a response to an emotion. In some instances, an act is called courageous because the agent showed presence of mind, and acted so promptly there could have been no time for fear. In other instances, the hallmark of courage is the coolness of the courageous act, where, seemingly, fear failed to arise at all. Once again, the different ways of defining courage and thus the difficulty in pinning down its meaning suggest more the nature of a philosophical problem, even if psychology is certainly involved as well.

Ernest Hemingway proposed a neat definition of courage: "grace under pressure." Aristotle struck a similar note in defining courage as a kind of balanced deliberation in a tight situation. Most of us, at first exposure to this idea, think it represents a curiously intellectualistic account of courage. The model we probably think of as the paradigm of courageous action may be more of the "blood and guts" variety—steely determination or bold, hotheaded aggressiveness— that seems the opposite of intellectual calculations or deliberations. There thus seem to be at least two different conceptions of courageous action, and it may depend on one's own moral preconceptions which one is preferred. These reflections immediately lead to a problem.

Is the bold rush to attack in difficult or uncertain circumstances a courageous act even if it may not be clear that it is the product of cool deliberation? There seems to be a sort of paradox here. On the one hand, many successful military strategists, notably Suvorov and Rommel, have emphasized that a dangerous situation such as battle is extremely fluid and uncertain and that boldness is therefore generally a good policy. On the other hand, a reflex of boldness in a situation not calling for it can be reckless (foolish). Moreover, in some fluid and uncertain situations a policy of caution is clearly sensible. Consider the following instance, however, from the account of McGarry (1977).

When a gasoline tanker collided with two trucks on the outskirts of Edmonton on March 30, 1974, gasoline flowed freely across the highway and into the ditch. The tanker driver was thrown into this ditch, his right leg almost severed. A crowd of confused people, some of them injured, milled around. Only Ken Bishop leaped from his car to help the tanker driver, at the same time warning the others of the danger of possible explosion the gasoline. Then the gasoline exploded, and produced a wall of flames surrounding the injured man. The explosion also hurled Bishop through the air and set his clothes alight. Rolling in the snow to extinguish the flames, Bishop returned and dragged the injured man clear of the blaze. Bishop suffered second-degree burns over 40 percent of his body, and was unable to return to work for a year. He was awarded the Cross of Valor for his heroic act.

In this case, one person boldly attacked the dangerous situation, while others milled around ineffectually. It is a nice question of interpretation, however, whether this promptness to act could be better described as a quick-witted action based on a sound perception of the danger and an altruistic desire to help someone in trouble, even in the face of that danger. Therefore, a hot-blooded charge into danger, although present here, is not itself the mark of a courageous act. It is, rather the quick perception of the right thing to do and the willingness to do it, even at great personal risk. Other cases also suggest that considerable care is needed in evaluating acts of courage that involve a bold or aggressive rush.

One sees in descriptions of the actions cited for the Congressional Medal of Honor (COVA 1973) many instances where a soldier freely exposed himself to massive and continuous enemy fire in a sudden, bold, one-man assault on a position. Often the attacking soldier had many near misses and wounds, yet went on, staggering, bleeding, and disregarding bullets going through his clothing. Yet, even though some position is won or some contribution to the advance is made by such a bold assault, if the advancing soldier was killed one hesitates to conclude that the attack had all the characteristics of courageous action. It can hardly be denied that such an attack is fearless or intrepid, an extraordinary act. Yet one wonders: What was the real reason for it?

Why the hesitation? Is it that what could have been an act of thoughtless fury lacks the deliberation and purposefulness of the acts of highest courage? Or is it that the act seemed so dangerous as to approach the suicidal? Could it be that when the risks taken are so fearsome one begins to question the rationality of the act? When asking these questions it is well to remember that boldness, at least in some—even apparently hopeless—situations, does sometimes work out surprisingly well.

In June 1944, in France, an American infantry battalion was pinned down by firmly entrenched enemy forces on high ground. Supporting fire proved futile in dislodging the enemy, so Sergeant Frank D. Peregory single-handedly advanced up the hill under heavy fire and discovered a trench leading to the main enemy fortifications. According to the description (COVA 1973:658), Peregory plunged into the trench and, by himself, attacked a squad of enemy riflemen with hand grenades and bayonet. After killing a number of men, and forcing over thirty others to surrender, he eventually captured the enemy machine gunners, enabling his battalion to advance.

This extraordinary aggressiveness might seem reckless almost to the point of foolhardiness, but it worked. Attacking a large number of determined enemy soldiers all by oneself in this fashion stretched boldness to the point that one might begin to question the rationality of the act. Yet Peregory seemed to be in control of the situation, and his extraordinarily bold tactics cleared the line of advance. For this action, he was awarded the Congressional Medal of Honor.

This act was a bold and aggressive voluntary risk, a timely act that caught the enemy off balance, an act that was intrepid and brave. We have to concede that it was strategically sound because it worked. Thus we certainly cannot deny that it was a courageous act. But do we think it courageous because of its sheer audacity and fearlessness? Or is it that, in retrospect, we concede that audacity in this instance turned out to be the practical, wise solution to the stalemate?

The view of courageous action as a sudden outburst of will manifested in aggressive action should immediately be countered by the fact that some of the most courageous acts are deliberated through a period of solitary reflection and are quiet acts of high principle. Far from being aggressive, such an act or refusal to act may be a deliberate forfeit of one's own interest for the sake of others.

In February 1945, Lance-Corporal David Russell was an escaped prisoner of war living with an Italian peasant, Guiseppe Vettorello. Russell was captured, beaten up, and chained to a stable wall by the German commanding officer, who told him he would be shot if he did not identify his benefactor. Russell refused to inform. After several days of internment and beatings, he was shot by his captors on the grounds that when captured he was wearing civilian clothes and carrying a map and, therefore, was a spy. After the war, the local community showed its gratitude by erecting a memorial over his grave. Russell was awarded the George Cross in 1948. The *London Gazette* notice of 24 December 1948 concludes: "There can be no doubt whatsoever that Lance-Corporal Russell, in the midst of his enemies and in the face of death, bore himself with courage and dignity of a very high order" (O'Shea 1981:29).

This instance and others like it, where a prisoner refused under torture and threat of execution to give information that would have endangered others or led to their deaths, is a special kind of courage. This is the lonely courage of one "in the midst of his enemies and in the face of death" who undergoes the inner struggle of deliberation and acts freely on his principled decision despite the terrible threat. It is an integrity that cannot be overwhelmed by the most fearful assaults on the individual alone.

This kind of act seems to me an amazing tribute to the human species. It is one thing to disregard danger in the heat of action, quite another to resist the sure threat of death alone on principle. The quiet courage to freely permit one's own destruction in lonely and terrible circumstances of pressure, to act in accordance with one's principled deliberation, seems a uniquely difficult type of act.

I will define courage as an excellence of practical action both through skills of execution and through deliberation that enter into human actions. The goal is to amplify and clarify this definition while balancing it against alternative conceptions of courage. A definition of this sort can never be purely stipulative; it is more a normative guideline that can be defended or refuted philosophically.

1.2 *Courage as a Problem in Ethics*

Much recent and traditional moral philosophy is duty centered; consequently, actions that go "beyond the call of duty" have proved difficult to explain or account for in ethics. Acts not strictly required by duty—these include many acts of mercy, generosity, consideration, and politeness as well as acts of courage and heroism—have received surprisingly little systematic attention by ethical philosophers. The classic example is Kant, whose approach is based on the idea that any act is right only insofar as it corresponds to one's duty. Hence for Kant, supererogatory acts—acts beyond the requirements of duty—are of dubious or questionable moral value apart from their conformity to duty. Small wonder then that in the context of modern ethics courageous acts seem obscure or problematic when it comes to understanding the basis of their moral commendability or excellence.[5]

By contrast, courage as a morally excellent quality of conduct was readily comprehensible in the framework of Greek and Roman ethics. Classical ethics is axiological rather than deontological. That is, its basic concepts are goodness, virtue, and perfection, as opposed to duty, right, and justice. The axiological approach is more concerned with qualities of noble character or personal excellence. In Greek ethics, courage was readily accommodated to the ideal of virtue (excellence, *arete*) as one form of personal merit in conduct. We will see, for example, in Aristotle's ethical theory, courage, like all virtues, is defined as a *mean* or *moderation* between extremes of conduct.

The problem is that Greek ethics represents a framework that seems alien and out of line with respect to both modern social practices and recent ethical theory. As Heyd (1982:38) points out, social interaction in the ancient world was based on what is called a "gift relationship" rather than the highly commercialized notions of personal transactions which now seem to be dominant as models of relationships. The Greek practice was to expect a return from an act of giving, possibly a worthier gift that would cement friendship or assert the reciprocator's worth and merit. But the importance of this notion of voluntary giving in civic and social life has, in modern times, been superseded by ideas of obligatory fulfillment of specific duties and contracts. Thus, generosity, benevolence, and nobility, so important to the Greek ideal of the good man's contribution to society, no longer occupy center stage for moral ideals of conduct.

According to Hands (1968:40), the Greeks had no system of taxation in our sense. Instead, the wealthy were expected to contribute to public funds voluntarily when there was a need. By contributing generously to something of public benefit, the affluent person could demonstrate his virtue as a citizen of the community. But this notion of virtue seems somewhat out of place in the context of modern values, where "charitable donation" is thought better if carried out anonymously. A display of "public virtue" in the Greek sense might today be thought a conspicuous display of wealth or power, perhaps even demeaning to its recipients. What generosity or benevolence may be seen in such personal acts of giving is likely to be strongly tinged with a feeling that the rich person should not really have the right to possess more money than the rest of us, or to dispose of it at his or her personal whim.

To the Greeks, the notion of personal merit or worth deriving from generous or courageous acts over and above the requirements of law or strict duty made perfectly good sense as virtuous conduct. But to the modern sensibility, the notion of virtue as personal excellence carries strong connotations of a suspicious elitism. The notion that some persons have higher moral standards of personal conduct than others strongly offends our "democratic" preconceptions of perfect moral equality for all persons.

The notion of courage as a quality of personal merit made perfect sense in the context of Greek ethics. Courage is a moderation between excessive fear and excessive (foolish) confidence, and the exercise of the virtue of courage displayed or added to the personal merit of a man.

In the modern context, courage as a moral notion is shot through with dissonance and fails to find an assured place in the scheme of values, even though it continues to exert a strong hold on our intuitions about what is admirable conduct. We seem to have the idea that what mainly matters is whether one does one's duty or not. Where courage is supererogatory—beyond duty—the personal merit attaching to the courageous act seems to border on glorification of the ego and comes uncomfortably close to a fanatical or irrational hero worship. But where courageous action is in conformity to duty, under dangerous or difficult circumstances, we seem almost incapable of seeing the real value in it; the important thing may seem to be whether or not the requirements of duty were in fact met. How the act was carried out, or what were the obstacles or circumstances in which it was carried out, seem elusive or questionable as matters of moral obligation or value. Either way, courage as a moral quality seems elusive and dubious.

The dilemma is reflected in our ambivalence about courage as a valuable quality. We often praise courage in eulogies and other public addresses on civic or moral qualities. And popular culture, for example, in movies ranging from *High Noon* to *The Americanization of Emily,* is very often woven around a preoccupation with the theme of courage as a moral quality. But if, as we seem to think, courage is such an admirable quality, we are strangely silent when it comes to analyzing what it consists in, or to trying to systematically encourage our young people to attain it.

I remember being strongly moved as a youth when we read the story of Glenn Cunningham in literature class. As a boy, Cunningham had badly injured his legs in an accident and the doctors said he would never walk. He persisted, and was able to walk, then run, and eventually became an Olympic runner.

This act still seems to me courageous, but from the point of view of philosophical justification of my intuition, it may be appreciated why some would question its moral value or its place in ethics. Many men have become Olympic runners. That may be a good thing to do, but it is not morally valuable or meritorious in itself. What was so courageous about Cunningham's achievement?

What seems special is the unusual difficulty of his circumstances. It was terribly difficult for him to carry out his objective, and such a goal would even have appeared impossible to everyone when he began. But here is the question that some would pose: What is it about the difficulty of carrying out a certain objective that makes it better than if the act of achieving it was less difficult? It is true that one needs more determination to carry out a more difficult objective. But determination is not always good in itself. One can be determined to carry out a selfish or evil action as well.

Suppose you have two acts, A and B, where A is relatively easy to carry out but B is very difficult or dangerous to carry out. Yet, both

A and B are equally valuable in themselves as outcomes. Is it any better to have carried out B than A? In particular, if we were to say that carrying out B was courageous, whereas carrying out A was not, what moral value makes the carrying out of B any better? Traditional ethical theory appears to lack any theoretical resources for approaching this sort of question.

The ethics of virtue has traditionally adopted the viewpoint that virtues are qualities of character. Virtue ethics, in this view, may be contrasted with the other parts of ethics having to do with actions or what we ought to do. For example, Mayo (1958) suggests that the old-fashioned word 'virtue' is concerned with qualities of character, with what people are. He draws the contrast as one between "doing" and "being." The moral question for virtue ethics is "What shall I be?" as opposed to the rest of ethics, where the main question is "What shall I do?" Accordingly, virtues are defined as dispositions or traits of character.

According to Beauchamp (1982:149), the primary concern of virtue ethics is the question of "character-centered judgements which assert that a *person* or *character* is good or bad, virtuous or vicious, praiseworthy or blameworthy, admirable or reprehensible." According to Beauchamp, virtue ethics represents a challenge to utilitarian and deontological ethical theories, because these types of theories offer accounts of what we ought to do, as opposed to the kind of persons we ought to be.

The basic argument of this book will be opposed to this traditional viewpoint. I will argue that courage, as a virtue, is primarily a property of individual actions. I argue that each action should be judged on its own merits as courageous or not. Thus, the primary question for a virtue ethic—at least in regard to the virtue of courage—is whether a particular action is courageous. I argue that this judgment is a matter of how the action was carried out, which entails studying the practical reasoning behind the action—the way the agent carried out his intentions in the specific circumstances of the action.

Since intentions enter into practical reasoning, judgment of an act as courageous does involve, to some extent, an evaluation of the agent. But properly considered, I will argue, judgment of the courage of the person is not a question of the person's psychological propensity or disposition to act in a certain way. Judgment of a person as being courageous is a matter of evaluating the commitments of the agent, his position or stance as expressed by his actions, and the deliberations that produced those actions. The study of these deliberations and actions, however, is a question of practical reasoning—a normative question, not a psychological question of dispositions.

Judgments of cowardice, although they also involve practical reasoning, are legitimately psychological in a way that judgments of courage are not. I will argue that a cowardly action is necessarily an action taken out of fear. But a courageous action need not be defined in terms of the psychological property of fear. A courageous act is one in which, based on the good intentions of the agent in attempting to realize a worthy goal, he or she overcomes great danger or difficulty—whether afraid or not. Thus, once again, I will go against tradition. My argument will be that courage and cowardice are not opposites, as properties of actions.

Despite this opposition to the traditional conception of virtue as a property of character, I will argue that there is a sense in which virtuous actions do model a person-oriented ethics. Much ethical theory has been concerned with principles held to be universalizable, that is, they apply to all moral agents, at least in principle. However, judgments of the courage or cowardice of actions in many cases are not universalizable, as we will see. They are often "beyond the call of duty" and represent the agent's own personal merit and individual excellence of conduct. They represent values of the individual's conscience and personal commitment to ideals and aspirations. The proper method of their evaluation is therefore the personal consistency of an agent's deliberations and action that reflect his moral position as an individual.

1.3 Rejection of the Moral Value of Courage

The basis of utilitarian ethics is that the best action to perform among a set of alternatives is the one with maximal utility (benefit, happiness). On such a view, the fact that a course of action is known to be very difficult or dangerous is a good reason for *not* doing it (disutility). However, according to the viewpoint of maximization, if the act is altruistic and the benefits for others outweigh the pain and sacrifice to the agent, it would be mandatory for the agent to carry out the act. This might conflict with Heyd's (1982) quite reasonable thesis that many acts of heroic courage are beyond duty and therefore optional, in the sense that failure to act would not be morally culpable. Hence there are systematic reasons why, on utilitarian ethics, the value of a courageous act may be hard to justify, or even to perceive, in many cases.[6]

Moreover, utilitarian ethics tells one to choose the best outcome. The way in which an outcome was brought about, whether skillfully, deliberately, courageously, and so forth, may not necessarily count in the value of the outcome in utilitarian calculations. The value of courage as a moral quality therefore seems rather elusive in the utilitarian view. And in fact I know of no systematic attempts to elicit the moral value of courage from this standpoint.

According to Kantian ethics, the moral necessity of actions derives from the commands of the moral law. The test of an act's morality is its universalizability. An act is moral only if done for the sake of the moral law (from duty). For Kant, the results of the act are morally irrelevant—utilitarian factors are dismissed. But the person's real motive in performing the act, apart from reverence for duty, is also morally irrelevant; only those acts done from respect for the moral law have moral worth. Acts that merely accord with duty may have no moral worth as such, unless they are done from duty, as manifestations of a good will.

This too leads to a certain opacity when it comes to understanding the moral value of acts of courage. Many acts of courage are beyond duty (supererogatory). But Kant accepts the trichotomy now familiar in current deontic logic—an act that is neither permitted nor forbidden is morally indifferent. As Heyd (1982:51) points out, there is very little room, if any, in this scheme of things for justifying the special value of acts that go beyond the requirements of duty.

One kind of justification of the value of an act of courage is that such acts are performed with a noble objective (intention) in mind. The good of the intention therefore justifies the worth or value of the courageous act. But, in the *Groundwork of the Metaphysic of Morals* ([1785] 1964:68), Kant explicitly rejects this basis for the moral value of an act: "That the purposes we may have in our actions, and also their effects considered as ends and motives of the will, can give to actions no unconditioned and moral worth is clear." It is not the purpose of the act but the maxim or principle by which it has been decided that is what makes the action of moral worth.

Accordingly, in Kant's ethics, a courageous act can be of moral worth insofar as it corresponds to the dictates of one's duty. But the value of courageous actions, over and above other more usual incidents of doing one's duty, is not an unqualified good for Kant. Courage is described as a quality of temperament that may be good and desirable in some respects, but bad and hurtful in other respects (ibid., p. 61).

According to Urmson (1958), this trichotomy of classification of acts of moral worth is inadequate to the facts of morality. He argues that room should be made in ethical theory for heroic or saintly acts that are beyond the requirements of duty yet call for a positive moral evaluation or commendation. An act is heroic "if it is a case of duty done by virtue of self-control in a context in which most men would be led astray by fear or a drive for self-preservation" (1958:200). Urmson's paper was a bold and innovative criticism of the failure of traditional moral theories to cope with supererogatory moral qualities like courage.

Urmson's definition of 'heroic' raises the question of whether there is a difference between courageous actions and heroic actions. It also raises the question of whether heroic (courageous) actions are acts of duty, or acts beyond the requirements of duty.

Many acts of courage are clearly beyond the reasonable requirements of duty. For example, in October 1944, Captain James M. Burt was commanding a company of the 2d Armored Division of the U.S. Army. In the attack on Aachen, infantrymen ran into heavy small arms and mortar fire. Burt moved forward on foot beyond the infantry positions and, as the German troops concentrated their fire on him, he directed his tanks into good firing positions. Mounting a tank, he continued to direct the attack under severe fire. Painfully wounded, he maintained his post until the German guns were knocked out. On numerous other occasions during the next few days of the battle, Burt left cover and directed the course of battle from exposed positions in advance of his troops (COVA 1973:510).

This sort of conduct clearly represents actions beyond the requirements of what would be considered the duties of a company commander. Presumably, no officer would ask a soldier to undertake these kinds of risks, and it is noted (ibid.) that Burt's disregard of personal safety was so evident that the men serving under him were visibly inspired to overcome the wretched conditions of the bitter battle of the Aachen gap. This seems to reflect the presumption that Burt's actions went beyond what would be considered the regular duties or expectations of someone in his position.

Other courageous actions seem to be more in the line of duty. When Sergeant Murray Hudson of the Royal New Zealand Regiment was supervising live grenade practice in February 1974, he noticed an NCO who had armed a grenade. He ordered the man to throw the grenade, but there was no reaction and the man appeared to have frozen. Hudson died attempting to wrest the grenade from this man's hand and throw it over the parapet. As an experienced soldier, he fully knew the risk he took. This was an act of sacrifice in devotion to duty. Its courageousness lay in Hudson's devotion to duty over his concern for his own safety. His act also expressed altruistic concern for the other soldier. (See O'Shea [1981:32], and discussion in chap. 7.)

In fact, in many instances it is hard to say precisely when an act is done as required by one's duty or falls beyond the bounds of duty.[7] Yet it does seem that not all courageous acts are clearly supererogatory. Some acts seem to be in the line of duty, but the exemplary way they are carried out, or some other aspects, make them courageous.

In New Guinea in July 1944, Staff Sergeant Gerald Endl saw through a clearing of the Kunai grass that the platoon he had assumed command of was about to be hopelessly trapped by an enveloping movement of Japanese troops.

> In the face of extremely heavy fire he went forward alone and for a period of approximately ten minutes engaged the enemy in a heroic close-range fight, holding them off while his men crawled forward under cover to evacuate the wounded and withdraw. Courageously refusing to abandon four more wounded who were lying along the trail, one by one he brought them back to safety. (*COVA* 1973:548)

He was killed as he carried the last man back in his arms. For these actions, Endl was posthumously awarded the Congressional Medal of Honor.

Were these actions beyond the call of duty? Or were they the acts of a man who conscientiously carried out what he considered to be his duty? It is difficult to arrive at a definitive answer. And perhaps it does not matter insofar as the courageousness of the act is concerned. Even if these were acts of duty, they are courageous because of the desperate circumstances, the skillful and exemplary way they were carried out, the presence of mind and determination they showed, and the altruistic self-sacrifice shown by Sergeant Endl.

It therefore seems we should say that while it is clear that many courageous actions are beyond the requirements of duty, a case can be made for the claim that not all truly courageous actions are clearly supererogatory.

Much of Kant's problem with the morality of acts of courage stems from their supererogatory nature: if all morality is in conformity to duty, then acts beyond duty appear to have no moral value over and above their being done from duty. Yet even the question of knowing what is distinctively meritorious about courageous acts done in the line of duty remains for Kant. As Heyd (1982:55) suggests, Kant's answer is ambivalent and indicates considerable suspicion of courage as a moral virtue.

Denigration of courage as a moral quality is not altogether unexpected in any ethical theory that stresses scrupulous fairness, equal distribution of goods, or ideals of strict equality of merit and worth. For a courageous act is a sign of outstanding personal excellence, or unusual merit in standards or skill in carrying out a noble objective. An act of courage is in its way a demonstration of inequality, of moral superiority. Ethics in recent times has become virtually obsessed with strict notions of fairness and equality, and increasingly, it seems, less and less room is left for the moral value of virtues like courage or gallantry.

This theoretical bent toward an "economic" and "democratic" view of ethics as equal distribution of goods is mirrored by a popular suspicion and cynicism about anything that seems to derive value from heroic excellence. As a result of the influence of the social sciences, altruistic acts are no longer likely to be taken at face value, and may be thought to be irrational in one way or another once deeper motives are explored. To many of us, then, courage as a virtue may seem but a tattered remnant of outdated ideals of chivalry—a macho-military quality that has outgrown its usefulness in civilized society. To some, courage is not a virtue but only an indelicate reminder of violence, war, domination, or other unpleasant conditions.

Perhaps another reason that courage today seems to many to be an absurd or outdated virtue is the growing lack of cohesiveness in social structures and group purposes. In vast modern industrial societies, the individual feels anonymous and often loses identity with the community as a group. This phenomenon in North America has often been remarked upon. Twenty-six bystanders watched as Kitty Genovese was brutally murdered on the street, not even one calling the police. The current expression is "Nobody wants to get involved." A kind of moral anomie is described by Camus in *L'Etranger*—an individual fails to feel even the smallest sympathy or emotion at the death of another. The attitude seems to be a moral aimlessness, a lack of purpose or feeling beyond one's own egoistic interests. To one in this frame of mind, courage—taking personal risk to try to save another or to help the group or community in time of trouble—seems simply an irrational risk, no gain at all.

Perception of courage as a nonvirtue is often particularly linked to a rejection of military actions of any sort. As I will suggest, an act's value as courageous is tied to its purpose as a noble expression, an enactment of some worthy objective. In war, the fate of the entire community is at risk. Therefore, the conduct of the soldier who defends that community must presumably be viewed as an expression of his commitment to the values of the community and its needs. If the community is perceived by the individual as valueless, however, the act of courage, or any altruistic deed, must be seen as absurd. Thus, to one who is alienated from community values, courage is a quality to be denigrated and ridiculed. Perhaps there is a kind of logic to such a view: if the objective is not perceived as worthy, no act to attain it should properly be described as courageous. For the vandal, who expresses his alienation by destroying community property, the soldier's act of self-sacrifice hardly makes sense.

During and after the Vietnam conflict, a denigration of military courage was widespread. No doubt this stemmed from the perception of many that this war was not necessary for the defense of the United States. At any rate, there was certainly a lack of strong feeling of a clear, well-defined goal and, as a result, the conflict failed to have a strongly defined purpose in the public consciousness. Courageous acts of sacrifice were therefore perceived by many at the time as being of little worth.

Hence courage in a military context is in particular strongly tied to one's view of the conflict in question as, say, an imminent threat to a community with which one strongly identifies. Where there is a loosening of the tie that binds the individual to the purpose and interests of his or her own community, the diminution of courage as a quality of excellence is consequential. In a selfish and egocentric group, valiant acts of risk to defend the group must be greeted as hypocritical. Such acts may be encouraged by the egoist in a cynical way, not because they are deeply valued. They may even be privately ridiculed by such a person.

At present, in many Western countries morality must be seen as a function of plurality of different principles and views, often in conflict. Minority groups and special interest groups of many kinds see their own particular objectives as more important than overall objectives of the community to which all belong. An act thought to be courageous by one group can therefore be seen as simply misguided by another group that has conflicting objectives in relation to the former.[8] Hence any act that is widely altruistic, or that involves sacrificing one's special interests to those of the community as a whole, no longer qualifies as a courageous or worthy action because its purpose has been too diluted.

Perception of an act as courageous, it seems, may be strongly tied to ideologies or group values. To the skeptic, the link with ideology merely suggests the propagandistic nature of exaltation of courageous heroes. According to this viewpoint, courage is a negative quality.

1.4 Supererogation

Courage, we have suggested, is thought to be an especially commendable quality of an action because, in many instances, the action is a sacrifice or an accomplishment of good beyond the requirements of duty in a particular situation. Yet we do often tend to think of ethics as being concerned with strict rules of duty, and supererogatory concepts like courage thus would seem to have no rightful place in it.

Actions beyond the requirements of duty are, in an important sense, optional or discretionary rather than strict dictates of moral rules that would make nonperformance forbidden or blameworthy. Many moral qualities of actions have this discretionary character—for example, generosity, mercy, and politeness. This whole class of supererogatory acts provides a problem for ethical theory. Stemming from Urmson's pioneering paper, there have been a number of articles on this problem. A comprehensive treatment of this subject, which has not received the attention it deserves, is given in Heyd (1982).

Heyd (ibid., p. 115) proposes a definition of the class of supererogatory acts. An act is said to be supererogatory if and only if it meets these four requirements:

1. It is neither obligatory nor forbidden
2. Its omission is not wrong, and does not deserve sanction or criticism—either formal or informal
3. It is morally good, both by virtue of its (intended) consequences

and by virtue of its intrinsic value (being beyond duty)
4. It is done voluntarily for the sake of someone else's good, and is thus meritorious

This definition of supererogation will turn out to be quite congenial to my definition of courage, both because it makes supererogation an attribute of actions rather than of traits of character and because it requires a supererogatory act to be good as specified in (3). Subsequent chapters in this work, especially the later ones, consist largely in spelling out the notions of actions, intentions, and consequences which are appealed to by the definition above.

We will see that some definitions of courage do not require that a truly courageous act must always be carried out with a good intention in mind. However, according to my approach, a courageous act must be based on a good intention. Hence my approach fits in nicely with the general structure of Heyd's account of supererogation above. Of course, if you agree with my proposal that courageous acts need not always be beyond duty, then (1) and (2) above will not fit every courageous act. But insofar as courageous acts are supererogatory, Heyd's account of supererogation can be most helpful in showing us how courageous acts can be of positive moral value.

According to Heyd, individual life plans and projects are important in a morally balanced picture of the relationship between personal ideals and considerations of social or public good. He argues (ibid., p. 174) that persons are not exclusively tools for the promotion of public welfare—we are entitled to be somewhat different from each other, and some may be entitled to have different ideals or higher standards of personal conduct. This is an argument for a limitation on the scope of duty on the grounds of individual autonomy. Heyd's conception rejects the notion of the individual as a ceaseless obligatory worker for the welfare of others, a conception that often seems to be the ideal of utilitarian ethics. By contrast, personal autonomy can allow for supererogatory acts that are not universally required but express the agent's own personal values.[9]

One might think that supererogatory acts, like acts of courage, should need no justification as possible objects of moral value. But it is not difficult to see why a preoccupation with the requirements of duty has eclipsed them as a subject of importance to moral philosophy. Supererogatory acts are often optional, matters of personal rather than public standards, and perhaps, therefore, easy to think of as inessential frills.

As Davis (n.d.) has pointed out, however, supererogatory acts need not always be heroic in stature. They also include many everyday virtues such as politeness, generosity, consideration, and the willingness to be helpful beyond the requirements of duty.[10] With these qualities, life among one's fellows can be delightful and rewarding. Without them—in a society where everyone makes a point of doing only what is required—life would be a nasty and frustrating business. If each person insisted on rigid adherence to his or her rights, never giving an inch more than the strict requirements of duty, everyday life would be unproductive and exasperating to a degree that is hard to imagine.

James Evans has pointed out (personal communication), for example, that many legal contracts in business are much more open-ended and flexible than one's notion of "contract" might suggest. Circumstances of a situation often change in ways that cannot be anticipated or that are too numerous to be specified in advance. Goodwill and constructive, freely given concessions by both parties are therefore most often essential to reaching an agreement. A strict legalistic insistence on the finer points of rights or dues can be highly counterproductive in practice. The smooth flow of everyday contractual relations in business and government is more dependent on supererogatory acts than one might initially realize. Everyone could be counted on to do their duty in a morally perfect world without supererogatory acts, but trust, cooperation, or goodwill beyond the requirements of duty could not be counted on.

Let us take the practice of medicine as an example. In the most successful doctor-patient relationships there is a good deal of trust on both sides. Given the asymmetrical nature of the relationship— the doctor is an expert and the patient is an autonomous, decision-making client—trust, discretion, and cooperation are essential. This remains true even though both parties are self-interested bargainers to some extent, entering into the relationship in the expectation of some gain or benefit. Whatever the precise nature of this relationship is, it seems to involve a good deal of cooperation and empathy on both sides, over and above its strict contractual requirements, if it is to function smoothly.[11]

One could well imagine, for example, that patient-physician relationships would be very difficult or even impossible if neither party ever showed courage or gallantry in seeing through his or her part of a treatment. Many of the advances in medicine have come about through the sacrifice of dedicated researchers who labored long beyond the requirements of duty. Many medical treatments are painful and difficult, demanding determination and concessions from patient and family. Without courage and other supererogatory virtues, it is easy to imagine that many medical treatments could be nightmares of fearful anticipation and recrimination for patient and physician alike.

It may well be that many of the bioethical dilemmas concerning when to stop heroic treatment appear so problematic and nonsusceptible to strict ethical rules that are universally applicable precisely because of the supererogatory nature of this form of decision making. A type of treatment that one patient finds "heroic" or "extraordinary" may be acceptable and nonaggressive to another.[12] And one person's aspirations and ideals with regard to an appropriate level of difficulty and struggle could be very different from those of another. If these levels of personal expectation are discretionary and optional, we should not expect strictly universal ethical rules of duty or obligation to apply. It could be that our blindness to supererogation as a genuine locus of moral values has led us to misconstrue problems of discretionary, heroic therapy.[13] The standards involved could be personal (non-universal) yet, at the same time, moral.

Socrates acted out his personal ideals of correct conduct even to the point of unflinchingly and freely going to his death. Many of us might feel that such conduct was very well for one with such personal standards, but inappropriate for somebody else. One may conclude that Socrates' act was a purely personal, hence subjective, decision and therefore of no moral import. There is some point to this view. Supererogatory acts reflect a personal standard of conduct and are therefore not universalizable. It need not follow, however, that Socrates' heroic act was of no moral worth. He felt that it was the right thing to do because it preserved the laws of the state and, as a citizen, he was obliged to follow the law. On arguing the pros and cons with his students and friends, Socrates concluded that freely going to his death according to the dictates of the state was the best thing to do in the circumstances. One could argue against his decision, but it cannot be dismissed out of hand as of no moral import or as purely subjective.

The patient who struggles on because he feels that giving up too easily or contributing to his own death would take the decision "out of God's hands" may also be following a personal standard of conduct that he would not dictate to another. Yet, even if such a decision reflects his personal standards, it should not be assumed that it cannot be a morally significant decision of more than private import.

Supererogatory actions as a class deserve more recognition and study. With regard to the quality of courage, in particular, two aspects are especially important in considerations of moral value. The justification of acts of courage as being of special moral value stems, first, from the difficulty and danger or risk that is an essential part of any truly courageous act. If an act is terribly difficult or dangerous in the extreme, it may be unreasonable to expect any person to undertake it as a matter of duty or obligation. In some cases, therefore, the act should be regarded as discretionary or optional.

If the act is truly courageous, there must, second, be the intention of great good in carrying it out. If the courageous person chooses, in the urgency of the situation, to carry out the act, there will be, for example, a saving of life or a catastrophe averted. We could not expect anyone in such a situation to act, but if the person in question does, those who benefit—perhaps all of us—should be very grateful for this gift that was given at great personal risk or sacrifice.

Let us go back to the act of Staff Sergeant Erwin, who saved the crew of his plane by grasping a burning phosphoresce bomb in his arms and, despite his blindness and pain, managed to carry out a procedure to eject it from the plane. This was a singular feat that would surely be beyond the capability of most of us, even if we were bombardiers as well trained as he was. It would thus be inappropriate to cite such a heroic action as the correct requirements of duty for anyone in this, or a similar, situation. In the case of Erwin's action, both aspects of justification of moral value were met. The act was terribly difficult to carry out, and based on a good intention.

1.5 *Actions and Goals*

Courage is a valuable quality because it can tilt a dangerous or unstable situation away from catastrophe and toward good. A courageous act is one that makes a difference in a particular situation where there is potential for both good and bad outcomes.

An example provided by Robert Nola suggests that courage is a practical quality of thought and action.[14] Recently, in New Zealand, when the pilot of a small plane suffered a heart attack, a passenger with no pilot training or familiarity with aircraft found himself alone at the controls. By keeping his head, the passenger was able to follow instructions over the radio and eventually guide the plane to a safe landing, a feat that must have required considerable composure and deliberation. The fact that this man acted courageously and kept a clear head made the difference between disaster and a good outcome.

This courageous act, like Erwin's, demonstrates that courage is, first and foremost, a practical virtue, which is the view I will argue for. It is an example of practical reasoning, of deliberately carrying out acts that are the means to an end. In the case of courageous acts, the end is worthwhile or valuable, while the means are dangerous or difficult to carry out.

This approach to courage as a moral quality requires that we have some understanding of how actions are carried out as means to accomplishing the agent's intention.[15] Courage, it seems, has to do with how objectives or plans are carried out by means of actions. The branch of philosophy having to do with these notions is the theory of action. Our framework for understanding courage as a quality of human actions will, in the latter part of this work, be sought in the notion of practical reasoning, a topic in the theory of action.

Practical reasoning involves skills of judgment and discrimination in acting in particular circumstances. These skills are specific to a situation, and cannot be learned by following general principles that apply to all actions. Rather, they are learned, to a great extent, by looking to certain symbols or paradigms of action. We learn what courageous action is by looking at particular examples of actions that we judge to be courageous. True, there is a general structure of practical reasoning underlying these paradigms, but to fully understand what courage is we need to look at real practices of what Wittgenstein (1953) called "forms of life" in a community. These real practices can be shown to define a tradition of the moral life, sometimes a conflicting tradition that can be questioned through philosophical dialogue.

In my view, therefore, decorations for outstanding valor, such as the Victoria Cross and the Congressional Medal of Honor, provide us with much valuable information, just as the Carnegie Medal and the Cross of Valor, among others, provide us with valuable information on acts of courage from other walks of life. The Victoria Cross is the highest award for gallantry bestowed in England and the Commonwealth countries, and, of all Commonwealth honors, it is ranked highest in precedence. In the United States, the Congressional Medal of Honor is the highest award for valor. Though mainly given to members of the armed forces, it has been awarded to civilians. The Carnegie Hero Fund was established in 1904 by Andrew Carnegie to recognize outstanding acts of selfless heroism performed in the United States and Canada. It awards the Carnegie Medal for acts of heroism in which several conditions are fulfilled (Carnegie Hero Fund Commission 1979). There must be conclusive evidence that the person voluntarily risked his or her life in saving or attempting to save another person to whom no full measure of responsibility exists. This means that persons whose duty or vocation requires them to perform such acts are ineligible, including members of the armed services.

In 1972, the honors system of Canada was enlarged to include three awards for bravery. They are, in order of precedence, the Cross of Valor, the Star of Courage, and the Medal of Bravery. They can be awarded to anyone, whether a Canadian citizen or not, who has performed a courageous act that merits recognition by Canada.

The descriptions of these citations yield examples or case studies that are most helpful in focusing our vague intuitions. One could sometimes wish for more information about the intentions and actions involved in an act we think courageous. History and biography are good sources here. The philosophical analysis of courage as a moral quality stops short of full-fledged biographical or historical treatment, which is not necessary for our purposes. For once we get enough details of a sequence of actions in a set of particular circumstances, given some information about the agent's general intentions, we can reconstruct a plausible picture of the situation and the nature of the agent's reaction to it. Giving the agent the benefit of the doubt where gaps in our plausible reconstruction exist, we form some judgment of whether or not the act was courageous.

In some cases, we do not know much about the individuals or their deeper motivations. But what we do know about their reactions to the situations, as we have them described, lends the weight of reasonable presumption to our feeling that their actions represent high moral courage. We know enough to be reasonably justified in this presumption. I will argue that this sort of dialectical knowledge, by tilting the burden of proof to one plausible reconstruction and interpretation of a situation, is the best we can aspire to in our moral judgments of courage and cowardice.

1.6 Virtues and Personal Ideals

Of the virtues extolled by the ancient Greeks, courage is one that still has a strong hold on us. Much of our literature and drama is deeply concerned with the morality of courage. We have deep feelings about this quality of excellence in conduct, and we are moved by instances of it in particular circumstances. Why is it then such an elusive quality in moral philosophy?

Could it be that we are not able to understand or justify the moral excellence of courage as a category of morally commendable action because we simply do not know what courage is? We can perhaps identify courageous conduct in particular instances, but as a general quality that runs through all examples of truly courageous action, courage seems difficult to articulate.

A main argument of this study is that courage as a moral quality is best defined as deliberate, practical reasoning in turbulent and troubled circumstances—the calm in the eye of the storm. It is a challenge to argue for this thesis—as Socrates found in the *Protagoras*—because of the initial plausibility of the popular view that courage is intestinal fortitude, a strong will needed to overcome fear.[16] In this view, sheer "guts" is the important thing—reasoning or intellectual understanding is not only unnecessary, it can be an impediment to courageous action.

Moreover, there are several methodological difficulties in trying to gain an understanding of "courageous" as a moral term that applies to all actions we might judge as such. If virtues are personal ideals, as opposed to universal moral principles, could it be that any philosophical attempt to describe them in objective or universal terms could be misleading?

Principles of duty and justice, as we have seen, are traditionally thought by philosophers to have universalizability as a defining characteristic. What this means, presumably, is that rules of duty are codes that apply to everyone equally—they are universally binding on all moral agents. What is characteristic of the moral ideals and aspirations associated with the supererogatory ethics of saints and heroes is the very lack of universality these ideals embody. Such aspirations are highly individual to the person who holds them—other persons are not to be considered morally lacking because of failure to follow the same moral ideals.

What is characteristic, therefore, of a moral aspiration is its relativity to a specific person. Beauchamp (1982:170) distinguishes two kinds of moral goodness: one for persons who do what is required by duty, the other the uncommon morality within the reach of the individual of extraordinary talent or drive. The latter is based on ideals to which the rest of us are not bound. Hence, the individual sets his or her own personal standards. Others may admire this person for following these standards, but should not or need not themselves feel bound to follow them.

If the ideals of virtue are individual, who is to say that they are more than purely subjective values? Sullivan (1982:112) writes: "For the ethics of virtue and its allied tradition of practical reason, to imagine that one can transcend the horizon of one's own moral understanding immediately into a universal and 'objective' context of rationality is a serious error." According to him, such an attempt must narrow the understanding of human activity by ignoring the authoritative role of paradigms of good life practices and good persons in the analysis of virtue.

These cautionary remarks are important. They suggest that real examples and cases of courage are essential in any study of the ethics of courage as a virtue. The courageous actions themselves are part of the analysis of courage, not merely illustrations. In evaluating these real cases, there is risk of misunderstanding and error, for the reconstruction of the agent's practical reasoning is always an interpretation based on plausible assumptions and burden of proof.

Anyone who has actually confronted a dangerous or difficult situation must know that uncertainty and riskiness are all part of the problem of acting virtuously. It is quite possible to act on wrong information, yet turn out to have acted well, provided there was some reason to act in the way one did. In war, politics, or any important situations of moral uncertainty, the virtuous person must take a stand, adopt a position, even if it is not clear that he or she is right in the long run. As Sullivan (ibid., p. 112) puts it, "For those within the moral horizon, whose characters and vision of the world are shaped through fidelity to an understanding of virtue, the contingent and risky wagers about the good are in fact what makes life worthwhile." Judgments of courage, then, are in an important sense based on the agent's personal position that motivated the action.

Our judgment of whether an act is cowardly or courageous cannot help being conditioned by an element of luck that, in some cases, determines the outcome of the agent's course of action. The process of reasonably reconstructing an agent's presumed steps of practical reasoning, judging mainly by how he acted in real circumstances, must often proceed by giving the agent the benefit of the doubt. We can and should presume, in the absence of evidence to the contrary, that the agent knew what he was doing.

Slote (1983:56) gives an example to illustrate the general point that our moral assessment of an act done under conditions of uncertainty can vary, depending on the luck of circumstances. Suppose a sentry is given an order to kill all strangers on sight, but is unable to fire on an approaching pregnant woman with a toddler in tow. If she turned out to be as harmless as she appears, the sentry may be judged as commendable for his flexibility in intepreting the orders. If she turned out to be a spy, the sentry might be condemned for failing in his duty. It appears that our moral evaluation of the act could be conditioned by circumstances independent of the sentry's knowledge or control. In fact, then, common moral thinking does seem to be committed to judging a person's action as partly dependent on luck.

I think that, because we must make plausible judgments in reconstructing an agent's practical reasoning in particular circumstances, this element of luck is never entirely ruled out. There is always a certain looseness in judgments that proceed on the basis of plausible presumptions. This is not necessarily bad, however, for it means we should always be open to new evidence. It also means that the burden of proof should rest on those who would condemn an act.

This individuality of moral aspirations of the virtue kind of moral goodness is best modeled, I will argue, by the concept of a position in a game of dialogue. A participant in this game adopts commitments in dialogue which mark off his or her position in opposition to the position of another player. Each set of commitments is individualized to the reasoned convictions defended by that particular player. So considered, moral aspirations must be reasonably defensible by the person who holds to them. That individual person is obliged to defend his or her own convictions and to live up to them. Others are not.

A common opinion is that teleological judgments of ends and means allow for discussion of informal exposition but do not admit of strictly scientific explanation or deduction. Accordingly, teleological expositions are more properly a part of the humanities than the social sciences. Following a humanistic approach, our subsequent discussions of courage as a norm of action will take the form of a discussion or dialogue that challenges the reader's preconceptions and implicit assumptions. By making these assumptions surface, and by challenging and questioning them (and even sometimes justifying or defending them), I hope to engage in a dialogue with the reader which will lead to new knowledge about courage and cowardice as moral guidelines of human actions.

CHAPTER 2

Popular Images of Courage

THE MORE ONE begins to reflect on the nature of courage, Hemingway's definition, "grace under pressure," seems to become more appropriate. But the strangeness of this definition makes us wonder if we really know what courage is at all.

This work is about courage and cowardice, and is concerned with the reactions we have to situations in which these two properties appear strongly to be manifested. My arguments have to do with whether or how these initial reactions can be justified or refuted by appeal to the nature of courage and cowardice as coherent concepts of practical ethics.

A practical work of philosophy, as this is intended to be, takes as its subject matter familiar concerns of everyday life. Most of us have a deep familiarity with such topics on a practical level and, therefore, come to any philosophical consideration of them with strong views or at least strong preconceptions. Ultimately, it is these deeply imbued intuitions based on one's personal experience which provide the interest and also a good deal of the basis of argument for practical books or treatises in moral philosophy.

The doctrine that courage is a "virtue" no longer holds the same commonplace grip on moral intuitions as it may have previously. If virtue is defined after MacIntyre (1981) as a good of practical excellence, however, it takes on a compelling impact indeed.[1] For courage as a basic value category of practical conduct has a very strong grip on commonplace intuitions. The idea of courage conveys powerful feelings and responses. As we have seen, however, most of us would be hard put to articulate just what courage is as a quality of excellence in human action and character.

2.1 Two Views of Courage

One of the most common images of courage is that of the soldier in wartime attacking a hostile force with grim determination in a situation of extreme danger—the gung ho image of courage. There are probably strong overtones of fear, danger, and violence. This image immediately has a number of connotations. Some would say that courage is a barbaric macho quality, too often linked with lust for power or even killing one's fellow human beings. In this view, courage is by no means an essentially excellent or morally positive quality in itself. While possibly sometimes good, it may too often be turned to bad ends, even to the exaltation of morally corrupt political philosophies and the worship of force.[2]

In contrast, courage has often been thoughtfully praised as a virtue, even exalted as one of the highest forms of excellence of civilized human conduct.[3] How can we resolve this apparent contradiction? Is courage intrinsically good? Or is it a quality that is only sometimes good, a quality that on occasion can also be a property of acts that should be roundly condemned? The answer to such questions can only be resolved, it seems, by first offering some form of clear and justifiable "definition" of courage and then seeing whether the definition requires any and every courageous act to fulfill universal or only occasional normative requirements of goodness or excellence.

Such a quest for definition could be misleading. After all, if courage has to do with the handling, absence, or overcoming of the emotion of fear, perhaps an empirical, psychological account of it should be attempted rather than a peremptory normative or ethical analysis. Could courage be impelled by a characteristic motive of determination to conquer adverse circumstances, or a volition, a powerful will, to contend with danger? Psychologists, however, have never isolated any motive that corresponds to courageous behavior,[4] and philosophers are not inclined to regard volitions, or inner urges, as respectable explanations of human action.[5] It was once thought that the will was an internal impulse that could serve to explain behavior, in particular, voluntary human actions, but the lack of any empirical or conceptual account of such a force has led contemporary theorists to largely abandon volitional theories of mind.

Could courage then be defined in a more circumspect and negative way as simply the absence of fear? As we will see, the overwhelming problem with this approach is that the act of the foolish and reckless person who is entirely oblivious to a very dangerous impending situation would have to be defined as courageous. This is not in itself a promising approach. Perhaps, then, courage is some sort of positive response to a dangerous or fear-inducing situation. Instead of being motivated by the emotion of fear, however, the courageous person is driven forward by anger or a daring aggressiveness. Even if we must give up the idea of a unique courage-causing volition or motive, some violent emotion or passion such as anger can perhaps be associated with it as a characteristic.

A nice distinction made by Aristotle is that between the truly courageous action and the act produced by pain or anger.[6] Aristotle's conception of courage requires that the agent have a noble goal and that he use practical reasoning to obtain it. The person who acts in a rage is driven by passion—not at all by clearheaded practical reasoning—and therefore, by Aristotle's definition, his act could not be courageous even if his anger drives him to accomplish a fearful deed. Moreover, although the action might have favorable consequences, if carried out in the heat of anger or pain, it cannot have been done for the sake of a noble goal. There is no element of purposive reasoning to intentionally bring about a good end if the act is perpetrated in a blind rage. Such an act might seem brave, but by Aristotle's definition—and by the account I will subsequently offer—it cannot be accounted a truly courageous action. Putting aside for the moment the finer points of definition, could Aristotle be partially right in that at least sometimes acts of courage are characterized by cool deliberation rather than hot-blooded impulse? Once again, Hemingway's characterization of courage as grace under pressure would seem to capture the Aristotelian model.

An interesting counterbalance to the presumption that courageous acts are violent, eruptive acts of daring or bloodletting is the reflection that the most inspiring acts of courage may be both calm and benevolent. Reverend John Foote, V.C., saved the lives of many wounded men while continually exposing himself to heavy fire during the terrible fight at Dieppe on August 19, 1942. According to the description with his citation, Reverend Foote's example inspired all around him: "Those who observed him state that the calmness of this heroic man as he walked about, collecting the wounded on the fire-swept beach, will never be forgotten" (Swettenham 1973:173). At the end of the engagement, instead of staying with the evacuating landing craft, he courageously walked to the German position, voluntarily allowing himself to be taken prisoner so that he could look after those destined for prisoner-of-war camps.

Psychologists have noted that a major determinant of fear in combat is the example of others—both fear and calmness are contagious.[7] Thus, an example of calm behavior under fire can have a very powerful effect on group behavior. Calmness or coolness is also a hallmark of practical reasoning in a bad situation. Contrary to some initial presumptions, calmness rather than violent rage may therefore be more characteristic of the courageous act.

The other striking characteristic of Reverend Foote's exemplary conduct is altruism: he continued to risk his life to help those in need. Such an altruistic purpose is one of the strongest marks of the nobility of, and is characteristic of, the courageous act.[8]

This case is particularly striking because of the contrast it evokes. A man calmly and capably went about his work of ministering to those in need in the midst of what surely was one of the more vicious and desperate battles of the war. Courage is not always driven by rage or violent emotion.

The Greek view of courage embodied in the accounts of Plato[9] and Aristotle takes the courageous person as one who engages in thoughtful, practical deliberation and coolly acts in the way that is calculated to most successfully achieve his noble purpose in a particular situation. This conception may seem overly coldblooded or intellectualistic by current preconceptions. Many of us probably equate courage, at least initially, more with bold and even violently passionate action that is conducted as a bold and rapid response to a dangerous situation rather than through calculated reflection. This passionate model of courage found its official exponents in more modern times. Two nineteenth-century writers, Thomas Carlyle and Friedrich Nietzsche, adopted a philosophy of heroic vitalism constructed around a courageous hero of lightning and frenzy, a man of bold actions based on a will to power.

Carlyle, striking a pre-Freudian note, believed in the primacy of the unconscious and, in his theory of action, exalted intuition above reason. Carlyle thought of a crude, directive mass of energy as being the mainspring of human motivation, a sort of "mental volcano" (see Bentley 1969:57). This was coupled with a Social Darwinism that suggested courageous action should be bold and aggressive striving. Nietzsche also postulated as a moral model a superman who sacrifices pleasure for the sake of greater power. Like Carlyle, he felt that the

Christian virtues of charity, meekness, forgiveness, and patience are stagnant or decadent models of virtuous action. Rather, the heroic vitalist superman should be bold, proud, and hard, something like a bright and violent explosion of creativity. Thus, on both these views, courage seems to be equated with bold determination and a frank confrontation of the fearful, rather than cool calculation or careful judgment. In many ways, however, Nietzsche's position stressed reason as opposed to unconscious striving. Nietzsche was struck by the dangers of the Darwinian analogy between man and animal. The kind of competition he viewed as the will to power included artistic creation and intellectual achievement. The end of morals is power—but a power of creative activity. Hence rationality and dignity, the need to rise above the level of the animals, is a necessary aspect of Nietzsche's will to power.

Schacht (1983:324) notes that for Nietzsche, spirituality arises out of the ferocity and anarchy of the instincts when they are "taught new employments." Thus, in man, the animal drives of ferocity and anarchy are spiritualized into the development of traits of shrewdness, clarity, and logicality. Hence Nietzsche is not an irrationalist: we need reason to sublimate our animal impulses into an analytical instrument of the will to power.

Nietzsche's aphoristic style of writing led to many interpretations of his philosophy which equated it with Carlyle's cruder philosophy of Social Darwinism and exaltation of intuition unshackled by reason. Although there may be some basis for such a comparison, it seems quite wrong to interpret Nietzsche as a philosopher who glorified political power or power in a physical sense. On the contrary, Nietzsche is a strong advocate of moral or spiritual courage, integrity, and independence of rational thought. It is Carlyle's conception of courage, not Nietzsche's, that should properly be contrasted by the Greek view of courageous action.

2.2 The Two Views Compared

Though there is some basis for the Carlyle conception of courage in the way we do evaluate acts of courage, there are also contrary cases, even military ones, where altruism and charity are the qualities that appear to make the act so remarkably courageous. The heroic vitalist conception is egoistically oriented to the overpowering will of the agent. But as we saw in the case of Reverend Foote, altruism is sometimes more the mark of courage.

One of the ennobling aspects of an act of courage is that it brings us out of ourselves and transcends our usual motives for self-concern and self-protection. Sometimes characteristic of a courageous act is an almost casual lack of ordinary concern for oneself in the preoccupation with others or external circumstances. Indeed, psychological research (see Rachman 1978) suggests that diversionary activities or preoccupations in the face of perceived danger has a fear-reducing effect. Certainly, acts that we perceive as being remarkably courageous are often linked with a quality of disregard for self.

Andrew C. Mynarski, remaining alone with a tail gunner in a burning Lancaster bomber over Cambrai on June 12, 1944, was so preoccupied by his efforts to free the trapped gunner that he paid no attention to the flames consuming his own clothing and parachute. Eventually, after the tail gunner indicated nothing more could be done, he reluctantly went back through the flames to bail out. "There, as a last gesture to the trapped gunner, he turned towards him, stood to attention in his flaming clothes and saluted, before he jumped out of the aircraft" (Swettenham 1973:183). Strangely, although Mynarski later died from his burns, the tail gunner, Flying Officer George Patrick Brophy, survived the crash, and lived to give an account of the incident.

What was particularly courageous about Mynarski's act? He failed in what he tried to do, and it might even be said that he acted unwisely in so delaying his exit to try to save one other person. What is most moving to me is precisely this evident disregard for his own person in his concern for his trapped friend. The tail turret is a lonely place to die and is feared by many airmen as a place to be in combat. The selfless sympathy that drew this man to his trapped comrade so dominated his quite reasonable and legitimate interests in his own fate that one cannot help but be drawn strongly to him. A heroic disregard for self is the best way to describe his act.

Other cases also suggest that courage is not merely bold determination or the aggressive attack fueled by violent volitions. Sergeant Erwin's feat—saving his crew by throwing a burning bomb from the plane—was accomplished by keeping a remarkably cool head in a frightfully dangerous and painful situation that would drive most of us to despair. His act was accomplished through keeping his composure, and carefully and practically reasoning his way through a difficult, tricky procedure. That called for the highest kind of courage, in my view, and his act was certainly not characterized by a bold, aggressive, and fearless onrush fueled by hot-blooded emotion. On the contrary, it was his cool deliberation of action in this most terrible and hopeless situation that makes his act so admirable and remarkable as a virtuous and exemplary feat of valor.

Carlyle's notion of courage as violent boldness of action is simply off the mark in this sort of case. Though Sergeant Erwin's action was certainly bold, or at least showed a willingness to do something nearly all of us would shrink from, valor is more than just whatever boldness was shown by this act. There are other qualities that make for the act's special courage. The fact that he cared enough about saving the aircrew to carry out such a fearful job, deliberately, at terrible injury to himself is surely important. Carlyle's view of courage seems to be very one-sided at best, and seems to miss the important points about acts of great valor.

To a certain extent, Carlyle retained elements of the Greek conception of courage. In his view the courageous man is pragmatic in that he recognizes facts squarely and acts boldly. However, there the parallel with the Greek view ends. Whereas the Greek view emphasized moderation, caution, reflection, and temperate practical judgment, Carlyle equated courageous action with intuition as opposed to analytical reasoning, and stressed speed and boldness of judgment. According to a series of lectures given in 1838 (see Bentley 1969:24), Carlyle thought Socrates to be "the emblem of the decline of the Greeks" and castigated his "wire-drawn notions about virtue." Carlyle concluded that the healthiest periods of history are those of action, not those of thought.

However, even in some of the most remarkable cases of military courage which initially suggest bold aggressiveness, when more soberly considered, may also illustrate someone acting with practical resourcefulness in the face of a desperate situation. Rather than someone boldly or unthinkingly charging ahead, the picture is one of somebody being stuck in a bad situation and helping his platoon or company out of that situation by an unusually effective but also bold response. What may initially seem simply like a bold, emotional, intuitive burst of action may really be a skillful and deliberate response to a desperate emergency.

Courage is a response to dangerous or difficult circumstances. Real danger often appears suddenly, and sometimes a particular person is singled out by the circumstances as a kind of pivot point in a volatile situation. On his action defeat or victory, good or evil, may depend. Occasionally, in such a situation a person singled out may respond not only effectively but also heroically, far beyond what anyone would or should expect. Because such a person can be singled out as a pivot point by circumstances not in his making or control, courage is sometimes—contrary to what some claim—a highly democratic virtue. These people do not have glory "thrust upon them," at least entirely, for it is their reaction to the situation, coming from within, that shapes the hard circumstances thrust at them.

A bitter firefight developed around three farm buildings held by German troops at Mooshof, Germany, February 25, 1945. During confused fighting with many casualties, Sergeant Aubrey Cosens took command of the four survivors of his platoon, his officer also having been killed. Covered by his platoon, he arranged to follow a tank that burst through the side of the farmhouse. Despite desperate fire from the German defenders, he plunged through the hole created by the tank and shot his way from room to room, clearing the farmhouse. Seeming invulnerable, "Cosens charged the second and third buildings alone, routing the defenders despite a hail of machine gun and small arms [fire]" (Swettenham 1973:193). After the action, on his way to report, he was shot by a sniper and died instantly. Cosens was awarded the Victoria Cross posthumously.

What stands out in this description of Cosens's actions is not only the determination to take the position and the practical execution of the undertaking but also the extraordinary response of one man in a desperate emergency.

Many military citations for courage in combat do conform to the Carlyle-Nietzsche model of the soldier who suddenly attacks in a violent frenzy, risking almost certain death to boldly rush forward and kill remarkable numbers of the opposing troops. In one characteristic example of this sort, a soldier stood up in full view of enemy troops and steadily advanced while firing. Disregarding the bullets that flew around him, he steadily advanced, eventually killing more than twenty of the enemy soldiers. With rifle fire and grenades, he continued his apparently suicidal assault and somehow survived while succeeding in routing the entire enemy position. For this act, he received a citation for conspicuous courage beyond the call of duty.

But was this act truly courageous? Here is where I begin to question the wisdom of those who judge and evaluate citations for courage. This particular action could have been courageous if its results were particularly significant and if the intention of the attacking soldier was to bring about these significant consequences. Let us suppose that his intention was to stem the flow of casualties caused by repeated assaults on a position where the attack had been stalled for many days. In war, it is well known to strategists that the element of surprise can be very important. By this line of argument, one could claim that this one-man surprise attack was truly courageous.

But need it have been so? It all depends on the intention of the soldier who boldly attacked. If he acted from rage, boredom, violent revenge, or a lust for heroism, I would not be inclined to think his action truly courageous in the proper moral sense of the term. Some citations of heroism in combat are in fact filled with bloodthirsty claims of derring-do such as he "blasted the enemy," "emptied his carbine into so-and-so," or "killed thirty-five Japs," reminiscent of the best juvenile comic-book language. I think that is unfortunate, for it demeans courage as a moral quality. Moreover, I think that it is just where this Carlyle-Nietzsche conception of the "bold attack" gets hold that this sort of homicidal language begins to get linked with courage or bravery of actions.

Sometimes, for example, in military citations for courageous acts, it is stated that the morning after the attack, such-and-such a number of dead enemy troops were found around this man's position. Is this meant merely as evidence of the desperation of the struggle, or is it really a glorification of the power to kill? I am very suspicious about such bloodthirsty reporting of actions, and find negative implications.

Any claim of heroism is, by its nature, intrinsically open to the suspicion that a person acted from wrong motives, for example, desire for fame. Bold violence of action is not always courageous. Much depends on a person's intentions in acting.

In both Carlyle's and Nietzsche's doctrine that the vitalistic hero is above conventional morality there is a rejection of Christian morality and a glorification of power for its own sake. This form of success worship and hero worship can be a very dangerous doctrine politically. It is contrary to democratic ideals and, as its critics have alleged, may have contributed to the rise of the Nazi movement in Germany.[10] Any form of hero worship can be dangerous because there is a tendency to substitute emotional urges for rational thinking and practical deliberation. Such a substitution can entail a sort of thoughtlessness or mental anesthesia. Instead of asking oneself, Is this act truly good or worthwhile? one may instinctively follow a role model that embodies questionable, but emotionally appealing values. Youth are particularly susceptible to graphically drawn images of power or domination over others embodied in fictional or historical role models. The political use of such models to gain popular support for aggressive foreign policies is well known.[11]

What can be objected to in Carlyle's exaltation of courage as a blind vitalistic force is its embodiment of what might be called the barbaristic view of courage. According to this probably quite common conception, courage is typified by violent acts of bloodshed perpetrated in rage or revenge, the base element or motivation being a kind of aggrieved truculence culminating in a burst of aggressiveness—the "incredible hulk" reaction.[12] If this is one's definition of courage, or at least the intuition behind it, then of course courage is an unworthy quality that should not even be tolerated, much less encouraged or exalted. But is that how a civilized society should define courage? I do not think so, and the argument of this book is toward a rejection of such a definition of courage.

The Carlyle view made courage out to be something that could be quite bad, whereas Aristotle's account makes it so that courage must, by definition, be a good thing. Such an opposition suggests that the project of defining courage contains a fundamental problem. If the definition is to have normative force in deciding ethical issues of what acts are truly courageous, how can we build a normative requirement into the definition without begging the question, unfairly pulling ourselves up by our normative bootstraps? By defining courage as a good thing, Aristotle seems to preclude a negatively normative evaluation of his own definition. We return to this problem subsequently.

2.3 Courage as a Heroic Quality

Urmson (1958) distinguishes between saints and heroes. An act is *saintly* if it is a case of duty done through abnormal self-control in a context in which most men would not do the right thing, being led astray by self-interest or inclination. An act is *heroic* if it is a case of duty done through abnormal self-control in a context in which most men would be led astray by fear or a drive for self-preservation. Presumably, what we have been calling "courageous action" would be equivalent to what Urmson calls "heroic action." By Urmson's account, then, both saintly and heroic acts are matters of unusual self-control, only the drive to thwart each being characteristically different.

Where Urmson's account of heroic acts differs from the usual is in allowing for the heroic deed par excellence, the supererogatory act. In addition to calling a person saintly or heroic because he does his duty in difficult contexts where most would fail, as above, he adds that we may also call a person a saint or hero in an "above-the-call-of-duty" sense. There is the heroic action of the doctor who does his duty by staying with his patients in a city with plague. But there is also the case of the doctor who volunteers to join the medical team in that city. The difference Urmson has in mind is akin to the difference between the Military Medal and the Victoria Cross (ibid., p. 202).

Notable here is the thesis that courage is *heroic* if the courageous act is beyond the requirements of the duty of the agent in a situation. Many courageous acts are done in the line of duty, where doing one's duty may be very dangerous or difficult. But there are supererogatory actions that may be too difficult or dangerous to require anyone to do as an expected duty.

Sometimes the line between duty and what lies beyond expected duty is elusive and hard to fix precisely. But in some situations, the participants are quite clear on where the line is drawn. In one Victoria Cross citation, a navy pilot pursued his determination to persist with close-aiming the delivery of a bomb under antiaircraft fire from a ship, beyond the degree his comrades expected or required of him. In this instance, he went beyond the requirements of duty in order to secure his end of disabling or destroying this ship. His act was therefore courageous, but in the heroic dimension. He took a risk that pilots were not expected to in this situation, although, of course, normal expectations demanded an incredibly high risk.

The pilot in this case, Robert H. Gray, was attacking a destroyer through a cone of defensive fire from the ship and from shore. According to the description from Swettenham (1973:199), this pilot's action of holding his Corsair aircraft on course while it was being ripped apart by shells, right up to a distance of fifty feet from the destroyer, was "beyond the limits of ordinary courage." The point made is that it would have been quite acceptable for Gray to have released his bombs from a safer altitude even though the chances of hitting the target would not have been nearly as great. No doubt the pilots themselves had a fairly precise idea of just how close one would have been expected to go in this situation.

The presumption that courageous acts are sometimes good acts that are nevertheless beyond the requirement of duty is not a problem for moral philosophy except for those theories, like Kant's, that rule that all and only morally good acts are ones that conform to duty. According to Kant's view (1785:67), conduct only has real moral worth if it conforms to the requirements of duty and if done from duty. Kant's theory proposes that an action done from any other motive or inclination than duty, however benevolent or amiable, has no real moral worth. For Kant, the real moral weight of the action must be sought in the "maxim" or policy of which the act is an instance. Thus Kant thinks of virtues like courage as mere accoutrements of popular morality with no serious weight in ethical theory. Whether an act is done from a courageous motive is for Kant no true indication of its moral worth, as such.

We will see ultimately, however, that courage is not itself a motive.[13] Hence it is quite possible that a courageous act might be done out of duty in some instances. Perhaps the reason Kant tends to denigrate courage as a moral quality is that courage is not itself an end of action. Rather "courageous" is a property of how an act is brought about. 'Courageously', the adverb modifying a verb that conveys some human action, refers to the way or manner in which the act is brought about. Kantian ethics, however, regards the rightness of acts exclusively in terms of the end of the act, the manner of carrying out an act being secondary or even morally trivial.

But is such an approach consistent with the way we do and should evaluate human conduct? I will argue that it is not. Sometimes the fact that a certain objective was realized with cool practicality in a tight situation is a mark of our commendation. What we commend is how the action was carried out—the manner of its execution in the circumstances. Such evaluations may be more a part of practical than theoretical ethics. But I will argue they are legitimate ethical judgments.

Prichard (1912:59) also sees morality and virtue as independent. A virtuous act, by Prichard's account, must be done willingly or with pleasure, not from a sense of obligation but from a good desire or emotion. Thus, Prichard defines a courageous act as one where the agent prevents himself "from being dominated by a feeling of terror, desiring to do so from a sense of shame at being terrified" (ibid., p. 60). This definition is an interesting departure from the modern trend of defining courage negatively as absence of fear, since a positive motive of shame is identified as a defining characteristic.

However, the definition, presuming that is what it is meant to be, is a dubious one. For many an act of courage cannot fairly be described as having been committed exclusively (or even partly) from a motive of shame. Indeed, in actions of heroic virtue, there should be no shame involved at all in forgoing such an act. Had Gray not descended to such a level of proximity to ensure the destruction of his target, there would have been no shame in fulfilling his duty of attacking from the expected level.

Courage thus may not be a matter of ethical theory defined as the evaluation of moral ends in Kant's sense. Nor should courage be defined as some sort of moral or psychological motive. Rather, courage has to do with the practical deliberations and actions utilized to carry out the action in question. It is a question of practical ethics. Courage is sometimes in conformity to duty, sometimes in acts beyond duty. The true morality of the courageous act resides, however, in how its normatively positive end was carried out. Thus the proposition that courageous acts can be beyond duty, I will argue, can be accommodated to moral philosophy.

Too much of an insistence on the "letter" in matters of responsibility, as with rights, can be unproductive, divisive, and not a sign of moral correctness. Walking along a street in Auckland, I saw an elderly gentleman who had stopped his car in the middle of the road to pick up his fellow bowls player whom he noticed walking along the sidewalk. It was evident that both were going to the bowling tournament down the street—both were fully dressed in white in the customary form for lawn bowling. A young man in the car behind (with a surfboard on it) was held up by this quite needless obstruction of traffic while the other elderly gentleman got into the car. I looked at the face of the young man in the other car to see if he might be irritated, but his expression was one of genial tolerance. The elderly man was in the wrong, for he could have easily pulled over closer to the curb in front of the parked car he was adjacent to. But the young man did not insist on the point, and I thought that he showed an admirable moral quality of tolerance by his easy conduct.

It could be for reasons based on the intuition of this sort of observation that Heyd (1982) is led to conclude that there is more to morality than the morality of duty. Heyd remarks that even if a society could survive where its members strictly adhered to all the rules of behavior but never went beyond those rules—for example, by generous conduct, not strictly required—this society would somehow be morally deficient. "Our objection to such a society is analogous to our judgment of an individual who never forgives, who is never charitable in his dealings with others, and who always and without exception insists on his rights" (ibid., p. 179). Goodwill and benevolence need not be strictly matters of rights and duties.

2.4 *The Hero as a Moral Model*

The foregoing discussion may conceal an important ambiguity. While it is true that the terms 'heroic' and 'courageous' often overlap, and may even be used equivalently in some contexts, we should also consider them separately. Can an action be courageous without necessarily being heroic? Can a person be a hero on grounds other than courage? It would seem so, in both cases. For example, a child could be courageous in not crying and maintaining a dignified composure during a difficult or painful medical treatment. We might not say this was heroic or that the child is a hero, although we might not be inclined to strongly deny it either. Albert Einstein's scientific achievements were heroic, and he remains a hero for scientists, even though his scientific achievements were not necessarily courageous actions. Once again, however, we might not want to deny that Einstein's dedication to science involved a kind of courage.

We are working toward an analysis of courage, but what should we say about trying to define the concept of a hero? Is a hero a sort of person, or should we more properly speak of heroic actions?

Although courage is primarily an attribute of actions, so I argue, heroism is primarily an attribute of persons. At least, on balance, I am inclined to argue this way, even though there are many difficulties and uncertainties in trying to formulate a morally adequate conception of the hero. I think the best conception is that the hero is the person who has formulated and followed his own special ideal of conduct, or high standard of conduct, or at least carried out that ideal of conduct in his actions. The hero has carved out a certain stance or position, and then individually lived up to this level of aspiration in a way that others can admire without necessarily following.

The hero's code or ideal is thus individualized to himself. Others are not bound to follow it, though they may admire the hero's dedication. This does not mean that the heroic individual is a law to himself, that he can violate the petty rules set for lesser persons, or something of that sort. The general codes of morality he follows are the same as those set for everyone. However, the individual rightly perceived as heroic is the one who follows the dictates of his standards of morality beyond the point where anyone could be excused for falling back. In so venturing, however, the heroic person may, in some sense, be setting higher standards. Hence he may be asked to defend the reasonableness of his conduct, to justify his unusual stance. The riskiness and contingency of heroic action is reflected in the expression "taking a stand." Moral action based on one's personal values and perception of a situation defines a position that can be challenged.

Carlyle speculated that each age must find a hero in order to prevent its civilization from falling into moral chaos and destruction. Yet, if Aristotle is right that "courage" is defined by its end, as an act of noble purpose, then how each civilization views its conception of the good will be modeled in its chosen heroes. If this approach is correct, then it follows that chosen heroes can fulfill the important function in a civilization of cementing together the dominant moral values that guide its members' beliefs and actions. By the same token, a decadent society would presumably choose "heroes" that reflect its evil goals and values.

To say someone is a hero or a saint does seem to have some long-term implications over and above any single act carried out by that person. According to Beauchamp (1982:172), a saint must, as a requirement, have a character that consistently disposes him "to proper deeds over a long period of time." By contrast, Beauchamp thinks that a hero can become a hero "instantly," by a single act. Yet he concedes that we would be likely to deny that a person is either a saint or a hero if he was a person of bad character, or acted badly on other occasions.

In my view, the concept of heroism becomes very fuzzy and unwieldy once it is linked to long-term dispositions or habits and one is right to be skeptical about heroic persons, so conceived. Far better, I think, to view courageous actions or agents as models of excellence of conduct or personal merit. In the case of the attributions of a courageous person, I think that is best conceived as a matter of personal commitment or conviction, as expressed in one or several actions more fully documented by a biographical context. This biographical context is a matter of practical reasoning, not a matter of psychological dispositions or habits.

Beauchamp (ibid., p. 173) adds that it would be an error to think that saints and heroes are the only individuals who can serve as models of virtue. He suggests that a saint or hero is a person who possesses many virtues. However, parents or teachers could be, in many instances, good models of how to lead virtuous lives, without being saints or heroes.

Until we know more about what the virtues are, it is probably too soon to say very much about exactly what sort of person should best be considered a saint or hero. But I think the suggestion that a saint or hero is one who exhibits many virtues over a long period is probably not too far off the mark. Whatever saints and heroes are, they should be the upper strata of real-life models of excellence of conduct and personal merit.

As far as courage is concerned, it can be good to learn from real examples of courageous conduct as a moral model of excellence of action in dangerous or difficult situations. One problem with copying the actions or characteristics of a model, however, is that external features may be copied without the copier grasping the moral essentials of the situation or the issue. Hence critical reflection and practical judgment must be included as part of the "model" that is emulated or held up as an ideal. Thus the practical reasoning that is part of the documentation and description of any truly courageous act must not be left out. For courage is always a matter of practical judgment in how to respond to particular circumstances. No two sets of particular circumstances are ever perfectly identical. Hence there can be no rote procedure for emulating a model which will always lead a person to act courageously in any situation.

The kind of sustained critical reflection needed to perceive the best path of conduct in the complexities of real life tends to be better developed with the maturity of experience, however. Therefore, the notion that practical wisdom can sometimes be guided through critical discussion between those who are less and those who are more experienced in the difficulties of acting well or rightly in difficult situations is an idea that should be given serious weight. Sometimes, too, tradition in the form of literature, biography, folklore, and so forth, is an important way of passing on the moral insights of practical wisdom from one generation to another. Thus the thesis that one can learn about courage as a virtue through real-life models of exemplary conduct—when properly qualified—has a reasonable basis of justification.

2.5 The Pitfalls of Heroism

In a skeptical and morally relativistic age, we may scoff at heroes as quixotic or impractical idealists. The "Greatest American Hero" is a sort of superman who bungles, who is earnest and tries to do right, but who is always crashing into buildings or being taken for a mentally disturbed person.[14] Yet, in the end, despite his frailties, he does achieve good results. Perhaps this could be a healthy recognition that nobody is perfect. Perhaps too it could be that North Americans are not willing to recommend altruism too wholeheartedly and are suspicious of anyone who seems to claim to be superior to others. Whatever the precise sociological lessons of heroism, we can be assured that a society's choice of heroes is by no means morally trivial.

Perhaps one reason heroism seems discreditable or suspicious is that the curiously arbitrary way the "hero" seems to be selected for popular attention discriminates against many ordinary, unnoticed persons whose acts are equally or more courageous, but may be "undramatic." Nadia Lindner makes a thoughtful point: "When I think of heroes, I think of someone who quit drinking after twenty years of being an alcoholic, or another who managed to rise above a rotten childhood. People who have been heroes in their own private way."[15] In fact, examples like these may require outstanding, truly heroic determination and self-control, with very beneficial results for society. It has sometimes been said that the greatest medical problem in North America is drug abuse. If more individuals had more self-control and courage of personal conduct, imagine the impact for society on this sort of important problem. However, because examples of this sort of "private courage" are not conspicuously altruistic or strikingly dramatic in their obvious effects, there is a tendency to overlook them, or even not perceive them as "courageous."

Imagine awarding a medal to someone who has quit drinking after being an alcoholic, or to someone who has overcome an unhappy childhood. Most people would probably scoff at such an award, since the "courageous" person selected would probably seem somewhat inferior, as opposed to the superior type of person we like to equate with "courageous" or "heroic." I am suggesting then that we should rethink this sort of judgment and try to resist an uncritical tendency to acquiesce in the *pedestal effect* in our choice of heroes. Because heroism, as it is publicly perceived, tends to draw people together, the tendency is to seek out an idol whose acts or personal attributes have exclusively positive qualities, or qualities that are perceived to be positive by the whole group. This pedestal effect may, however, result in a somewhat capricious choice of heroes, excluding those who may not appeal for some adventitious reason that should really not count for much in our correct assessment of their deed.

At any rate, this effect may serve as one good explanation for our tendency to be suspicious of, or skeptical about, heroes who receive a lot of publicity. What I am suggesting is that such skepticism may in some cases be quite morally justifiable, given the possible fallacies inherent in the selection process that seems to be operative.

Indeed, there is a danger of the *ad populum* fallacy implicit in the selection of popular heroes. This fallacy consists in the inference to the conclusion that a proposition is true, based on the premise that everyone believes that it is true.[16] But "everyone's belief" can change, or be found erroneous, and hence no popular belief can be sacrosanct —not even judgments of popular heroism. Hitler was once perceived as a popular hero by the German people, certainly at least by many of them. That perception was subsequently shown to be incorrect. Napoleon, now evidently considered heroic, was once thought despicable. The point is that *belief* in heroes may be more a function of popular taste than moral justification.

Another possible explanation of present-day cynicism about heroic courage concerns the media and mass popularity. One way, it seems, to achieve good in a democratic society is to mobilize public opinion and support behind your cause. Any conspicuous act carried out possibly for a good end, however, often has a way of getting caught up in such a massive groundswell of media coverage that the original purpose of the act may become difficult to evaluate. Did the person really do it for altruistic reasons, or in the crush of all that publicity, can we not help but suspect a wish for adulation or attention? Moreover, any act undertaken to mobilize public support runs the risk of being the very sort of *ad populum* appeal that is normally the very opposite of moral courage, the courageous opposition to popular pressure to "go along" with the morally dubious proposition. What the broad public immediately recognizes as a conspicuously courageous act may tend to reflect the gut emotional appeal of a superficial patriotism or some other "glamorous" aspect, rather than any deep moral worth of the act. Once an act becomes so highly publicized, it seems to become harder and harder to reach any clear evaluation of its true moral worth.

Ken Taylor, the Canadian ambassador in Iran, became a hero overnight by taking six fugitive Americans into the Canadian embassy during the time that American embassy staff were being taken hostage in Iran. Was this an act of heroism? It was certainly an act of courtesy and duty, and as such is highly commendable. The public response, the awards and so forth, subsequent to the event in the United States, certainly suggested the act had heroic status. Taylor himself modestly denied it, however, claiming that he did what he had to do professionally and instinctively, in the line of duty. Perhaps it was a courageous act, but one suspects that the massive groundswell of public attention that lifted this man to the status of a popular hero may have been as much due to the fact that the act fulfilled a kind of ideological need of the moment than to an outstanding courage that prompted it. It is hard to say, however, how history will judge such acts in the future.

In the case of the Terry Fox Marathon of Hope there seems to be a good case for a courageous act. For those who may not know, Fox was a young man suffering from cancer who set out, with an artificial leg, on a run across Canada. Although he failed to reach his destination, his act took truly outstanding determination in formidably difficult circumstances, and achieved a notable mobilization of public support for cancer research and treatment. Moreover, Fox seemed to be a sincere man who was doing his best in a very bad situation in which most people would give up. He didn't have to do what he did—his act was beyond any requirement of duty—and that makes its valor even greater.

But it is hard not to be a little skeptical about the public reaction to his actions. The whole idea of an appealing young person under the threat of death running a countrywide marathon on an artificial leg is one of such a massive, popular emotional impact that one wonders: Why did so many people find it so notably courageous? What nerve did it touch? Can we analyze it by means of an evaluation of the purpose of the act and the difficulty of the circumstances? We recall that the means to the end of raising funds for cancer was precisely the mobilization of public contributions attained through publicity of the act. At least one takes it that this was the noble purpose of the act, not just reaching Vancouver in the marathon run. But, perhaps more important, Fox's purpose could have been victory over himself, a quest for inner excellence. This very personal type of intention is hard to evaluate, precisely because of its elusive and subjective quality. Perhaps the attempt to do something, anything, in the face of a remorseless and unbeatable disease is courageous.

The intense spotlight of public scrutiny and personal emotion of certain acts makes their evaluation more difficult. And that, I think, is why as a counterpart to exaltation of these public personages, there is also an element of public cynicism about them. The word 'hero' has even become used in a derogatory way by some, to refer to someone who purposely seeks public attention whether for honorable motives or not. This usage is by no means salutary, but one can see the reason for skeptical or cynical responses to courage when it gets swept up in the massive but sometimes superficial coverage of modern communication systems.

One problem with the pedestal effect is that it demands perfection of the hero. Yet, as Aristotle observed, a man may be virtuous in one way while not being particularly virtuous in another, for example, the courageous man may be intemperate. Perhaps it is even less misleading to talk of courageous acts rather than courageous persons. That is, while courage may be a general character trait of some individuals, it is quite possible that even a person who is courageous may occasionally act in a cowardly fashion. However, the very same individual act of one person surely cannot be both courageous and cowardly.[17]

Even more strictly speaking, it may be better to say that some individual act-description cannot be both cowardly and courageous. For example, Smith's pulling the trigger may have been courageous—he was trying to defend his family—but his shooting Jones may not have been courageous at all, since it was accidental and he was really trying to shoot Robinson. The problem indicated here is that different descriptions of the same act may have different properties of moral accountability.[18]

As soon as we try to extrapolate from the courageousness of a single act, or description of that act, to the general courageousness of some individual as a heroic model of courage, we run into many pitfalls and fallacies. The tendency to aggrandizement has an obvious appeal, but runs the risk of becoming preposterous. No man is a hero to his valet, it is said, and given the kind of ubiquitous investigative reporting of public figures today, it is easy to uncover the feet of clay.

Although a certain distrust or skepticism about "courageous heroes" is no doubt at times a healthy attitude and a properly inquisitive moral stance, if it is carried to the point of a wholesale denigration of courage as a value, a moral weakening can result. Such a weakening, often accompanied by statements of moral relativism, can function as an excuse for immoral or asocial conduct. For example, a pregnant woman might decide that the pain, danger, and sacrifice of carrying her pregnancy to term is an inconvenient and therefore negatively "heroic" act.

A "courageous hero" may be defined as a person who has committed a courageous act, or better, someone who has shown a consistent disposition to act courageously over a period of time. Dispositions are long-term properties, however, so a person could be courageous with respect to one action and then later demonstrate cowardice in another instance. It is therefore simpler and better to concentrate first on defining 'courageously' as a property of a single action. Even if an act is heroically courageous, then, it need not follow that the agent is a "courageous hero" in the sense of being always or usually disposed to act courageously.

The problem of maintaining the proper critical perspective on heroes and acts of courage can only ultimately be solved by embedding a theory of practical reasoning in a context of reasonable dialogue to justify an agent's position in acting. This means that the notion of moral virtue must be part of our conception of courage.

But we can certainly appreciate why the difficulty of keeping the proper perspective has led commentators to adopt the view that the hero is not a morally worthy person. For example, Hook (1943:153) wrote that "we must rule out as irrelevant the conception of the hero as a morally worthy man, not because ethical judgments are illegitimate in history, but because so much of it has been made by the wicked." Certainly, we can be wrong and misguided in choosing heroes for reasons that turn out to be superficial and, in some cases, morally open to criticism and refutation. But I do not think we need to abdicate to the untenable position that heroes should not be chosen or evaluated on moral grounds.

This leads us to the general problem of building a normative clause into any definition of courage. Since it is a central and recurring problem of this work, it is well to define its nature clearly at these early stages of the discussion: this is the problem of the courage of the villain.

2.6 Courage of the Villain

There appears to be fundamental disagreement about whether a good purpose in acting is an essential characteristic of a courageous act. Aristotle, and following him Aquinas, required a good end as one characteristic requirement of courage. Geach (1977:160) is also obdurate on this point, stipulating that an act of facing danger or affliction should not be called virtuous or courageous if done for a worthless or vicious cause: "Endurance or defiance of danger in pursuance of a wrong end is not virtuous and in my book is not courageous either." Von Wright (1963:53) takes the opposite side, claiming that a "self-regarding" virtue like courage is not necessarily useful from a neighbor's point of view: "The courage which burglars or robbers display can be much to the detriment of their neighbour's welfare." It is less clear where others stand on this issue, but it appears that some would tend to go to von Wright's side. Wallace (1978:78) requires only that the courageous person believe that what he does is "worth the risk it involves." This requirement would seem to allow an immoral aim in acting courageously, provided the agent thinks the act worth the risk.

One way out of the problem is to say that courage is not always virtuous. One might concede that although an act of villainy can never truly be a courageous act as such—exemplifying the virtue of courage—we might still say that a coolly executed act of villainy in the face of danger "took courage." This is the tack taken by Foot (1978). She argues that courage is a word that names a certain power like "solvent" or "corrosive." Arsenic is a poison, but that does not mean that it always acts as a poison wherever it is found. "Similarly, courage is not operating as a virtue when the murderer turns his courage, which is a virtue, to bad ends" (p. 16). Foot's position on this question is an interesting sort of compromise. An act of villainy, for example, murder, may "take courage," even if we hesitate to describe it as a "courageous act." Could we say that it is courageous in a certain respect only, without being fully characteristic of a courageous act?

In one way, we shall have to reject Foot's solution insofar as it takes as fundamental the notion of courage to be a character disposition. As noted in the previous section, we want to define 'courageously' as it applies to individual actions. In the end, however, we will adopt part of her suggestion by recognizing the distinction between an act that was done courageously and one that took courage to bring about.

Ultimately, however, this move by itself does not resolve the problem of the courage of the villain. For the fearless individual action of the burglar in extricating himself from a dangerous situation still leaves us with the dilemma of whether or not it can or should be called courageous. Only after developing a full definition of courage can we resolve this problem.

To consistently defend the requirement that a courageous act have a good end seems to involve us in more realistically troublesome cases than just the abstract problem of the "courageous burglar." If, to be courageous, an act must be done out of duty, be beyond duty, or at least be done for the clear purpose of the betterment of humanity, it is hard to see how we could truly call Sir Edmund Hillary's conquest of Everest courageous. However, given the risks and difficulties involved, most of us would be inclined to call it a courageous act, probably a highly courageous one at that. Perhaps this is only a reflection of our presumption that there is nobility in such a feat, or at least that the purpose of the act must have been good. No doubt rock climbers can at least try to explain to the rest of us precisely what this good purpose is.

There is quite a serious puzzle in trying to evaluate truly heroic acts like the climbing of Everest, skiing down Everest, and other notable feats of daring, skill, and achievement. They are truly heroic acts, in some sense, yet it may be difficult to discern a good or truly commendable intention in every case. One always wonders: could not the intention have been an egotistical need for individual attention, a wish for publicity and fame? Moreover, it is hard to justify an altruistic intent in such acts.

Is altruism always necessary for an act to be truly courageous? Are heroic acts always courageous? I think the answer to these two controversial questions is no. Even so, heroic acts such as the first ascent of Everest pose a problem. They do seem to be courageous, and are certainly called courageous. They are certainly dangerous and difficult. But what is their noble purpose?

The first answer is that the purpose of such an act could simply be the victory of the protagonist over himself. However, while I am sympathetic to this answer because I feel that self-discipline is intrinsically good, I do not find it sufficient. Instead of being engaged in an elusive victory over oneself one could be trying to do something more worthwhile. To me, such achievements pale beside those of the tireless medical researcher, one selflessly dedicated to cultural achievement, saving lives, or sacrificing one's own life to others in times of danger.

The second answer, which I find more convincing, is that we very often simply don't know the benefits (side effects) of an action. Space research, for example, has generated surprising benefits for medical technology and health research. Hence if we set out to do something very difficult, even if our intentions may not be too clear, sometimes the benefits can be better than anyone might expect. A challenge to do something difficult stretches abilities to their fullest, and that always seems to have remarkable benefits. So, choosing to do something very difficult should perhaps be called courageous even if the agent's intention is not too specific or conspicuously well intentioned other than the attempt to try something difficult. Perhaps when we gain a better idea of what courage is, some of these puzzles will be a little less opaque.

A definition of courage, then, could be useful in helping us to unravel and decide on realistic cases where we have difficulty in backing our arguments that an action is truly courageous or not. We often have disputes and conversations when trying to morally evaluate actions in order to decide just how commendable a certain act should be thought to be. In giving medals, citations, and other commendations, we must try not to be blinded by the morally superficial aspects of a situation, and clearly justify our feelings that a particular reported act is truly and properly courageous. Only some form of general definition of courage can make such arguments cogent or rationally defensible.

To pursue the definition of courage in ethics we are really asking how to justify courage as a good quality of actions if or when it is good. Can courage be intrinsically bad, or is it merely a good thing that can lead to bad results? Courage may seem to some an exotic, chivalrous, or purely military virtue of no utilitarian value in itself. Geach (1977:152) quite commendably points out, however, that without the courage and endurance of much of the workers of the mines and mills in the lumber and fishing industries no country could be built or continue to function. The value of courage, then, may be that it enables us to struggle with a difficult, less than perfect, and sometimes dangerous world. Fortunately for many of us, our favorable circumstances do not require that we act courageously to achieve our ends. But such a security can be illusory.

One noted problem in practical ethics today concerns dying in the institutional setting of a hospital, now a commonplace occurrence. Because of the ethical difficulties implicit in the unilateral withdrawal of life-support systems and aggressive technologies by hospital staff, patients must now be prepared to take some part in this type of decision. Walton's (1983) recent case studies show that in fact the best handling of such a process of decision making takes the courage of thoughtful deliberation by a patient who faces the greatest risk, even the certainty, of personal destruction. As Aristotle remarked, death is the most formidable risk, and therefore courage in the face of death is the highest form of courage. Thus courage may be needed by all of us, not only those in high-risk occupations, and is therefore not a quality to be lightly dismissed as of no utilitarian value to most of us.

Courage is one of those unfortunate qualities that only emerges or is necessary in circumstances of catastrophe, in the violent conflict of war or other bad situations. Some identify the evil circumstances with the quality needed to confront those circumstances, and mistakenly conclude that courage itself is an evil, that is not a positive virtue. It is as if anything connected with evil is tarred by the same brush.

Such an inference is incorrect. Courage is a quality that is found in a good human response to an evil situation. It thus flows from the free will of human agency bending itself to salvage some good from catastrophe. It is an unfortunate truth, often remarked on by theologians, that some kinds of goods must flow from evil. These are second-order goods, like the qualities of perseverence and resilience, that can only emerge from the trials of adversity. Thus it is often noticed that courage is a difficult virtue, and an unpleasant one for the unfortunate person who has to show it. Nothing in all this means, however, that the quality of courage is itself intrinsically bad. In one respect, courage is a nobler quality because its attainment must always be in difficult circumstances. To overcome difficulties and obstacles is a very human quality.

CHAPTER 3

Existing Accounts
of Courage

HERE SOME OF the best known and most promising attempts to define courage will be surveyed. Rather than conducting a historical survey of what philosophers have written about courage, which remains to be done, we shall simply try to gain some wisdom by looking at what are from our point of view some of the more suggestive and interesting proposals. In the end, they will all prove more or less inadequate to our purposes, but each of them, especially the two major attempts at a general definition, will give us much insight on how to proceed. Only two of the great philosophers, namely, Aristotle and Aquinas, have had a good deal to say of a constructive nature on attempting to define courage. Generally, the subject appears to have been neglected in moral philosophy.

What there is does, however, constitute a good basis for further inquiry. Indeed, Aristotle's discussion of courage seems so sensible and central that it would be hard to imagine a plausible normative analysis of courageous action that could deviate too much from his basic ideas. In fact, both my own analysis, in chapter 4, and Wallace's definition, studied below, are basically Aristotelian in their general flavor, although each sharply deviates from Aristotle's definition in certain respects. The same can be said of the account given by Aquinas.

3.1 Plato on Courage

The Platonic dialogue on courage, the *Laches*, begins with a conversation between Socrates and two generals, Nicias and Laches, on the art of fighting in armor. Eventually the subject gets around to courage, and Socrates asks the main question, What is courage? Laches' first answer (190e) is that the courageous man is one who does not run away, but stays and fights at his post. Socrates astutely questions the generality of this answer by pointing out that although it is the function of the heavily armed soldier in the line to fight from a fixed position and not run, the cavalry soldier "fights flying, instead of remaining." (191a).

Trying to be more general, Laches puts forward his second hypothesis (192c) that courage is a sort of endurance of the soul. Socrates responds that sometimes endurance can be foolish, and when Laches agrees that courage is noble, both of them turn to the hypothesis that courage may be defined as wise endurance. Socrates, however, points out by some further canny questioning that there may be some opposition between courage and wisdom. The skillful diver who descends into a well may be less courageous than the man who performs a similar act but has no skill in diving. Using a military example, Socrates puts the question as follows.

> Again, take the case of one who endures in war, and is willing to fight, and wisely calculates and knows that others will help him, and that there will be fewer and inferior men against him than there are with him, and suppose that he has also advantages in position—would you say of such a one who endures with all this wisdom and preparation that he or some man in the opposing army who is in the opposite circumstances to these and yet endures and remains at his post is the braver?[1]

Laches thinks that the foolish endurance is the more courageous, but, as Socrates reminds him, this answer contradicts their previous assumption that courage is a noble quality.

This dilemma is quite an interesting one. For if courage is a matter of practical reasoning and nice judgment, then how can the poor strategist who has got himself into a tight situation act courageously, even if he fights valiantly to get out of it?

Perhaps the dilemma can be resolved, to some extent, by specifying more precisely what the "act" consists of that is or is not alleged to be courageous. Getting into the tight situation may have been foolish—or at least not the result of good practical deliberation—but then getting out of the situation could be courageous. The problem only arises when the two actions are put together into one longer act-sequence: Was the action of both getting in and getting out, taken together, courageous or not?

The problem is analogous to the golfer who makes a bad shot and puts his ball in a sand trap, but then makes a brilliant shot from the trap onto the green. Was his play overall bad or good? The question may be an instance of the "many questions" fallacy, for example,

"Have you stopped beating your wife?" No matter how one answers, one is committed to something one doesn't like.[2] Certainly what is shown is that we have to be very careful in specifying how an action is described when we use the phrase "courageous act."[3]

Next, Nicias takes his turn and ventures a new definition: courage is the knowledge of the grounds of fear or confidence. Like the previous definition, this one makes courage a matter of practical reasoning. Socrates responds that such a doctrine could never allow that an animal could be courageous, since animals do not appear to have the power of practical reasoning. Nicias responds that there is a difference between courage and fearlessness, and that in his view animals can be fearless, but never courageous, because courageous actions are wise actions (197c). However, Socrates has pointed up a genuine difficulty of any account of courage as excellence of practical reasoning, for it is moot to what extent such an account can contend with the common view that animals can be courageous.

Concluding the dialogue, Socrates criticizes Nicias' view as being limited strictly to the future, for fear and confidence pertain, he argues, only to future events. As usual, the dialogue concludes with all three participants agreeing that they do not really know what courage is.

Although Plato has not offered a positive theory of what courage is, he has already voiced the opposition between the common view of courage as some sort of positive mental property of endurance and the Greek view of courage as practical reasoning. Moreover, he has indicated that practical reasoning is not just a matter of wisdom, experience, or purely technical skill, if the less experienced diver may be the more courageous. It is evidently some sort of skill that blends factual knowledge of a situation with moral qualities in reacting to that situation that is the mark of courage. Plato leaves us with the puzzle of how to characterize such a process of deliberation. An elaborate ethical theory encompassing precisely this notion is offered by Aristotle.

3.2 Aristotle on Courage

To fully understand Aristotle's definition of courage, it is useful to sketch the basic framework of Aristotle's ethical theory. This framework begins with the distinction between the means and the end (goal, aim, or purpose) of action. According to Aristotle (*Nicomachean Ethics* 1113b3), the good of man, the ultimate end of human action, is the use of his reasoning power in accord with virtue or excellence. Any action is properly accounted as virtuous only if, first, it has a good or noble end, and, second, it is thoughtfully carried out by the application of a man's reasoning in a particular situation, to carry out that end. Thus a courageous act must have a noble end, but the means is also crucial. To be truly courageous, an act must be reasoned out and executed thoughtfully and carefully by its agent.

Aristotle's ethical approach strikes an antiquated note to modern ears for two reasons. First, for Aristotle, courage and temperance are "virtues." The Greek concept of virtue, or trait of excellence in character, is one that has not survived in any clear or readily intelligible form in modern times, either in philosophy or the common parlance of ethical conversations. Whether it can or should be rescued is debatable.[4] Yet the notion that courage is strongly tied to our evaluation of the practical deliberations that go into the execution of a human action is very much worth preserving and investigating. The second reason Aristotle's approach seems antiquated is that the notion of purpose or goal, although implicit in much modern biological theory, is notoriously difficult to define with logical precision and often strikes the modern reader as a signal that any scientifically acceptable form of definition is foregone.

There is, however, much of interest in what Aristotle has to say about courage as a virtue. We begin by asking: What for Aristotle is the difference between the responsible action of an adult and the behavior of an infant or chimpanzee? Why is the action of an adult thought to be controllable by law or social convention in a way that the behavior of the infant or chimpanzee is not? The answer Aristotle would give is that the behavior of the infant or chimpanzee is motivated by drives or "passions," such as hunger or anger, but the voluntary action of a responsible adult can also be influenced or controlled by its own internal springs of activation. This internal monitoring of action involves the awareness of different possible consequences of a situation, awareness of a choice among these consequences, different ends worth attaining or avoiding that can be related to these possible alternative consequences, and a deliberate act of judgment to make a choice and act on it. This entire structure of mapping a particular situation onto an agent's mental choice-structure of deliberation in acting is called Aristotle's theory of practical reasoning.

In its simplest form, the structure of inference characteristic of practical reasoning is described below. A and B are events or states of affairs—it does not matter at this point which you prefer—that represent possible results of actions.

Unless I do A, I can't do B.

I want to do B.

Therefore, I must do A.

This type of reasoning, according to Aristotle, is a practical matter, a question of expediency, and therefore differs from scientifically exact reasoning. For there are no invariable laws of practical reasoning—instead, the kind of reasoning to be demanded varies with the subject at hand.[5]

According to Aristotle's ethical theory, practical reasoning is a matter of judgment and therefore requires a certain steering of the middle way between extremes. Courage, then, is a matter of practical judgment. The man who fears everything, whose fear is excessive, never makes a stand, and is a coward. The man who fears nothing at all, whose fear is nonexistent, will face up to any danger, and is therefore a fool, an idiot. Virtue, then, is a kind of moderation in one's deliberate course of action based on one's reasoned appreciation of the situation in question (*Nicomachean Ethics* 1106b36). The excellence of courage consists in the judgment that steers the perfect middle way between the extremes of excess confidence and deficiency of justifiable confidence produced by fear or hesitation.

Now we can proceed to Aristotle's definition of courage given in the *Nicomachean Ethics* at the beginning of Book III. *The courageous man is one who acts to fulfil a noble end in the face of truly fearful danger, yet moderates his fear appropriately to the danger of the situation.* There are

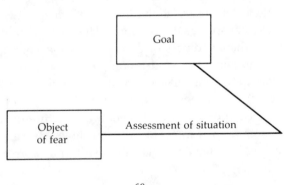

three requirements to this definition, each of which corresponds to an aspect of the agent's situation. Each of these three aspects requires certain elaboration. Above, we saw that Aristotle's model of practical deliberation involved several elements. The bottom box represents the particular situation as the agent perceives it. As indicated above, in the case of courage, the main fact to be confronted by the agent is a particularly dangerous or truly fearful situation. Thus the first requirement of Aristotle's definition of courage is this.

1. *Right Object:* the courageous man fears what he ought to fear. Aristotle comments on this requirement by, first, pointing out that there are things that we ought to fear, such as disgrace. It is honorable to fear disgrace, and ignoble not to fear it. However, there are other conditions, like poverty or disease, that we perhaps ought not to fear so much, because they do not tend to depend on our own conduct so much. The courageous man will experience fear—he is not an insensitive brute. He will fear disgrace of himself or his spouse or children. But he will not fear some minor pain or inconvenience, as a child might. Interestingly, Aristotle thinks that death is the most terrible thing for anyone to fear, and therefore the courageous man most nobly displays his quality in the face of death or an emergency that involves death.

2. *Right Manner:* the courageous man displays a fear appropriate to the danger. He regulates both his feeling of confidence and his action by his own reasonable assessment of the situation through practical deliberation. The person who is overconfident in the presence of a fearful thing is simply a fool, and often a braggart who blusters and makes a show of bravado but who does not really know where to take a stand. According to Aristotle (*Nicomachean Ethics* 1115b28), this sort of person tends to bluster as long as he is safe, but to run when the real danger comes. Overconfidence is not courage, but neither, of course, is underconfidence, displayed in an excess of fear. The coward is despondent and hopeless because he is frightened at everything. Courage, then, lies in the mean, or middle, way. As Aristotle puts it, "the courageous are keen in action, but quiet beforehand" (*Nicomachean Ethics,* 1116a6).

3. *Right Motive:* the courageous man acts to fulfill an end or motive that is noble. It is important for Aristotle that courage be a virtue or excellence, and therefore the purpose of a courageous act must be

truly good. Although there might be a certain resoluteness or other qualities in the man who confronts danger for an ignoble end, Aristotle would not call such an act "courageous." For example, to purposely seek death as an escape from poverty or other personal difficulties is, according to him, more the act of a coward than a brave man (*Nicomachean Ethics*, 1116a14). In such a case, Aristotle comments, the end is not a noble death but only an escape from one's problems. Aristotle's stand on the courageous villain issue is unequivocal.

This closes for now our outline of Aristotle's definition of courage. It is a very fundamental analysis, and of course much more remains to be said. We will return to further elaborations, refinements, criticisms, and discussions subsequently. Aristotle elaborates further on his analysis by outlining five types of action that are improperly called courageous even though they may initially seem so. Each of these five elaborations involves refinements that we need to return to in subsequent case studies.

Aristotle makes a point similar to Plato's suggestion[6] that the less experienced diver who accomplishes a task of diving similar in difficulty to that of the more experienced diver should be considered the more courageous of the two. Aristotle distinguishes between the truly brave soldier and the mercenary soldier whose boldness rests on his superior experience and skill in battle. The mercenary may seem more courageous, but actually the reason he seems cooler in battle is that he has less fear, because of his experience. If the mercenary sees what he thinks is real danger he will run, unlike the truly courageous man, who fights for honor, not money.

Having attained some grasp of the Aristotelian definition of courage, let us move on to outline several other accounts that introduce new variations on the same theme.

3.3 Aquinas on Courage

Aquinas gives an account of courage, translated as 'fortitude' by the Dominican Fathers, in his *Summa Theologica* (Part II of the Second Part; Question 123). This account consciously follows Aristotle in defining courage as a virtue that "makes its subject good and renders its work good" (II.-II., Q123, A. 1). Aquinas then adds that the term 'fortitude' can be taken in two ways. First, it denotes firmness of mind, which is a virtue or underlies every virtue. Second, 'fortitude' can be taken to mean firmness "in bearing and withstanding those things wherein it is most difficult to be firm, namely in certain grave dangers" (II.-II., Q123, A. 2). This second definition appears to accord very well with our subsequent account of courage as a response to situations that are either difficult or dangerous. In other ways, however, Aquinas's account does not seem to be so consistent with ours, unless "firmness of mind" could be analyzed as what we will later refer to as "determination."

Aquinas quotes Aristotle as writing that courage is about fear and daring, but then seems, to some extent, to question this hypothesis. He writes that the virtue of fortitude is "to remove any obstacle that withdraws the will from following the reason" (II.-II., Q123, A. 3). He adds, however, that withdrawal from an evil that entails difficulty belongs to the notion of fear. Thus he seems to be saying that courage is primarily about facing difficulties or obstacles and secondarily about facing fear (II.-II., Q123, Answer). However, a little later in Q123, Article 3 (Reply to Objection 2), Aquinas writes:

> Dangers and toils do not withdraw the will from the course of reason, except insofar as they are an object of fear. Hence fortitude needs to be immediately about fear and daring, but mediately about dangers and toils, these being the objects of those passions. (P. 199)

Here, he seems to suggest that courage should be defined primarily in terms of the "passions" of fear or daring, and only secondarily in terms of danger or difficulty. This apparent ambivalence reflects a general problem in any attempt to define courage, and we should subsequently have many occasions to comment on the problem.

In the seventh article, Aquinas goes on to discuss whether the brave man acts for the sake of good or through habit. He argues (II.-II., Q123, A. 7) that if the brave man's proximate end may be to "reproduce in action a likeness of his habit" (p. 205), he may still have an ultimate end of acting for the good. This discussion suggests that while courage may be based on habit, ultimately understanding why an action is courageous in a fuller sense may involve reference to the agent's ultimate intention in acting. Also suggested is a distinction between direct implementation of long-term goals in an action. An action is typically a sequence of actions and intentions that may be complex to evaluate.

In Q.123, Article 9, Aquinas asks whether anger has a role to play in courageous action. He notes that the Stoics excluded anger and other passions from the soul of the good man. However, Aquinas remarks that the Stoics may have been thinking of immoderate passions. But if the passions are in the command of reason, it can render action more prompt. It is concluded that it is all right for the brave man to employ moderate anger for his action, but not immoderate anger (p. 210).

On the whole, then, it seems that Aquinas would reject the view of courage as a daring act of intuitive emotion. Rather, he thinks of the notion of courageous action in terms similar to those of Aristotle— it is a matter of practical reason making a sound judgment on a dangerous situation, and not giving in to excessive or irrational emotion.

For similar reasons, Aquinas thinks that courage is not the same thing as fearlessness. In fact, he concludes (II.-II., Q126, A. 1) that fearlessness is a vice. His reasoning is that everyone naturally loves his own life. And if a man fears death or harm less than he should, it can only be because he lacks love, because he lacks comprehension that he can be harmed, or because of an egotistical pride. Hence it is clear that, for Aquinas, courage is not to be equated with fearlessness.

Also rejected (II.-II., Q127, A. 1) is the notion that courage can be identified with daring. Aquinas defines daring as a passion. Consequently it can be indulged in to excess. Courage is the moderation of a passionate response through reason. Hence sheer aggressive action through boldness or daring is not the same thing as courageous action.

3.4 *Von Wright and Foot on Courage*

According to von Wright (1963:145), courage is a trait of character connected with how one chooses particular actions where the good of some person is involved. Von Wright thinks that knowledge relating to the beneficial and the harmful, "practical judgment," is also involved. Third, passion or emotion namely, that of fear, is an essential feature (ibid., p. 147).

The role of courage, according to his account, is to counteract or eliminate the obscuring effect that fear in the face of danger may have on practical judgment. The courageous person is the one who has learned to control or subdue his fear in the face of danger (ibid.). The courageous person "has learnt not to let fear paralyse him, not to get panic-stricken, not to lose his head because of fear, but to act coolly when facing danger. In short: he has learnt not to let fear obscure his judgment as to what is the right course of action for him" (ibid., 148).

Von Wright's account seems to be basically Aristotelian, except for certain critical differences. For one thing, unlike Aristotle, von Wright fails to require goodness of the action as the prerequisite for it to be courageous. For another, he defines courage in relation to fear, whereas Aristotle defines it in relation to fearful danger. This may seem a small difference, but soon we will see its significance. Other than that, von Wright does not add much to, or deviate much from, the traditional Aristotelian definition.[7]

According to the account of Foot (1978), courage, like other virtues, is a *corrective* that enables one to resist temptation or overcome a deficiency of motivation. In the case of courage, the temptation is to give in to one's fear, even where that is not the right thing to do. In using the emotion of fear, this account is similar to von Wright's.

Immediately this account raises a certain problem. If courage is the overcoming or mastering of fear, does this mean that the greater the fear, the more courageous the man? Or is the more courageous person the one who has less fear to overcome? As Foot (1978:10) puts it: "Who shows most courage, the one who wants to run away but does not, or the one who does not even want to run away?" This problem poses a standard difficulty in trying to define courage.

Foot suggests that the problems raised by this difficulty have not all been solved, but she does make a number of relevant and interesting remarks. First, she suggests that the emotion of fear is not a necessary condition for the display of courage. For example, a man may show courage who risks death or a great harm even if he does not tremble. Perhaps part of the problem here is how we define 'fear'. Even though the man does not tremble outwardly, must he not show some fear of the potentially disastrous risk if his act is to be truly courageous? The question, then, is the extent to which "fear" can be an intellectual apprehension as opposed to an emotional reaction. Thus it seems that significant questions about defining courage rest on what we mean by 'fear.' As Foot also notes, what is fearful for one, for example, claustrophobia, need not be fearful for another.

A certain opposition on this score can be detected in the views of Wallace and Foot. Wallace (1978:78) writes, "Someone who sees no peril in what he does is not acting courageously." Foot (1978:12) appears to contravene this thesis in her claim that "the emotion of fear is not a necessary condition for the display of courage." Perhaps the apparent difference resides in a distinction between "seeing peril" and "experiencing the emotion of fear." One may see peril, that is, intellectually appreciate danger, without necessarily reacting in a way that need be described as the emotion of fear. At any rate, the term 'fear' as a description of a type of reaction to a perceived situation calls out for further clarification, if courage is to be defined in relation to it.

One key distinction necessary to emphasize is that fear may be irrational or at least unjustified, whereas if one "sees peril" it would seem to be implied that the danger is real. Indeed, the difference here is between a psychological reaction (fear), and an objective factor (danger) that is perceived. Which way should Foot go? Or, like Aristotle, should she utilize both concepts in defining courage? Let us pass on to a third, much more detailed account of courage.

3.5 The Wallace Analysis of Courage

Wallace (1978:chap. 3) offers an analysis of courage centered around analytical definitions of 'courage' and 'cowardice'. Wallace approaches the project by defining 'cowardice' first, since he takes the approach that the two terms are opposites and considers 'cowardice' more fundamental: "Cowardice is a tendency to be motivated by fear in certain ways, and courage, rather than being a tendency to be motivated in a particular way, is the absence of this tendency characteristic of cowardice" (ibid., p. 77). Wallace's theory takes some of its flavor from the "motivational theory" of character traits defended by R. B. Brandt which asserts that traits of character are dispositions of a "want-aversion" nature.[8] On this approach, fear, and presumably, therefore, cowardice, may be described as an aversion, since the coward is one who is disposed in certain situations to act on the motive of fear. Courage, however, on this approach, is not a disposition to act from a certain type of motive, but is rather the absence of the coward's disposition to act from fear.

But Wallace does not entirely agree with the theory that courage is a purely negative quality. He notes (ibid., p. 61) that courage also has a positive aspect because it is a positive capacity for acting rationally when certain motives incline one to act otherwise. Therefore, Wallace (ibid., p. 77) can describe courage as "the positive ability to cope rationally with fears and to face dangers." Thus courage seems to have some positive content over and above the absence of cowardice.

Nonetheless, Wallace still thinks of cowardice as the more positive quality, at least in one respect. He thinks that cowardice is a tendency to be motivated by fear in a certain way; therefore, one has some idea of the kind of motive involved in any cowardly act. He thinks, however, that courage is not itself a motive, or a disposition to act on a particular type of motive. In this way, courage is unlike generosity: "to say that a certain act is fully characteristic of the virtue generosity is to be given some idea of the purpose or motive behind it" (ibid., p. 77). By contrast, the courageous man does not do what he does on the prompting of a "courage-motive." Wallace concludes that from the viewpoint of the motivational view of character status, courage is a negative or privative state.

For these reasons, Wallace is led to formulate separate definitions for cowardice and courage. His definition of cowardice consists of a set of four conditions (ibid., pp. 70–74) for agent A and actions X and Y.

(i) A is doing X rather than Y.
(ii) A knows or believes that he has some reason to do Y.
(iii) A is doing X rather than Y because he is afraid to do Y.
(iv) *Either*
A believes that his doing Y would be worth the risks it involves.
Or
If A does not believe this, his not believing this is due to his being *excessively* afraid of the risks of doing Y.

This set of conditions is alleged by Wallace (ibid., p. 74) to be necessary for A's doing X to be cowardly. It is also supposed to be sufficient, except in two special cases: (v) where the risks of doing Y are so terrible that nobody could be expected to face them, or (v) where it would be foolhardy for A to do Y. To sum up, then, according to Wallace's account, the coward is one whose excessive fears prevent him from taking a risk he believes worthwhile.

The definition of courage given by Wallace (ibid., p. 78) is essentially an opposite of cowardice: the courageous man is the one who carries out an act that he believes is worth the risk even though he believes it is dangerous. More fully, A's doing X is courageous if, and only if:

(a) A believes that it is dangerous for him to do X.
(b) A believes that his doing X is worth the risk it involves.
(c) A believes it is possible for him not to do X.

(d) The danger A sees in doing X is sufficiently formidable that most people would find it difficult to do X.

(e) A is not coerced into doing X by threats of punishment that he fears more than the danger of doing X.

Wallace discusses other possible emendations and refinements, but these five clauses form the basis of his definition.

One class of counterexamples to the above definition is posed by the problem that mere belief, as required by clauses (a), (b), and (c), does not seem to be enough to bar certain types of irrational or ill-considered acts which would not be considered courageous. Five types of acts are especially noteworthy. (a) The act of the misguided fanatic: he believes his dangerous act of igniting himself with gasoline is worth the risk because it will further the cause of white supremacy. (2) The act of the idiot: he believes his dangerous act of putting his finger in a live electrical socket while standing in water is worth the risk because it will save him the time-consuming effort of using a nearby light bulb to test the circuit. (3) The act of the reckless one: he believes his dangerous act of charging right into the field of fire of a machine-gun emplacement is worth the risk it involves because he wants to emulate a John Wayne movie. (4) The act of the schizophrenic: he believes telling his psychiatrist there is a world conspiracy is dangerous because his enemies have him under surveillance, but thinks it is worth the risk. (5) The act of the gambler: he believes that gambling his family's life savings at roulette is dangerous, but believes it is worth the risk. The problem posed by all five of these types of acts is that they meet conditions (a) through (e) above, but do not constitute acts that we could rightly call courageous.

Another problem with Wallace's definition, pointed out by John Bishop, takes us back to the question of the courageous villain. It could be that A's action is immoral, even though A believes his doing it is worth the risk it involves. Take the example of the soldier who takes certain risks in combat fully knowing that his action may likely result in death for two of his comrades. But let us say that he believes this risky course of action will also attract a lot of attention and almost certainly win him a citation. Suppose this soldier believes getting the citation is worth the risk it involves. Suppose further that he successfully carries out the action and is not killed himself, but his two comrades are killed. By Wallace's definition, we have to say that the soldier's act was courageous. But was it necessarily a courageous act?

I would say not, if its intention was the immoral objective of self-glorification. Hence Wallace's definition is wide of the mark because it is too inclusive.

Eventually I will suggest that the best way to deal with these problems is to require that the beliefs in question be justified by the agent's appreciation of his circumstances. But to flesh out such a requirement, we will have an account of practical reasoning in a situation in which an agent arrives at a rational decision. Another possible counterexample to Wallace's definition of courage is posed by the observation of Geach (1977:161) that sometimes the bravest thing is to do what the agent rightly believes is the safest thing. According to a legend related by Geach, Alexander the Great was on one occasion left alone on top of the wall of a hostile city when a scaling ladder broke behind him. He jumped down among the enemy troops, eventually to be rescued by his own men. However, as the story goes, he would have been killed by enemy spears and arrows if he had stayed on the wall, and he would also have perished if he had jumped among his own men.

This story may pose a problem for Wallace's definition of courage because of clause (2), which requires that the courageous agent believe his act to be dangerous. No doubt, whatever Alexander might have done by any of his three choices was dangerous, and believed by him to be dangerous. As it turned out, however, at least according to the story, the course Alexander believed to be the least dangerous turned out in fact to be the least dangerous. So, relatively speaking, it is false, or at least misleading, to describe the actions of the story by saying "Alexander believed it was dangerous to leap among the enemy troops." Such an action may have appeared superficially to be the most dangerous option to most individuals in Alexander's situation. But presumably the point of the story was that Alexander had the coolness in a nasty situation to figure out that such an act was really in the end the safest available course to take. His act was courageous, yet he did not choose the most dangerous alternative.

In defense of Wallace's definition, it should be added, however, that Alexander may well have believed that jumping among the enemy troops was indeed dangerous, and that most people would find it difficult to do it. Still, in this instance anything Alexander did or failed to do would have been dangerous, and therefore the danger involved must be treated as a relative matter. He did the thing he believed to be least dangerous, and that took courage. This story seems to provide a counterexample to any analysis that rules the following condition as both necessary and sufficient for the performance of a courageous act: the agent chooses the more dangerous alternative over the less dangerous where the former is thought worth the risk.

Von Wright (1963:148) appears to make a similar point when he notes that the man of courage "may sometimes rightly choose to retreat from danger rather than to fight it." However, he adds (ibid.) that such a choice does not terminate in an act called virtuous, so "to retreat from danger is never an act of courage." The point is well made that the courageous man's choice is not always the courageous act. But does von Wright mean to say that the decision to pursue the safer course can never be a courageous act? If so, he and Geach are in strong disagreement.

Another difficulty for the line taken by Wallace and von Wright concerns the following sort of case. A man avoids a fight even though justifiably confident he would win it, and endures some public scorn as a result. He reasons, justifiably, however, that it is not worth violating his principles against unnecessary violence in order to remain popular with the group who scorns him. Presuming that in this instance the course chosen by the man turns out to be the safer one, Wallace and von Wright have to say his act (or omission) was not courageous. Yet I think many of us do persist in our belief that many actions of this sort can be highly courageous.

At any rate, it would seem that some of the finer points of Wallace's approach to defining courage need to be explored more fully.

A further problem with Wallace's definition is his requirement that the act in question be "worth the risks it involves," according to belief of the agent. As we have already seen, there are difficulties with mere belief in this clause, but there would still be a problem if we changed clause (b) to

> (b') A is justified in believing his doing Y is worth the risk it involves.

Consider the case of A, whose surgeon has told him that there is a 90 percent chance of remission if a tumor is removed, but a much greater likelihood of fatality if nothing is done. Suppose A justifiably believes it is dangerous for him to have the operation, but he justifiably believes it is worth the risk it involves, and he justifiably believes it is possible for him not to have the operation. Given all this, even if A decides to have the operation, we are not likely to think of his action so much as courageous as simply sensible. Of course, if A is really afraid of surgery, it may take courage for him to arrive at this decision and stick to it. But if he were not unusually afraid of it, I think we may not see his decision to pursue this course of action as particularly courageous. In short, pursuing a gamble that is worth the risk, even if it involves some danger, may not necessarily be courageous.

It is for this reason that the additional requirement (d) must be added to Wallace's definition. Wallace's requirement (d) follows Aristotle's suggestion that the brave man is fearless toward what is formidable or terrible for the majority. It stipulates that the courageous act must be formidable enough that most people would find it difficult to do in the circumstances. This is clearly a sensible requirement, but may not cover certain instances of courage very well.

Rachman (1978:244 f.) reviews the case of a middle-aged woman who had strong irrational fears of disease, germs, and dirt. She had become so frightened of possible contamination that she came to avoid contact with other people altogether, spending her days in one sequestered room of her house in a chair she scrubbed down with disinfectant several times each day. After much discussion and internal struggle, she chose the treatment option of "flooding"—a rapid and uncomfortable method of exposing the patient directly to the feared stimulus repeatedly—to slower but more comfortable methods. The first few sessions were particularly difficult for her. She was very frightened, and experienced obvious adverse reactions to the program of increasing contact with dirty objects and situations. Despite the severe emotional toll of these sessions, she persisted with the program to the end. Rachman (ibid., p. 245) comments that in his opinion she "displayed commendable courage," comparable in his experience to the courage shown by professional boxers, combat troops, and firemen.

It is hard to deny the claim that this woman acted courageously, but clearly (d) is not met. For it would be quite false to assert that the danger she saw in carrying out her treatment was sufficiently formidable that most people would find it difficult in the circumstances to do what she did.

Another difficulty with (d) concerns a possible instance of moral courage where a parliamentary leader decides to act in the interests of the broad majority of a country against a small but powerful interest group he belongs to which will unseat him for his independent act. It could be that he finds this act difficult because he strongly identifies with this unpopular minority group, and being a member of it himself, he rightly thinks that the majority will be satisfied with his act, but will not approve of him personally for having done it because of their distaste for all members of this minority.[9] In such a situation, it may well be the case that it is not true that the majority would find it difficult to carry out this particular act. In this case, then, (d) would be false.

Much depends here on what is meant precisely by "in the circumstances" in (d). Another person precisely like this heroic dissenter would presumably feel the same degree of formidable danger. So if the "most people" in (d) "in the circumstances" are supposed to be exactly like this particular person *in all respects*, then they too would feel the danger "sufficiently formidable." But I take it that is not what (d) requires, or should require. What (d) seems to mean is that the danger must be thought sufficiently formidable by the broad majority of people, many of whom may be quite unlike the courageous individual in question.

This is a curious problem about morally courageous acts that we could call the *paradox of the courageous act for the majority within a minority*.

3.6 Values and Practical Virtues

Since what we have now covered is the best of the received doctrines on courage, the reader might well begin to wonder why there is such a paucity of good material. Certainly Wallace's definition is an admirable ground-breaking piece of work in contemporary philosophy, but no doubt because of its very originality in the context of twentieth-century moral philosophy, it poses rather than resolves a number of basic problems in trying to define courage.

Could it be that there is some feeling on the part of moral philosophers that courage is not a proper subject for normative investigations? Certainly we saw in chapter 1 that there is danger in postulating definitions of courage that might have suspect moral or political implications. However, there has also been a feeling that the study of so-called virtues such as courage is not properly a part of ethical theory.

It seems, then, that what we are engaged in trying to do in defining courage may be partly a problem of moral philosophy but it also seems to involve elements of practical reasoning in objective circumstances (of risk or danger), and perhaps also elements of psychology (fear as an emotional response). Could it be that such an attempt to engage in practical ethics is too ambitious? Are we trying to do too much all at once and mixing up too big and heterogeneous a bag of ideas for one clear and coherent analysis to cover? Courage is in some sense a practical notion, as we have begun to see. Could it be that it is too practical for us to gain any clear theoretical grasp of it as an abstract concept? Some have thought this.

Prichard ([1912] 1966:60)[10] took up the thesis that the goodness of a courageous act stems from its good motive, the emotion of shame at being dominated by terror. Thus the goodness of a courageous act is different from the goodness of an act in the strict moral sense, by which Prichard means an act done from a sense of obligation. A courageous act, by this account, is not done through a "moral motive proper" (ibid., p. 60). Prichard gives the example of the doctor who might tend his patients out of a sense of duty, or from an interest in his patients, or in the exercise of a skill. Only the first is a moral motive proper, the remaining two being virtuous acts but not properly moral acts in the strict sense. As Cunningham (1981:133) notes, Prichard's approach indicates a striking metamorphosis in the traditional concept of moral value. Here virtue seems to be relegated to a secondary place in ethical theory.

This kind of ambivalence about courage as a moral quality can also be found in Kant's *Groundwork of the Metaphysic of Morals* ([1785] 1964:61).

> Intelligence, wit, judgement, and any other *talents* of the mind we may care to name, or courage, resolution, and constancy of purpose, as qualities of *temperament*, are without doubt good and desirable in many respects; but they can also be extremely bad and hurtful when the will is not good which has to make use of these gifts of nature, and which for this reason has the term *'character'* applied to its peculiar quality.

Certainly there is a danger of emulating morally dubious "heroes" as models of courage, but can it really be true that courageous actions are sometimes bad or hurtful? Perhaps Kant's assumption that this is so stems from his prior presumption that courage is like an emotion, a quality of temperament or character. But should courage be so defined? I will argue that it should not. At least, I will argue that the notion of character, as a category in which to include the concepts of courage, can lead to an improper account of courage, if character is a matter of dispositions. Whatever one is to say about Kant's interpretation of courage as a quality of temperament, he clearly sees it as a secondary good of mixed value—not an unqualifiably good quality.

Moore (1903) carried this critique a step further. He strongly criticized Aristotle for constructing a confused ethics around the proposition that virtues are good in themselves. Moore (1903:175 f.) argued, quite to the contrary, that virtues have no intrinsic value whatsoever. To give an example, Moore confesses that he is honest, in the sense that he habitually abstains from thieving, even in situations where others might be tempted. Thus Moore, we may say, has the virtue of honesty. Yet he adds that none of his performances of the duty of honesty have the smallest intrinsic value. This sounds paradoxical, and is perhaps meant to, but what Moore seems to mean is that honesty is of no intrinsic value as an end; it is a useful quality, and is good as a means to ends that have intrinsic value. Thus, perhaps all Moore meant to say is that virtues are concerned with how actions are brought about by practical deliberation (means) rather than with pure ethics as such (ends). This thesis is not paradoxical, or at any rate not nearly as paradoxical as it initially seemed.

Nonetheless, Moore (ibid., p. 176) concluded that Aristotle was greatly mistaken to take the exercise of the practical virtues as having intrinsic value, and insists that virtues are only good as means. Moreover, Moore went on to argue that a virtuous disposition is not better as a means than a nonvirtuous disposition, and that a virtuous disposition has no value in itself (ibid., p. 182). Such a view tended to "encourage the eclipse of virtue" as Cunningham (1981:133) puts it. Also, by defining virtue as a "disposition," a very difficult idea to define, Moore doubly denigrated the notion of a virtue as a serious concept of moral philosophy.

Recently, however, there has come to be more of an incentive to study practical virtues that are good as a means as the study of biomedical ethics and other more practical areas of ethics have come to be seen as legitimate areas of study.[11] Once one takes up a more practical approach to ethics, it is more easily appreciated why the way something is brought about is not morally trivial or neutral.

Let us review our present findings to see how we might proceed. The basic problem for the von Wright, Foot, and Wallace definitions is that by relating courage to purely psychological factors of belief, they lack normative force. The basic problem with Aristotle's approach, by contrast, is that by building in a normative requirement, he begs the normative question posed by problems such as the courageous villain. It seems that a definition of courage is partly normative, yet another part of it has to do with practical deliberation or perhaps psychology or a mental element of some sort. Can these two aspects be sorted out so that out of the inadequate definitions of Aristotle and Wallace a successful definition can be created? This is the project of the next chapter.

We will continue, then, in the belief that it is possible to engage in ethical inquiries that have to do with practical questions of means, rather than ends, as values in themselves. We elect to venture where Prichard and Moore feared to tread.

Prichard's driving a wedge between virtues and the "proper moral motives" of obligations had an interesting implication, which he drew in the case of courage.

> It is untrue to urge that, since courage is a virtue, we ought to act courageously. It is and must be untrue, because, as we see in the end, to feel an obligation to act courageously would involve a contradiction. For . . . we can only feel an obligation to *act;* we cannot feel an obligation to *act from a certain desire,* in this case the desire to conquer one's feelings of terror arising from the sense of shame which they arouse. (1912:61)

Although what Prichard says here is partly right, it is too strong. The proposition 'We ought to act courageously' cannot be universally true for the reason that courageous action is sometimes above and beyond the requirements of duty. However, it is incorrect to venture that we ought never to act courageously, that an obligation to act courageously would have to be contradictory. If a soldier is obliged to hold his position, and if that means acting courageously, then he ought to act courageously. Of course if he can't act courageously, then of course he is not obliged to do something he can't do, but he may be so obliged if he can do it.

Prichard is partly right, however, because there is a difference between the types of acts prescribed or allowed by ethics and the practical question of assessing responsibility for how an individual act of this or that type is actually carried out. Thus the general act 'holding the position' may be required by duty if the soldier is ordered to do it. But once he has done it, the question of whether he did so courageously is a separate question requiring a more detailed analysis of the soldier's deliberations and his own perceptions of the situation.

CHAPTER 4

Basic Structure
of the Courageous Act

It is a curious sort of obstacle we have found in attempting to define courage that we have to decide whether to define it as a good or commendable quality, or whether we should try to define it in a neutral way and then, separately, argue whether or not it is a good quality. If we, like Aristotle, take the first line, we may be criticized for begging the question of whether courage is truly a virtue or excellence. But if we, like von Wright, Foot, and Wallace, take the other option, it seems we are doomed always to come up with a "definition" that has no normative force and can never be adequate to our moral usage of 'courageous'. This sort of obstacle is common to ethical studies, and is worth exploring more fully at a general level.

4.1 The Definition as Normative Requirement

Definitions of terms like 'courage', 'person', or 'death' have the property of being open textured: they may be clear enough in everyday paradigm cases of usage, but can admit of inexactness in applying to borderline cases. Such borderline cases can in fact coincide with substantive moral dilemmas, for example, is a fetus a person? Aggressively stipulating the meaning of a term, and thereby attempting to undermine the position of one's opponent in moral disagreement by attempting peremptorily to impose word usage prejudicial to the adversary's case, tends toward the fallacy of begging the question.[1]

   An elementary illustration from Bentham: the argument 'This doctrine is heresy, therefore it should be condemned' is said to commit the fallacy of question-begging epithet. Such an argument is unfair and fallacious insofar as it is an attempt to quash a request from the supporters of the doctrine for substantial moral arguments for condemning it, when such substantial argument is required to shift the burden of proof.

So we see that substantive moral disagreements cannot be resolved simply by the stipulative redefinition of inexact concepts when the inexactness of the concept leaves open the possibility of stipulating otherwise and taking the other side of the moral issue. The lesson is that the definitions themselves may be ethically "loaded" with moral presuppositions, and therefore a definition may need to be backed up by appeal to moral principles and an examination of specific instances. Mere definition cannot always settle the disagreement.

What is meant when we talk about the definition of an ethical concept like 'death'? What is most often required to move an ethical discussion forward is not the "ad hoccery" of a purely stipulative definition, but rather an explication or analysis of the term which is consistent with agreed-upon assumptions of the discussion. Moreover, a real, as opposed to a nominal, definition is applied to individual cases by means of empirical criteria. One must be careful not to confuse the abstract definition with the criteria, even though the two may be linked by intermediary principles. Let us give a brief example.

Some would characterize the death of a person as the irreversible cessation of experience for that person. To make this characterization into a defensible definition, exponents of it need to tell us what more precisely they mean by "irreversible cessation" and "experience." It may not be easy to do this, but that is no reason to opt out by merely stipulating what is meant, quite arbitrarily, or to brush off any attempt at greater clarity or precision by dismissing it as possibly question begging. True, a real definition has real ethical implications. For example, it might arguably tend to fit better with brain-oriented criteria for death than with purely cardiorespiratory traditional criteria, especially in cases where a ventilator is in use. But that may not be a good and sufficient reason for rejecting it out of hand as question begging, even if one has a predisposition to favor the traditional criteria.[2]

The point is that there may be substantive moral and scientific arguments for adopting a definition. It need not be a purely stipulative move. A good definition is a target that indicates what it is that the criteria are supposed to determine.[3] Insofar as the target is clearly articulated, it can have a legitimate function in shifting the burden of proof in moral arguments, and should not always be lightly brushed aside.

Most definitions of courage, like Aristotle's, have a moral requirement built into the definition. By Aristotle's account, an act can only be truly courageous if it has a good end. However, some definitions, like Wallace's, avoid a built-in normative requirement securing the true goodness of courage by phrasing each clause in terms of what the agent believes to be the case, or believes to be good or worthwhile. But, precisely because of its lack of normative force, Wallace's definition succumbed to a battery of counterexamples, failing to distinguish between courageous and foolish acts. If, as it seems, we are thrown back on a normatively loaded definition, how can we avoid the inevitable question of begging the question of what acts are truly courageous?

Hare (1963:187) objects to the practice of taking a "specialized moral word" like 'courageous' and firmly tying its evaluation to its description. Hare thinks this practice is a kind of unfair tactic against the opponents of the proposed definition, for it leaves them no good choice. If they do not evaluate highly a certain kind of act, then they have to give up the word 'courageous' to describe it. If they continue to use the word, however, they are committed to certain evaluations. Acquiescing in such a tactic, according to Hare, commits one to a kind of naturalism in ethics, being forced to argue from a description to an evaluation.

Hare (ibid., p. 187 ff.) gives two examples he thinks are parallel. First, he imagines, suppose you have a person who was not inclined to commend those who act to preserve the safety of others by disregarding their own. Such a person should be entitled not to have to use the word 'courageous' to describe such an act "just because it incapsulates the attitude to which [he does] not subscribe" (ibid., p. 189). He should be allowed to use the "morally neutral" expression, "disregarding one's own safety in order to preserve that of others." The attempt of the evaluative definer of courage to press this man in argument is, according to Hare, similar to another case. Suppose a naturalist puts forward the following argument for despising blacks: "If, he might argue, a man has curly hair and a black skin and thick lips, and is descended from people with similar features, then we cannot deny that he is a nigger" (ibid., p. 188). The parallel lies in the same passage here from factual propositions about skin color and so forth to the evaluative proposition that so-and-so is a "nigger."

Hare is arguing that building positive evaluations into a supposedly descriptive word like courage is just as prejudicial and unfair as building nasty evaluations into a supposedly descriptive term like "nigger," as defined above.

What Hare has shown is that we have to be very careful here not to fall into the trap of attempting to define a highly loaded evaluative concept by fooling ourselves that we can avoid value-laden terms in the *definiens*. We must be clear about what we want to do with a definition, how we want to deploy it in moral argumentation, once we've fixed it by stipulation. Thus Hare's warnings reinforce our remarks above about the danger of question-begging definitions.

What Hare has not shown, and should not be taken to have demonstrated, is that it is always unfair or impossible to define 'courage' either normatively or nonnormatively. Hare's naturalist would offer an inadequate and incorrect definition of 'nigger' as a report of conversational usage without adding that it is a highly pejorative term as part of the definition. That is, an evaluative clause, in this instance a negative "red flag," would have to be included. Similarly, anyone who tried to define 'courageous' act as 'an act done by an agent as a necessary means to some end' would produce an inadequate and incorrect definition if he failed to add the normative requirements that the end be good and the means formidably dangerous or difficult. A nonevaluative definition would not be 'courage' as we know it, but only some part of it. Similarly, Hare's naturalist may define 'black person', but at best gives only a part of any adequate definition of the term 'nigger'.

A basic problem with Hare's parallel between defining 'courage' and 'nigger' stems from an ambiguity in the term 'normative' (or 'evaluative' if you prefer). One thing that might be meant by a non-normative definition of 'courage' is one that makes no mention of any normative concept whatsoever. This would be a strong sense of 'nonnormative'. Another sense might refer to a definition that has no requirement of real normative force, even though it may make mention of normative concepts or terms. For example, the way in which Aristotle defines 'courageous act' requires that the purpose of the act be noble. Thus, to be courageous, the act must be truly good. However, Wallace's definition only requires that the agent believe that the act is worth the risk. By this requirement—although a normative concept is mentioned, for example, 'worth'—there is no real normative force. That is, the act does not truly have to be worth the risk, the agent merely has to believe it so. The force of the requirement therefore is not truly normative but only psychological.

Is Wallace's definition "evaluatively neutral" by Hare's lights? I do not know. I do know, however, that 'nigger' unlike courage, does not admit of this ambiguity, and there Hare's parallel breaks down. If Sue says that Bob is a nigger, we cannot infer that Bob is truly contemptible. We can at best infer something to the effect that Sue believes Bob to be an object of contempt. That is the difference, then. 'Courage' may, and in my view does, properly have normative force. But 'nigger' does not. Thus Hare's analogy fails, and is quite misleading.

Despite Hare's masking of it, I think the real issue is whether 'courage' should be defined normatively—with real moral force—or non-normatively in the sense that it may contain moral terms in its definition but does not have truly moral force in its implications. Hare is quite right, however, to warn against begging questions in moral disputations on courage. The best definition should separate the normative elements from the nonnormative.

4.2 The Psychological Element

A major theoretical difficulty in defining courage is to clearly separate the normative from the psychological elements. Naturally, from a viewpoint of empirical psychology, it would be nice to define 'courageous behavior' exclusively in terms of observable events like bodily signs or chemical processes. However, such an account, while it might be quite useful for psychology, would not by itself give an answer to the question 'What is courage?' that would explain courage as a virtue or as a positive quality or moral worth. Much of what we seem curious about in relation to courage is the question of what is particularly commendable about courageous acts. This is a normative question, one about what ought to be done or what we should reasonably expect a person to do in certain circumstances.[4]

Experimental psychology could perhaps define 'courage' as a functional relationship between sets of stimuli and responses.[5] That would enable us to better predict certain responses from other stimuli, but in itself would not tell us why courage is, or is not, an exemplary quality of human action. Nor would a normative analysis of 'courage' serve to help us predict how an organism responds to fearful stimuli.

We are not saying that these behavioral and normative questions are altogether unrelated—one hopes they would be mutually connected. But it is important to carefully distinguish between them in posing the question 'What is courage?' with clarity.

Much of the confusion concerning these two viewpoints stems from the terms 'motive' and 'purpose'. The former term is often given a psychological meaning and the latter is usually thought of as a purely normative notion. But, often the two words are mixed together, sometimes even serving as synonyms for each other.[6]

It is a presumption easy to acquiesce in, especially in the context of empirical psychology, that courage may be equated with the absence of fear. For example, Rachman (1978:240) reports that according to some studies, people adapting to air raids in wartime became increasingly courageous as they became more experienced. Such a way of speaking is open to question, however. Socrates asked who is the bravest, the skilled person who engages in a dangerous task or the less skilled one who accomplishes a similar task? In the *Laches*, as we saw, the answer given would be that the latter is the more courageous. In the Greek view, the courage is in the mastery of the fear, not just the mastering of the particular circumstances of the situation, which could lead to a lessening of fear. However, on the presumption that courage is simply the absence of fear, the people adapting to air raids could be correctly described as becoming more courageous. But from the Greek point of view, such a description might not necessarily be appropriate.

The presumption that courage may be defined as absence of fear has a tendency to lend a certain air of unreality or even absurdity to some discussions. For example, a study reported by Rachman (ibid., p. 241) claims to have found that airmen displayed significantly more courageous behavior than other combat soldiers. No doubt the Air Force was delighted by this finding, but it is presumptuous to think that such a blanket judgment about courageous acts could be made fairly.

One category of person who is surely fearless but not courageous is the one who simply fails to perceive or to acknowledge danger. Aristotle noted that the optimist or the ignorant person is indeed confident and may therefore appear to be brave. But this confidence is not because of any determination to pursue a noble goal, merely to a misapprehension of the situation. Gray (1967:106) comments on the phenomenon of the combat soldier who cherishes his conviction that he is perfectly impervious to the bullets and shells around him. This conviction, he suggests, is misnamed 'courage', for once their childish illusion is shattered by a wound, the shock and outrage of disillusionment is a tragic blow. The psychological readjustment may be harder than the physical recovery from the wound. This sort of person is actually a kind of naive egoist who may become a cowardly and useless soldier once his myth of invulnerability is shattered.

It begins to seem, then, that courage should not be tied essentially to the emotion of fear at all, von Wright and Foot to the contrary. It does not seem to matter so much to the courage of an act whether the agent in fact experienced the emotion of fear or not. What matters is whether or not the act was truly dangerous or difficult. But this factor is quite independent of the psychological state of mind of the agent. What matters is that he or she responds to the situation in an effective way, whether fearful or not. True, fear is a potent obstacle to practical reasoning and effective action. But fear is not the only obstacle the courageous person overcomes. A disabled person who overcomes his or her disability by determination, persistence, and ingenuity may correctly be called courageous even if fear was not the main problem, or even a problem at all.

Rachman (1978) reports that almost all studies and surveys indicate that it is only a tiny proportion of people who think they never experience fear, even in very threatening situations. He suggests, however, that wartime evidence shows that most people are adept at coping with fears, and within this courageous species of person, there is a subgroup who are outstandingly competent (ibid., p. 237). Certain wartime jobs demand conspicuous courage, including bomb-disposal work. A study of American astronauts by Ruff and Korchin (1964) indicates that it is not fearlessness that accounts for their competence in dangerous work, but self-control, and an experience that gives them a feeling of mastery over their work. Ruff and Korchin indicated that these astronauts readily admitted to fear, but in space their anxiety levels were not high because of their confidence in training and technical readiness. Observations of parachute jumpers also have indicated that successful execution of jumps tended to lead to a subsiding of fear.

We conclude that although fear is often present in the initial stages of a courageous act, the emotion of fear is not, as such, an essential characteristic of the courageous act.

4.3 Risk, Danger, and Difficulty

Aristotle's conception of courage turns on the notion of the coura-geous man's practical reason calculating the seriousness of danger and, responding accordingly, making an appropriate decision. Wal-lace's definition of courage requires, in a somewhat similar fashion, that the courageous action be "worth the risk." But how should one calculate "risk"? According to Lowrance (1976), *measuring risk* is an objective but probabilistic pursuit, whereas *judging the acceptability of risk* is a matter of personal and social value judgment (ibid., p. 8). Expressions of risk are usually compound measures describing the *probability* of harm and its *severity*. For example, the usual way of calculating the risk of dying in an automobile accident is to divide the number of automobile deaths per year into the total population of the country. The risk to any particular individual then depends on his *exposure* to this risk—how much he is on the road, where he drives, whether he is accident prone, and so forth.

Under unusual or severe circumstances, our judgment of what is worth the risk or acceptably risky may vary considerably. If a situation is very dangerous no matter what you do or don't do, for example, war, then a risk that might seem unacceptable in peacetime conditions could seem more worth the gamble. Robert Graves, in *Good-Bye to All That* (1930, p. 164 f.) remarks that experienced front-line troops always have a carefully worked out formula for taking risks. The men he was with had the following formulas. To save life or take an important position, take any risk, even certain death. To take life, run a one-in-five risk, especially if the objective is more than simply reducing enemy firepower, for example, gaining fire ascendancy in danger-ously close trenches. Some units would take, say, a one-in-twenty risk to get a wounded enemy soldier to safety. Other units would take no risks for this; still others would go out of their way to kill enemy wounded. Taking a shortcut over the top where the enemy was not nearer than four or five hundred yards would justify a one-in-two hundred risk if you were in a hurry, but a one-in-fifty risk if you were "dead tired" (ibid., p. 165). In these matters, Graves adds, much depended on the *morale* of the battalion.

In many dangerous situations, risk may be unique and therefore no meaningful statistical measure may be applicable. Given Graves's remarks, it also seems likely that what is to be judged a worthwhile risk in particular circumstances may be impossible to realistically appreciate except for one familiar with these particular circumstances. Thus, if we take these notions of "worth the risk" and "practical reason" very seriously, it may be impossible to definitely tell whether a given act was truly "courageous" as opposed to a "normal risk" or a "foolish risk." Perhaps the best we can do in such situations is to rely on the subjective indication of what most people familiar with that type of situation would consider a normal risk *versus* a very great risk. Perhaps an example may illustrate some of these quandaries.

Gordon L. Bastian, a Canadian serving in the British Merchant Navy, was on watch in the engine room when his ship was torpedoed five hundred miles off Brest, March 30, 1943. The engine room became dark and water poured in, but Bastian remembered that two firemen were still in the stokehold, behind a watertight door adjoining the engine room. In opening this door, there was "grave risk of disastrous flooding" (Swettenham 1973:211). According to the description given in the *London Gazette* (August 17, 1943), Bastian "did not hesitate but groped his way to the door and opened it," with the result that the two firemen were swept in a flow of water to the engine room. Both men were injured, but were saved by Bastian who, although "himself half choked by cordite fumes," dragged and lifted them onto the deck. The description adds that this man "took a very great risk in opening the watertight door" to save both men. Bastian was awarded the George Cross.

This act was a courageous one, unquestionably—Bastian showed great presence of mind to act so quickly and ably in a confusing and dangerous situation. Moreover, he acted to save others in face of the grave risk to himself. But it is the nature of the risk in this case that poses some interesting questions concerning the nature of courage.

How great was the risk of "disastrous flooding" in opening the watertight door? We do not really know. Bastian himself probably knew better than anyone who might now try, in retrospect, to evaluate the situation. But perhaps he didn't even really have a very precise idea of the risk himself. Does it matter? If not, how can we arrive at an estimate of the risk, or whether the risk was acceptable or worthwhile? And is such an estimate consequently as necessary and important as both Aristotle and Wallace think?

What one's reaction to this case suggests is that, as things turned out, the risk was well worth taking. Thus, whether, in the grand scheme of things, Bastian's fortunate act succeeded more through luck than calculation does not really matter to its courageousness. When we look back over a past action and try to reconstruct the practical deliberations and perceptions of the agent in order to evaluate his responsibility for conduct, our picture is bound to be an incomplete speculation. In this instance, comparing the real risk to the agent's perception of the risk is guesswork at best. But that does not matter in the end. This selfless act was one that most of us would think to be quite risky, and the successful saving of two lives as a result justifies the risk as having been worthwhile.

Thus, grave risks, severe dangers, and formidable obstacles may all be objective factors that can be determined in specific cases of practical reasoning, even if calculating the precise extent of risk may be impossible. In defining courage, then, perhaps we should concentrate on relating courage to the objective notion of danger or risk, rather than on the psychological notion of fear.

Courage, I propose, has to do with the overcoming of an obstacle to gain some end.[7] The more formidable the obstacle, the greater tends to be the courage. Formidableness can consist in fearsomeness, where the obstacle is a danger or even a threat to life. But formidableness can also mean an obstacle that is very dangerous or difficult to overcome, requiring great determination and persistence, and where it may be easy for the person involved to lose heart or become hopeless.

The formidableness of the obstacle is one index of the degree of courage, but another mark of courage is the nobility or greatness of the thing one wants to achieve by overcoming the obstacle. If that end is altruistic, at the cost of self-sacrifice or great personal risk by the agent, the act is especially courageous. Thus there is a practical element involved—the nature of the action itself and the action to overcome an obstacle to its realization. Then there is the normative aspect—the end the agent has in mind to realize as the outcome of the act, and the formidableness of the danger or difficulty of the obstacle.

To accommodate all these intuitions about courage, we propose a two-part definition that separates the practical aspect from the normative. Note that 'fear' is not mentioned at all in the definition. Hence the definition of courage will not be essentially psychological at all. The subsequent definition of cowardice will be defined in terms of fear, however. It will follow, on my definitions, that courage and cowardice are not, strictly speaking, opposites.

4.4 Basic Definitions of Courage and Cowardice

To define the notion of a courageous action, we start with an agent *a* and some descriptions of states of affairs A and B.[8] We say that *a*'s bringing about A is a *courageous action* only if there exists some state of affairs B such that the following five clauses are met. The five clauses state the basic concept of a courageous action, and need to be supplemented by several derivative clauses some of which define special overtones of the basic definition and some of which define special kinds of courageous acts. The five clauses are divided into two parts. The first part, called the *practical reasoning base,* has three clauses.

(P1) In order to bring about B, *a* considers that it is necessary to bring about A.

(P2) *a* brings about A.

(P3) *a* could have not brought about A.

The practical reasoning base has to be interpreted and determined, in a particular case, against a framework of the rational appreciation of *a*'s act in retrospect by the evaluator of the responsibility or credit for the act. This evaluation is defeasible and takes place by practical reasoning. A defensible account must be given of what the circumstances of the act were, how the agent perceives the circumstances, and the extent to which the facts fitted the agent's estimate. It is presumed that there are different possible courses of events other than A or B and that the agent made some form of deliberation that accounts for his bringing about A as a necessary element in his plan.

Second, an *ethical matrix* is imposed on the practical base. The ethical matrix has two clauses.

(E1) *a* considers that B is [highly] worth *a*'s bringing about.

(E2) *a* considers that his bringing about A is dangerous or difficult [to a formidable extent].

The determination of (E1) and (E2) are very much matters of degree, in several respects. First, the greater the degree of each is present, the greater is the quality of the courageous act, and the more certain are we that the act is truly courageous. Second, there must be a relative weighting of (E1) and (E2) such that the worth of what is brought about outweighs the negative consequences implicit in the danger of (E2). The risk must be an acceptable one, otherwise the act could tend more toward the foolish than the courageous. Third, the worth of the act as specified by (E1) must be such that we have reasonably concluded that the agent's bringing it about in the circumstances in relation to the agent's position is defined by his actions and commitments. Hence (E1) and (E2) are "normative" in that they express the worth of the agent's intentions in relation to his reasoned position.

A key question is what is meant by the phrase '*a* considers that . . .' In our theory of practical reasoning, which will turn out to be the basis of this definition of 'courageous action', we will develop the thesis that '*a* considers that . . .' is equivalent to '*a* justifiably believes . . . in the circumstances.' Here, then, is a crucial difference between my own approach and that of Wallace. For Wallace, mere belief is enough. My own account of courage will require that the agent justifiably believes that his act is dangerous yet will have good results or benefits. Otherwise, in my view, the act need not be truly courageous. It is a matter of how the agent sees the situation, what his intentions are, and how he carries out these intentions in the particular circumstances by practical reasoning.

Wallace, however, is quite right to suggest that risk is involved in courageous action, and that the act must be worthwhile, or the risk acceptable. He is also quite right to suggest that danger is involved.

We could define a *crisis* as a formidably dangerous or difficult situation involving an agent. What we mean by 'involving' is that the agent is affected by the situation, or that he is contemplating bringing it about or bringing about some state of affairs related to it so that the danger or difficulty will affect him or others. Usually for the situation to be a crisis for this agent, he will have to have some justified appreciation of the extent of the danger or difficulty. In this sense (E2) could be equivalently expressed by saying that *a*'s bringing about A is a crisis.

Implementing both these clauses in particular cases is a normative matter that raises many problems characteristic of the concept of courage in particular, and other traditional ethical problems having to do with the general moral principles, duties, and particular circumstances.

It is disputable whether we should demand these five conditions as necessary for courageous action precisely as they stand, or require that the agent believes they obtain, knows they obtain, or justifiably believes they obtain. We prefer the latter, and will defend this preference from time to time, though not dogmatically.

Some might want to strengthen this set of conditions by adding a further stipulation to the ethical matrix to the effect that a must bring about A in order to bring (for the purpose of bringing) about B. For unless a's act of bringing about A is an intentional attempt to aim at B, the bringing about of B could be purely accidental or inadvertent, and therefore of no moral worth as an act of courage.

It is not clear, however, that such an additional requirement is always appropriate. Suppose that a soldier's only intention in defending his post under severe attack is to follow his orders to hold the position at any cost. His intention or purpose may not be to save the whole front from collapse, even if his valiant stand does in fact accomplish such an outcome. Yet we might think his act of grim determination in defense of his post is highly courageous. Moreover, the fact that it saved the front and many of his comrades' lives might add to our appreciation of the courageousness of the act. Yet the full worth of what he brought about by so acting was not his specific purpose or intention at the time.

But our evaluation of an action as courageous must take into account the state of the agent's mind at the time of the act in question, and in particular his awareness of the likelihood of B as a possible consequence of his act.[9] Therefore, to make the above basic structural definition workable, it will have to be set in a theory of practical reasoning. Moreover, the definition is basic in the sense that courage has a variety of overtones or peripheral meanings. The next several chapters will flesh out the basic definition by studying the overtonal meanings of courage and the nature of practical reasoning.

The definiton of a *cowardly action* also begins with a practical reasoning base. a's bringing about A is a *cowardly action* only if there is some state of affairs B such that these six conditons are met.

(P1) In order to bring about B, a considers that it is necessary to bring about A.

(NP2) a does not bring about A.

(NP3) a could have brought about A.

The ethical matrix consists of only one clause, specifying that a's bringing about B is a moral requirement.

(F1) It is a's considered duty to bring about B.

In this regard, defining cowardly action is simpler than courageous action, since it is not necessary to go into the dangerousness or difficulty of the act. Here, belief is enough. A doesn't have to be truly dangerous—a just has to think it is dangerous enough for him to be afraid. Accordingly, to define cowardly action, it is necessary to add a two-part *psychological matrix*.

(S1) a experiences fear.
(S2) Because a experiences fear, a does not bring about A.

Here (S1) is a purely psychological clause, requiring some fearful behavior or attitudes on the part of a. And (S2) requires a causal link between (S1) and (NP2).

We can now see why courage and cowardice are not direct opposites, and in fact are essentially different concepts. First, the ethical matrices are different. Courage, unlike cowardice, has to do sometimes with acts beyond the requirements of duty. Such a failure to act beyond duty may not be courageous, yet at the same time may not be cowardly either. The soldier who does not volunteer for an extraordinarily hazardous patrol may not thereby be acting in a cowardly fashion, even though he fails to act courageously in this instance.

Second, cowardice is partly a psychological concept whereas courage is not at all psychological in nature. Failure to carry out the requirements of one's duty may be for all kinds of reasons—laziness, inattentiveness, self-interest, and so forth. But it is only when the cause is the emotion of fear that such a failure should properly be called cowardice. Likewise, failure to act correctly in a difficult but not fearful situation need not exemplify cowardice—such a failure may be due rather to impatience or even laziness. Cowardice always results from fear.

With courageous actions, mere psychological belief that the situation is dangerous is not adequate. To be truly courageous, an act must overcome real difficulty or danger. The agent must be justified in his belief that the situation is dangerous for the act to be courageous. Courageous action has essentially to do with a deeper level of practical reasoning where we must assess the agent's understanding of the situation and its alternatives.

4.5 Objections and Replies

Courage is a purely normative notion and, therefore, there is no singular motive that provides its psychological mainspring. Cowardice is based essentially on the emotion of fear and, therefore, cannot be purely normative. The study of cowardice is a curious mixture of psychology and ethics.

We must now reply to the objection that our proposed definition begs the question of whether courage is a good quality because the ethical matrix requires that the outcome B must be worth bringing about. My response is that by separating the ethical matrix from the practical base, the definition divides rather than begs the question.

If you want to construct a nonnormative definition of courage, you take the practical base, and then add to it a nonnormative counterpart to (E2) which says that A is a difficult or dangerous obstacle in some nonnormative sense. The critical question here is what should be meant by 'difficult' or 'dangerous'. Previously, I argued that 'difficult obstacle', 'dangerous situation', or 'risk' could be defined in an objective (i.e., nonpsychological and nonnormative) way. If so, an objective formulation of (E2) could be added to the practical reasoning base, and the result is a nonnormative definition of courage. Alternatively, I have proposed to treat 'formidably difficult or dangerous' and 'acceptable risk' as frankly normative concepts, and therefore put (E2) in with the ethical matrix. Although I argue for the latter approach, I do not dogmatically foreclose the former. Indeed, our divided formulation of the definition allows precisely for that possibility. Hence the issue is not begged, but divided.

Why then did I put (E2) in the ethical matrix rather than putting an objective formulation of this clause in the practical reasoning base? Because ultimately I think that a fully adequate definition of courage must take into account that assessment of risk or possible danger is most often a subjective and partially normative matter in the evaluation of whether an act is courageous. The case of Bastian, and other cases we have looked at as well, bear out the thesis that assessment of the formidableness of risk depends on many subjectively normative factors.

Nonetheless, I am perfectly willing to formulate a purely practical (nonnormative) definition of courage as a possible competitor to my normative definition. To get it, just add the following clause to (P1), (P2), and (P3).

(P4) A is a dangerous or difficult thing to bring about.

In so doing, interpret 'dangerous' and 'difficult' in some objective way, without appealing to any normative concepts. Then drop (E1), thereby eliminating the ethical matrix altogether.

I would of course reject the objective definition so produced because it seems to me that there are many difficult and dangerous things we accomplish that should not properly be called courageous. For example, my getting into the office in the Arts Tower at the University of Auckland last Saturday was very difficult. The key would not work, and only after many persistent attempts was I able to jiggle the lock so that the bolt was released. However, I do not feel that it is correct or morally appropriate to say that my act of getting into the office was courageous.

No doubt, therefore, exponents of the objective approach need to specify some degree of difficulty or danger for the act to meet in order to qualify as "courageous." I do not see that such a project is very hopeful or sensible, but I would not dogmatically exclude those who wish to pursue it further.

It might be well at this point to mention again the other fundamental decision—whether courage should be defined as overcoming the internal emotion of fear or as overcoming difficult or dangerous circumstances. In the latter option, the sort of dangerous circumstances one would characteristically have in mind would be partly a matter of fact, to some extent external to the agent's psychology. Fear, by contrast, is essentially a subjective parameter contained in the agent's own mind, an emotion. Although I have argued against this latter option, it should not be rejected dogmatically.

Of course, there are intermediate options as well, and not all possible definitions need be precisely so polarized. One might, for example, want to define courage in terms of the overcoming of justifiable fear, or of fearful circumstances. Various compromises are possible.

Even within the dichotomy of fear versus dangerous circumstances, the resulting definitions of courage need not be purely psychological—as opposed to purely objective—in nature. It might seem to be so because fear, as an emotion, seems to be psychological, whereas the question of whether a set of circumstances is "dangerous" might be thought a matter of objective risk, calculated by some measure of the severity of an outcome and the probability that it will occur. But in the fuller definition of courage, for the act to be truly courageous, practical reason must determine whether the risk is worthwhile. And, as we saw, mere absence of fear by itself is not a very favorable account of courage. However, one can see the advantages many would perceive in defining courage either in a purely psychological or a purely objective (nonpsychological) way, with no references to mental perceptions or emotions.

Indeed, the tendency toward this dichotomy leads to a sort of paradoxical question, known to Aristotle and often asked subsequently. Who is more courageous, the man who carries out a dangerous act fearlessly or the man who carries out an equally dangerous act despite his considerable fear? Clearly, the answer depends on whether the obstacle to be overcome, to make the act courageous, is the dangerous or difficult circumstance or the fear in facing the danger. If the external obstacle is the thing of foremost importance in defining courage, then the fearless man may seem the more courageous, or perhaps both may be equally courageous. If the internal object of one's own fear is the most significant factor, then clearly the fearful man is the more courageous. The latter result could be called the case of the *courageous coward,* indicating the paradoxical nature of the tension between the two approaches to defining courage.

In the end, I argue that making essential reference to fear is the lesser definition, as opposed to citing the formidableness of the obstacle, risk, or danger. I have so argued because sometimes courage is simply not correlated with the presence or absence of fear at all. Rather, courage is related to the extent of risk, danger, or difficulty. But to some extent, a mark of courage is how one overcomes the obstacle.

In many instances, courage is defined by a positive element of determination or persistence in overcoming a difficulty. In such cases, the absence of courage would not necessarily be called cowardice; therefore, courage and cowardice are not opposites. Courage is more than merely absence of cowardice.

Warren Johnson is a professor of health education and physical education at the University of Maryland who was diagnosed as having diffuse scleroderma, a disease of hardening of the skin that his doctors described as degenerative, progressive, and incurable. His skin became hard and waxlike, he lost weight and height, his hair began to fall out, his back began to hunch, and his esophagus was damaged. His skin became sore to the touch, his joints painful, and later complications included skin cancer. Even shaving and brushing his teeth became impossible tasks.[10]

To the astonishment of experts, Johnson began an exercise program and slowly began to regain flexibility and coordination. This would literally tear his skin apart, and by the following day the disease would begin to constrict the tissues again. When dentists recommended removal of his teeth, he instead devised a method of stretching his mouth with tongue depressors which enabled him to continue eating and chewing. He has had the strong support of his family and has managed to continue running a clinic for developmentally disabled children. He has even written a book about his disease and treatment, with the theme of how to make the best of a bad situation, entitled *So Desperate the Fight: A Creative Approach to Chronic Illness.* His thesis is that people can take upon themselves a large portion of responsibility for dealing with serious illness if they learn more about how their bodies work.

We call Johnson's actions courageous because they show an outstanding determination not to give in to despair or hopelessness in an intimidating and excruciatingly difficult situation. Perhaps the courage of persons with catastrophic illnesses is a little different in nature from the more usual examples of courage cited where the imminent danger could be avoided by foregoing the noble end. Yet it often seems to me even nobler and more impressive, in its way, than the danger-confronting acts of combat or life saving of others that are more usually cited. Where the threat is directly to one's own existence and well-being, as in catastrophic illness or disability, the danger is more than just a risk or possible consequence. It is an actuality of the most proximate sort.

There are two objections to this interpretation, however, that remain to be discussed. One who doubts that 'difficult', apart from 'dangerous', should be one of the elements of a courageous act, might think that overcoming difficulties is more a matter of persistence or determination than courage. This objector might be inclined to conclude that Johnson's act was courageous only as he overcame fear that could have paralyzed his determination to go on living. My reply is that if there were no real difficulties in Mr. Johnson's problem, apart from his own attitudes or fears, then we should be much less inclined to call his actions courageous. Moreover, it is for the reason that these fears are justifiably based on real dangers and genuine difficulties and obstacles that an act in this situation is courageous. Fear itself can be a real obstacle or difficulty. An obstacle or difficulty is something that blocks an agent's practical reasoning and thwarts his ability to judge a situation realistically and carry out his intentions in that situation. Courage is the use of practical reasoning to remove any obstacle that prevents a person from carrying out good intentions that are possible and appropriate in a particular situation.

My reply here is somewhat reminiscent of the point made by Aquinas in the *Summa Theologica* (II.-II., Q123, A. 3): "it belongs to the virtue of fortitude to remove any obstacle that withdraws the will from following the reason" (p. 198). Aquinas goes on to mention that withdrawing from something difficult belongs to the notion of fear (p. 198). Hence, he seems to agree that courage contains the element 'difficult' as well as the element 'dangerous'. And he appears to also make the point that fear itself can be an obstacle or difficulty to reasoned action.

The second objection concerns the requirement that the objective of a courageous act must be a goal of moral worth. Now, in fact, people who fight hard to struggle against a disease have what could be described as a self-concerned objective. It is hard to see in what sense this objective is of moral significance. Consequently, in a case like Johnson's, we are forced to one or the other of two conclusions: either (a) Mr. Johnson's actions were persistent and determined, but not truly courageous, or (b) it is not always true that the objectives of a courageous act must be moral.

My reply to this objection is as follows. Either Johnson's objectives were moral, that is, of moral worth, or not. If so, his actions were courageous. If his objectives cannot be judged morally worthy, then his actions should not be judged as courageous. As the objection itself concedes, however, it is hard to know, in a particular case, whether the agent's objectives really are moral, of moral worth. Most of us would probably say that Johnson's actions were courageous, and leave it at that. I think this is a reflection of our reasonable willingness to give him the benefit of the doubt and presume that his intentions were of moral worth. Also, generally speaking, preserving one's life does have moral worth. As Aquinas pointed out (II.-II., Q126, A. 1), it is natural to love life, and love of life is of moral worth. For example, one's life and survival may be of potential benefit to others. Hence there is a reasonable presumption that a struggle against disease to save one's life may be presumed, in many cases, or usually, to be of moral worth.

The other part of my reply concerns the point that in any case of the actions of a real person, it is hard to know what the intentions in acting truly are. For example, in the case of a mountain climber who succeeds in a difficult and dangerous ascent, we may say that his act was courageous even though the climber's precise intentions in this act may never have been formulated in public. Many individual acts of courage seem to have the form of a private quest for personal meaning. Until we know more about the agent's practical reasoning in a particular act, and particularly his intentions, we may not be in a position to evaluate his action as courageous or not with confidence and on the basis of good evidence. We return to this problem in chapter 10.

Much of the problem here is that of determining what an agent's intentions were. However, once the evidence is in, we can make an evaluation. To be truly courageous, the act must be carried out with intentions that are of moral worth. However, plausible judgments are often made on the basis of burden of proof: we reasonably presume that the agent's intentions could have been of moral worth, unless there is evidence to the contrary.

Hence when I say that conditions (E1) and (E2) require that courageous action be an action that is of normative worth, I mean 'normative' in the sense of the agent's personal—but reasonable—standards of virtue in relation to his position. I do not mean 'normative' in the sense referring to duties that apply to all moral agents as such. Yet even though the term 'considers' is used in the statements of my basic definition of the courageous act, I do not thereby require merely that the agent thought, rightly or wrongly, that he acted for a worthwhile end. His act must have been done for a justifiably worthwhile end that therefore has genuine moral significance as a virtuous end.

Anyone who still objects that (E1) and (E2) cannot express true and objective normative worth as long as they contain the "nonobjective" word 'considers', must continue past chapter 8 on practical reasoning, in which it is argued that real normative worth can be established only in relation to an agent's reasonable position.

Parallel to the objections above, a counterpart objection can be raised against my thesis that a cowardly action requires that the act be done out of fear.

What about moral cowardice? Suppose a senator fails to support a bill he knows he should support, but knows also that supporting it would lose him some critical votes. Could he be described as a "moral coward"? He may not have been motivated by fear, but rather by what he realizes to be an immoral instinct for his own best interests over those of his constituents or his country. Would we not call such an act cowardly? If so, then defining cowardice in our way, to require the cowardly act to be done out of fear, is too narrow.

There is some question, however, of whether calling such an immorally self-interested act cowardly is to be taken literally, or more as a figurative extension of the real meaning of 'cowardly'. One might reply that the senator's act, or failure to act, was not so much cowardly as simply selfish. However, if he was really motivated by some fear of his own downfall, then his act may be called cowardly, but no problem is posed for the definition at issue.

Some of these possibly borderline cases call for fuller treatment. Let us move on, therefore, to a fuller account of some peripheral meanings of courage as a test of the new definition.

CHAPTER 5

The Outer Edges

NOW THAT WE have constructed a basic definition of courageous action, it is necessary to look at many borderline instances in which courage and cowardice are harder to define sharply. There are instances in which we might be inclined to call an act courageous where it does not fit our definition, at least clearly. In these cases, we need to expand or elaborate the definition in various directions. Thus, the basic definition has various practical overtones or secondary meanings that allow its application to specific acts of courage and cowardice.

5.1 Courage, Bravery, and Intrepid Action

The problem of the courageous villain has already been accommodated by the explanation that the ethical matrix can be withdrawn to produce an alternative nonnormative definition of courage. It was suggested, however, that although lacking a worthwhile end, an act could be said to "take courage" if it meets all the practical conditions. Now we need to see that an even more difficult problem than that of the courageous villain can be posed. We should now contemplate an act that shows all the practical characteristics of courage but is amoral; that is, it is not villainous but is simply amoral in the sense that it fails to be of any moral worth even though it is not positively bad. Let us say that such an act meets all the requirements of courage, including being a dangerous or difficult act objectively speaking, except (E1). But it does not have a positively worthwhile end toward which it contributes some necessary condition, so far as we can tell. Is such an act courageous? The problem is that many of us would be inclined to say so. However, the description of such an act will not meet the requirements of our fully normative definition of courage.

Gray (1967) was a professional philosopher who saw extensive wartime service in combat during the Second World War. His observations and insights into the phenomenology of courageous and cowardly actions in wartime conditions is an invaluable source of material. A very subtle paradox is posed by his combat experiences (ibid., p. 109) concerning a type of soldier whose fearlessness is not merely based on his illusion of indestructibility but rather on an indomitable will to power. According to Gray, there are a very few remarkably fearless warriors who have an extraordinary will to victory and iron nerve based on a fanatical power of faith in their own destiny. Such persons find their element in battle and seem to be able to use their own fearlessness, along with the fearlessness of others in the face of death, as a source of power through which they gain their distinctiveness. Gray observes, however, that there is an inhumanistic aspect to this type of soldier. He is contemptuous of others who are not like himself, thus he hardly recognizes other men as such and is "capable of walking over bodies, living or dead, without a qualm" (ibid., p. 110).

The paradox posed by Gray's very astute observation is this. Most of us, notably including the fellow soldiers of this powerfully willed man, would call him outstandingly courageous. As Gray puts it, "Battle appears to be their very element, and in that element men will not hesitate to pay them homage" (ibid.). Nevertheless, he suggests, it is not courage that such men display, not a human will triumphing over fate, but a kind of inhuman egoism. Some of us may well concede that the fearless fool who cannot conceive his own death is not courageous, yet balk at denying that this strong-willed man is courageous. For this man, according to Gray, is quite well aware of death. He just reacts to it in an unusual way.

The best way to resolve Gray's paradox is to make a distinction between courage and bravery. I propose that only a truly courageous act is valorous in the sense that it has a noble or worthy purpose or objective. If an act meets all the practical requirements of courage, but it is not determined that it conforms to the ethical matrix, then we call it an *intrepid act* or *brave act*. Thus, I am arguing that the powerfully willed soldier described by Gray may be brave but is not truly courageous. In other words, I am using the alternative (non-normative) definition discussed previously as a *definiens* for a brave act. To be truly courageous, an act must meet condition (E1) as well as all the other conditions specified. However, an act can be intrepid or brave (but not necessarily courageous) if it meets all the practical conditions of a courageous act but fails to meet (E1). This approach allows us to deal both with the problem of the "courageous villain" and this new problem of the "amoral soldier."

It follows, then, that an act that takes courage could be a brave act without necessarily being courageous. In effect, we are saying that Aristotle and Wallace are not necessarily in such direct conflict or disagreement as it may have seemed earlier. Rather, Aristotle defined courage and Wallace, his words to the contrary, defined bravery, or at least something more like what I now propose we should strictly call bravery rather than courage.

5.2 Determination and Presence of Mind

Sherman, the American Civil War general, offered the following definition: "I would define true courage to be a perfect sensibility of the measure of danger, and a mental willingness to incur it." In offering the second part of this definition, Sherman was returning to the idea of Carlyle and Nietzsche, elaborated in chapter 1, that there is a positive mental element in courageous acts.

I have so far largely resisted this idea, except perhaps for allowing that the element of practical reasoning does constitute a sort of "positive" factor in courageous action. It is now time to concede, however, that there are certain acts that we are inclined to think of as courageous partially because they do have certain positive characteristics pertaining to the mental state of the agent at the time the act was committed. One of these characteristics could be called determination and another might be described as presence of mind.

Sometimes the hallmark of courage is not so much calmness of deliberation or cleverness of practical reasoning as simply a grim determination or persistence to achieve an extremely difficult objective. This quality is sometimes called "grit" or "guts." Many cases of contending with disease, suffering, and medical catastrophe are of this sort. One military instance is that of Major Charles F. Hoey, who, on February 16, 1944, was ordered to take an enemy position in Burma at all costs. After a night march through enemy territory, Hoey personally led his company to the position. Despite his wounds, firing a Bren gun taken from one of his men, he reached the strong post first and killed all the occupants before being mortally wounded. The citation read: "Major Hoey's outstanding gallantry and leadership, his total disregard of personal safety and his grim determination to reach the objective resulted in the capture of this vital position" (Swettenham 1973:179). Hoey, a Canadian in the Lincolnshire Regiment of the British Army, was awarded the Victoria Cross posthumously.

In this case, the plan was straightforward and we have no reason to think it was marked by any special ingenuity. Nor was the objective outstandingly noble or altruistic; it was a matter of military necessity. In addition, Hoey had been given a direct order to take this position "at all costs." Therefore, in one sense, the act was not above the requirements of duty, but was rather a fulfillment of duty. Why then was the act correctly perceived to be courageous? Three aspects are noteworthy. First, the "grim determination" to take the objective. Second, the quality of leadership, personally leading the attack despite his wounds when nobody would have laid blame on the commander who stayed back and ordered his men to do the fighting. In this sense, the act was—contrary to the other sense noted above— beyond the requirements of duty. But this very act of leading the attack personally is indeed evidence of a truly awesome determination to achieve an objective in the face of overwhelming dangers and obstacles. Self-sacrifice is the third aspect.

One account that shows an extraordinary instance of determination and resolve to carry on to the very end of personal resources is the *London Gazette* chronicle of September 26, 1945, describing an action led by Charles Hazlitt Upham. Upham, a captain in the 20th New Zealand Battalion, was commanding a company of New Zealand troops in the Western Desert in Africa. He already held the Victoria Cross for exploits in operations in Crete in 1941. During this occasion in the Western Desert, his battalion had been ordered forward but encountered strong enemy fire. Without hesitation, Upham led his men forward in a determined attack.

Although Upham had been shot through the arm, he went—his arm broken—to bring back some men who had become isolated. He then led his men to beat off a violent counterattack, and through dominating the situation by personal leadership, consolidated a vital position.

> Exhausted by pain from his wound and weak from loss of blood, Captain Upham was then removed to the regimental aid post, but immediately his wound had been dressed he returned to his men remaining with them

all day long under heavy enemy artillery and mortar fire until he was again severely wounded, and being now unable to move, fell into the hands of the enemy when, his gallant company having been reduced to only six survivors, his position was finally over-run by superior enemy forces, in spite of the outstanding gallantry and magnificent leadership shown by Captain Upham. (Army Headquarters 1969:10)

For this action, Upham was awarded the Bar to the Victoria Cross. Since the Victoria Cross was instituted by Queen Victoria in 1865, only three Bars have been awarded.

Very often characteristic of courageous acts is a kind of presence of mind, a quick grasp of the situation and an active and dauntless intervention into the circumstances encountered. A good case study is that of the act of Charles Hudlow in saving four teenagers from the burning wreck of an automobile.[1] Seeing flames at the roadside, Hudlow stopped his car one evening in 1981 and came upon the burning wreckage of a car smashed against a tree. Although he had a fear of fire—his daughter had nearly died of burns from an oven fire—he tore his way into the car and managed to get two of the occupants to safety.

At that point, another man, Steve Kimball, also stopped to help. While he was helping, Hudlow climbed into the flaming car and pulled out another girl. Then, reentering the burning wreckage, Hudlow, with the assistance of Kimball, managed to pry the driver, who was pinned behind the steering wheel, out of the car. All the occupants of the car survived with severe injuries, and Hudlow himself sustained second-degree burns, a fractured chest bone, a broken tooth, and smoke inhalation.

One aspect of this incident which appears to be remarkable is the speed with which this man reacted to the situation, the aggressiveness of his assault on the burning car, and, in general, the alertness of his response to a dreadful situation. Kimball said of Hudlow's actions that "he acted as if he had done it all before."[2] According to the report of the incident, Hudlow admonished his own children, "If you see something that needs to be done, do it!"[3] The active nature of the intervention, the lack of hesitation, not only were necessary to the success of this feat but also represent a characteristic that makes the action especially valorous.

Cases of courageous acts such as those above do suggest positive characteristics of how the act was brought about by the agent in addition to the element of the formidableness of the danger or the goodness of the objective. In this sense, there does appear to be some evidence for the Carlyle viewpoint against the more Aristotelian approach. However, both determination and presence of mind do have to do with the practical deliberation that goes into the bringing about of an objective or outcome of one's act. Perhaps, then, if the Aristotelian type of definition adopted in chapter 4 can be supplemented by a theory of practical reasoning, such borderline cases as these can be accommodated to the definition.

Again and again, the theme is perceived that a mark of conspicuous courage is doing something in a situation that seems so hopeless most of us would give up. All of us know the despair of defective or failed equipment in a difficult situation. Frustration is not a good mood in which to confront a situation needing judgment, deliberation, or quick thinking. Yet, curiously, some people have been known to make incredibly determined attempts to "get on with the job" in the most hopeless and problematic situations and—even more strangely—have succeeded.

In November 1967 in Vietnam, Sergeant Sammy L. Davis was assisting a gun crew attempting to fire at a strong enemy ground assault. Only a river separated the Viet Cong attackers from the American position. A direct hit from an enemy recoilless rifle round hurled the gun crew from their howitzer, and Davis was blown into a shell hole. Disregarding strong enemy fire, he got up and aimed and fired the howitzer, blowing himself to the ground again. Still not discouraged, he returned to fire again when he was injured by an enemy mortar shell explosion. Getting up once more despite painful injuries, he fired again, and knocked himself down again by the recoil. After firing more shells, he negotiated an air mattress across the deep river to rescue three wounded Americans on the other side, even though he himself could not swim. After this successful action, he continued to refuse medical attention, and joined another howitzer crew until the Viet Cong attack was broken up (COVA 1973:831).

This situation did not seem too hopeful. After the blast that had thrown the crew from the howitzer, we are told that the artillery piece was "burning furiously," and that Davis was warned repeatedly to seek cover. He didn't. Almost certainly, most of us would have. Davis was awarded the Congressional Medal of Honor for this action.

The problem is not that the cases above fail to meet our definition of courage, for they clearly do meet it. Rather, the problem is that they seem to suggest additional dimensions of courage that may help us to more fully characterize acts of courage. Yet another dimension of courage is suggested by some observations of Gray (1967).

5.3 Constitutional Cowardice and Courage

It is the experience of many combat veterans that most soldiers feel fear, but that most also learn to manage their fear well enough to get the job done. Gray (1967:111) distinguishes, on the basis of his military experience, between what he calls the "occasional coward" and the "constitutional coward." The latter person simply cannot manage to endure personal danger with composure and feels that every bullet is intended for him. Such a person is easily identified in combat and becomes an object of contempt, a "coward." However, Gray adds that even the most elite troops or the bravest veterans may at some time flee in terror. Occasional cowardice is thus a different type of phenomenon from a constantly present trait or quality: "Cowardice in this [occasional] sense is, like rashness, a group phenomenon and greatly contagious" (ibid., p. 112). Occasional cowardice seems more like what Aristotle had in mind as the opposite of courage, for it appears to be a temporary lapse of practical reasoning due to some failure in certain circumstances to cope with sudden emotions. The cowardice of the constitutional coward, by contrast, seems to be a function of how he perceives the dangerous situation.

Gray (ibid., p. 113) observed that the constitutional coward tends to be constantly troubled by his own imagination—he sees potential danger everywhere and is constantly on the move to find a safer spot. He gives an example of a man in his unit who was constantly worried about his safety, even sleeping in a ravine full of red ants one night after a bombing instead of staying in a chalet with the rest of the platoon.

In answer to the query of what makes the constitutional coward so different from the average soldier, Gray offers the hypothesis that this type of individual lacks the sense of union with his comrades that the other men share. In a way, Gray's explanation suggests that the behavior of the constitutional coward is consistent with the inner logic of his beliefs. It is an observation of Gray's that most soldiers have a joy in sacrifice and will often give up their lives easily for the necessity of the group in combat. However, the constitutional coward is unable to understand this altruistic behavior. For him, the value of the group does not outweigh the value of his own life. This individual, as Gray puts it (ibid., p. 114), has one answer to arguments concerning his duty or respect toward his friends: "What do they matter if I am no longer alive to know about them?" Thus, this type of cowardice is not a lapse of practical reasoning in the face of a sudden emotional distraction, as the Greek view would depict cowardice, but rather it is uniform and consistent practical reasoning based on an unusually egoistic premise. If my premise is that my interests are much more valuable than anyone else's, even collectively as an other-group, then surely it would be illogical to risk my own demise for the possible benefit of the group. The failure here, according to Gray, is a deficiency of love, an inability to participate in the lives of others. According to him, the spectacle of the death of this sort of coward is a most unpleasant scene.

What Gray (1967) calls constitutional cowardice seems quite similar to what Wallace (1978) calls the type of cowardice due to excessive fear. To exemplify this type of cowardice, Wallace (1978:68) asks us to consider the hypothetical case of Smythe, who is terribly afraid of hurt or injury because she believes her affairs are not worth the risk of injury.

> She is convinced that it is worth suffering any frustration and humiliation in order to avoid the danger of pain and injury. She sometimes neglects her affairs, family, and friends, not because she is indifferent, but because she is so afraid of being injured, that all other considerations pale beside the urgency of avoiding this sort of danger.

To account for this species of cowardice, Wallace adds the fourth clause, concerning excessive fear of risk, to his definition of cowardice.

This account of cowardice does seem very similar to the description given by Gray of the constitutional coward. Both individuals risk disapproval or rejection of their fellows by an excessive fear of personal danger. But there may be a significant difference. Gray's coward tries so hard to avoid risk of personal danger precisely because he is not, at bottom, capable of concern with the lives of others. Note, however, that Wallace's Smythe neglects her comrades not because of her indifference but because of the intrinsic fear of personal injury. Thus Smythe, unlike Gray's coward, seems more motivated by a kind of excessive fastidiousness, a fear of the physical distress of personal injury. This seems more like a kind of lack of physical courage, and therefore seems quite different from Gray's soldier who even slept in a ravine full of red ants in order to be more assured of his safety from bombardment. Wallace (ibid., p. 68 f.) writes that Smythe does have normal concerns for obligations and commitments, but is excessively concerned about possible injury. Her perception is therefore somehow distorted because she overemphasizes danger, the injury looms too large in her imagination as a fearful threat to be avoided. Gray's coward perceives the situation accurately enough, but his reasoning is always colored by the high value he puts on his own life. Both are logical enough in their practical reasoning, but both start from an unusual premise that makes each give a high priority to avoiding danger. However, in one case the premise is a kind of selfishness or lack of involvement with others; in the other, the premise is a kind of distaste or abhorrence of personal injury. Smythe's failure is really an excessive preoccupation with details that most of us dismiss as minor nuisances in our concentration on the main task.

Indeed, one hallmark of courage may be focusing on the job or goal in mind instead of becoming confused by or bogged down in trivial details. Instead of worrying about small injuries that will eventually heal anyway, the courageous person plunges ahead with the goal firmly in mind of preventing some irreversible harm like the death of a person.

The opposite of the person who is cowardly through a worrisome fastidiousness about the smaller details of personal well-being is the individual who can display equanimity and even cheerfulness in the face of many painful annoyances, bodily catastrophes, illnesses, and injuries. A record of sorts in this line would appear to be attributed to Roy Reep, who was a sixty-seven-year-old fire dispatcher at the time a column was written about him in the *Hamilton Spectator*.[4] At age three, Reep's brother shot him in the face with their grandfather's pistol, and the bullet still remained in his neck. A playmate damaged the back of his head on a barrel when he was eight, and he sustained an injury he still feels. At eleven, his father accidentally split his head open with an axe. At age thirteen, he needed surgery to correct some results of his early gunshot wound.

As a young man, he suffered a pelvic fracture and internal injuries in a car accident. The doctors said he would not be able to walk again after he was put in a cast, but he now walks, runs, and plays golf. He was shot in the chest and arm by his inebriated wife (now deceased), and three years later the doctors removed a bullet after he experienced chest pains. He fell from a ladder, and as a result, missed a year's work. Subsequently, he went blind in one eye after an operation to remove a cataract. Reep has also had other "minor problems"—a hole in the roof of his mouth from his gunshot injury, blood poisoning in a leg and finger, the loss of a finger in a job-related accident.

Despite this continual succession of harassments, Reep reports that he has a wonderful life, that he has been lucky, and that "the most wonderful part is that I can run and I can play golf and I'm sixty-seven years old." He is described as being a cheerful person.

Constitutional courage and cowardice would seem to be kinds of physical courage and cowardice. At least the cases described above seem to pertain to bodily inconveniences and discomforts. Could it therefore be useful to make a distinction between moral and physical courage? Most of the cases we have looked at so far have involved physical danger and difficulty, but there are cases where the danger is not so much physical in nature but rather involves the loss of reputation, prestige, popularity, or some other negative outcome that does not involve direct physical harm or danger.

5.4 *Moral and Physical Courage*

It has been shown that a distinction should be made between *physical courage* and *moral courage*. Physical courage has sometimes been denigrated as a "purely physical" and therefore morally worthless quality. But, of course, it depends on how courage is defined. If physical courage is simply defined as absence of fear or absence of pain, then it may not be a morally commendable quality. But we have already argued against such psychologistic and normatively empty attempts to define courage.

A better way to make the distinction is as follows. Physically courageous acts are those specified by an optional interpretation (E2) in the ethical matrix, indicating that the danger or difficulty is primarily of a physical nature. An example would be the person who endures a debilitating or catastrophic illness or injury uncomplainingly and with dignity. A moving wartime illustration is given by Robert Graves.[5] He describes how Captain A. L. Simpson of the Royal Welsh Fusiliers had fallen mortally wounded twenty yards out from the front line. This officer was so highly respected that three men were killed and four more wounded in attempts to get him back. When his own orderly reached him, Simpson sent him back, apologizing for making so much noise. When found by Graves at dusk, he was dead, hit in seventeen places, his knuckles forced into his mouth to keep himself from crying out and possibly attracting more men to their deaths.

Morally courageous acts are those where the difficulty or danger, specified in (E2), is not so much an immediate threat to one's physical well-being as a threat to one's social standing, financial prospects, relations with one's colleagues, approval of one's constituents, and so forth. Here the threat is not directly or primarily physical, although physical illness or family problems may be one effect of something like the loss of one's job, one possible consequence of a morally courageous act. Socrates' persistence in his philosophical activities took moral courage, and, ultimately, physical courage as well.

An unusual case described by Gray (1967:185), which he calls a "revelation of nobility," combines both moral and physical courage in one act. The story is told by the Dutch of a German soldier, a member of an execution squad ordered to shoot innocent hostages. "Suddenly he stepped out of rank and refused to participate in the execution. On the spot he was charged with treason by the officer in charge and was placed with the hostages, where he was promptly executed by his comrades." This act of courage is outstanding because the soldier knew that his disobedience meant his death. Also, he had to overcome the inertia of belonging to the security of his own group of comrades, a strong link in wartime. Despite all these external constraints—an unusually strong combination—he responded to his conscience and moved forward to protest by his act of disobedience. Another factor is the effect of his heroism on the slayers and the slain, not to mention our own reactions to the incident, an effect that is even now inspiring.

Courage is given the literal description "guts" most appropriately when it involves heroic action in face of physical assaults or damage to the person. One action for which a man was awarded the Congressional Medal of Honor is particularly impressive. This act of courage took place during the Second World War in the campaign in Italy in June 1944. Caught in a massed ambush of enemy fire from riflemen, machine guns, and tanks, Private Herbert F. Christian of the U.S. Infantry, stood erect in a brightly illuminated area and signaled his patrol to withdraw. When his right leg was severed above the knee by canon fire, Christian continued to advance on his left knee and the stump of his right thigh, while firing his submachine gun. Advancing to within ten yards of the enemy, he reloaded and continued to fire, until he was killed by the concentration of enemy fire. By firing directly into the enemy position and drawing their fire to himself, he had enabled the other twelve men in his patrol to escape from the ambush.

This act combines so many qualities of courage into one action that it has an awesome quality. The act was one of self-sacrifice. It was a successful ruse in a most terrible situation, undertaken with such boldness and presence of mind that it took back the initiative from those who had prepared a careful trap. It showed a bold decisiveness in a deadly, intimidating, and hopeless situation, and a resolute persistence and determination to carry on in the face of grievous wounds and pain. It is a triumph of spirit over the worst situation, yet also an altruistic act of sacrifice voluntarily undertaken. Perhaps what it most graphically illustrates, however, is sheer guts—the capability to persist in the face of physical destruction.

Perhaps, then, the usual distinction between moral courage and physical courage is useful. But the two qualities are not mutually exclusive. Moral courage, like determination and presence of mind, is another aspect of the nature of courage stated previously. (More about moral courage in the next chapter.) Next, let us pose a common puzzle that also stretches the concepts of courage and cowardice at their outer edges.

5.5 Can Animals Be Courageous?

If courage could be adequately defined as simply absence of fear, then it would seem to follow that animals can be courageous. For nobody denies that animals can exhibit fear.

Some interesting light is thrown on this implication by the work of learning theorists on experimental trials with animals. Pavlov reported an experiment that gradually increased an electrical current applied to a very hungry dog each time the dog was fed. The experimenter found that after a while the dog reacted to the electric current by salivating, wagging its tail, and exhibiting other food reactions. In other experiments reported by Mowrer (1961:433), rats accustomed to running over an energized electric grill to get food would cross at much higher shock intensities than ones who had no previous experience of crossing it. Mowrer (ibid., p. 434) concludes that courage seems to be able to be acquired, and is a function of how hope and fear are balanced. Much fear and little hope gives a "cowardly" response; the opposite produces a "courageous" response. The use of the term 'courage' here perhaps seems acceptable if we think of it as being purely definable as an emotional reaction or lack thereof—that is, in purely behavioristic terms.

Another psychologist, Muenzinger, objected to the use of the term 'courage' in this context. Moreover, Muenzinger added, if we do not want to use the concept of courage in relation to the behavior of rats, would it not be inconsistent to use the "complementary concept of fear in rats?" (quoted by Mowrer 1961:435). As we have seen, anyone adopting the definition proposed in chapter 4 would regard it as an error to treat fear and courage as opposites, or "complementary concepts." But, for a behaviorist, who is not concerned with the cognitive component of courage, such an approach might seem logical. Indeed, Mowrer himself questions whether courage might be simply defined as the absence of fear in situations where it would be expected to be present (ibid., p. 435).

However, in a later note (ibid., p. 471), Mowrer shows some discomfort with the word 'courage' by posing the following problem. Consider two groups of rats. Each rat in the first group is allowed to press a food-giving bar one hundred times, each time receiving an electric shock. The second group is given the same food in response to the same number of bar pressings but is only shocked occasionally. The result is that after the one hundred trials it would be far less inhibiting to the second group of rats. The problem is: Do we say that the second group of animals has developed "courage" or should we say that they are perverse, rigid, foolhardy?

Mowrer says that the answer is that the rats are "courageous" if we wish the animals to ignore the shock. And the answer is negative if we wish to block the rats' habit. The answer, then, does not appear to be a function of the rats' behavior at all, but merely a function of our own response to it. In other words, our use of the term 'courageous' here is simply anthropomorphism when applied to rats.

Thus it seems apparent that there is a certain absurdity in attributing courage to rats. If courage is simply the absence of fear, how do we answer the question posed by Mowrer's problem? It seems we cannot, except by simply imposing our own subjective expectations on the situation, which is not a good way to proceed. If courage is defined exclusively as absence of fear, the definition will always have an aspect of vagueness about it that makes it seem trivial.

Does the question make more sense when considered in light of my definition of 'courageous act'? Perhaps a little. For if an animal can contribute to the bringing about of some worthwhile state of affairs by overcoming some difficult or dangerous obstacle through determination and persistence, then, analogous to previous cases of courageous acts, it would make a certain amount of sense to say that the animal had acted courageously. True, this move would mean a certain stretching of our basic definition. For it is quite disputable whether any animal can be justified in believing that the various clauses of courageous action are met. But sometimes acts performed by animals do seem very strongly to be plausibly described as courageous.

I recall reading of a not uncommon sort of case where a large dog had gnawed through a locked door to save a large family, including several children, from a house that burned down without warning during the night. The dog suffered severe splinters and bleeding from its mouth and was severely burned in returning to the blazing house several times to drag children to safety. It is hard in this case to withhold the term 'courage'.

Later (chap. 8), we will argue that an act of courage is an attempt to bring about a good end by means of practical reasoning. This type of reasoning implies that the agent acted by bringing about some means he or she considered necessary to bring about that good end. However, it is disputable whether animals, younger children, and other agencies not thought to be "competent" decision makers can act through practical reasoning.

I will argue that when we do perceive actions by children or animals as courageous, we make a judgment that it is "as if" the child or the animal were acting by forethought or practical reasoning to undertake a worthwhile objective. It may not be so, but by a kind of presumptive extension of reasonable action, we accord the animal or the child the benefit of the doubt, and may call their action courageous.

We will see later that cases of reflexive actions and cases of "courageous" acts by children and animals pose a problem for our analysis of courage, because our analysis requires practical reasoning. And that, in turn, seems to require competence in deliberation and reasonable forethought. But such problems can be dealt with.

5.6 *Altruism and Courage*

Heyd (1982:115) requires that an act be done for the sake of someone else's good in order for it to qualify as a supererogatory act. Of course, not all courageous acts are supererogatory. Yet it might seem that all courageous acts are altruistic. In my own view, an act need not be altruistic to qualify as being truly courageous. Yet it does seem that most truly outstanding acts of courage have altruistic elements.

Sometimes the altruism of courage is the selflessness of being concerned about others more than danger to oneself. In May 1945, on Okinawa, Private Desmond T. Doss was giving first aid during a night attack in open territory when he was seriously wounded in the legs by a grenade explosion.[6] Not wanting to call another aid man from cover, he tended his own wounds and waited for five hours. When two men came to help, the three of them were caught in a Japanese tank attack. Doss noticed a more critically wounded man nearby, and crawled off the litter so it could be used for this other man. Wounded again, in the arm this time, he bound up his own wound with a rifle stock and crawled three hundred yards over rough terrain to the aid station.

On September 4, 1974, Jean Swedberg, the switchboard operator at the Valnicola Hotel in Merritt, British Columbia, ran to alert the guests during a fire that was running out of control. She warned the first floor occupants, then went through the smoke to the second story, going from door to door. Aware of the danger, she continued through the blaze to warn the people in the last few rooms. However, fire sealed off her escape and a mass of flames consumed the building with the result that she lost her life in the fire. She was awarded the Cross of Valor (Honors Secretariat 1983). Here again the act was an altruistic disregard of self in attempting to help or save others.

Sometimes an act we recognize as courageous involves one person putting his or her own life at grave risk in order to attempt to save the life of another. In such a case, the act is altruistic, but different from cases where one person risks his or her own life to save many lives or where the purpose could be considered so noble or good as to "outweigh" the risk of a single life. Yet even where the risk is one-for-one, we may consider the act highly courageous.

On the morning of October 28, 1923, the U.S. Submarine 0-5 collided with the steamship *Abangarez* and sank in less than a minute.

Torpedoman Henry Breault reached the hatch and saw that the boat was rapidly sinking. Instead of making his way off the sinking submarine, he returned to the torpedo room to rescue a trapped shipmate, closing the torpedo room hatch after his entry. Both men remained trapped in the compartment until rescued by a salvage party thirty-one hours later. For this act of courage, Breault was awarded the Congressional Medal of Honor (COVA 1973:475).

Altruism in acts of courage has to do with what I have called the ethical matrix of the definition of courage. The service of others is obviously one form of noble objective or life purpose of commendable action. We could say that a courageous act especially marked by altruistic intent is an act of gallantry. Most truly courageous acts are gallant. That could be because most intentions to do something good involve an element of altruism.

Altruism is intrinsically connected with courage through the concept of a position. A position is one's personal stance on an issue, but a position in relation to action becomes especially significant if a large number of people adhere to it and are prepared to act on it. Hence it is characteristic of positions that one person's position can be identified with an "official" group position. By becoming a committed Catholic or a committed Republican, one shares a group position. The sincerity of one's commitment may therefore be challenged if one refuses to make some sacrifices to support the goals that are part of that collective position by undertaking action required to support the group effort.

A soldier who volunteers for an especially hazardous job shows his commitment beyond the requirements of duty, to his branch of the service, to his country, and ultimately to the cause his side fights for. If history decides the cause was unjust, his commitment to that position may turn out to have been unjustified. Positions can turn out to be indefensible, and therefore any action that proceeds from commitment to a position may be risky, in more ways than one. Commitment thus involves elements of "faith" and "luck." Choosing a position on significant issues almost always means taking sides with some group of adherents against an opposed group.

However, one's acts based on commitment will only be virtuous insofar as one's position is morally sound and reasonable. Having become committed to the group position, one must defend it insofar as one continues to judge it to be reasonable. Otherwise, it would not be courageous to sacrifice one's own interests to support the group position. In short, an act does not have to be altruistic to be courageous. But the nature of action done through moral commitment is usually to serve the group position, whether it be community, church, or country.

So strongly is courage linked to altruism that—so it seems to me—the essence of courage is commonly thought to consist in the taking of risk or the making of self-sacrifice for the purpose of saving or helping others. The Carnegie Hero Fund Commission has set down as the main requirement for the Carnegie Medal that the person performing the heroic act must have voluntarily risked his or her life in saving or trying to save the life of another person. Moreover, there must be no prior obligation or duty or reason for a special responsibility for the action. The medal is given for "selfless heroism." But I think many would equate that with courage, thereby defining courage as heroic altruism of action.

Courageous acts are often acts of saving, or attempting to save, the life of another person. Hence one might also be led to conclude that acts of courage always involve self-sacrifice or altruistic risk with the purpose of saving a life. I have held, however, that courage should not be identified exclusively with either altruism or life saving in every instance. Striving for a conspicuously good purpose in the face of danger or personal risk comes very close to being always life supporting, life saving, and altruistic. For any act of great good usually turns out to have altruistic implications. Yet I think some cases of courage are only altruistic in an incidental way.

Stephen Hawking is a professor of mathematics at Cambridge University who has received the prestigious Franklin Medal "for his revolutionary contributions to, among others, the theory of general relativity, astrophysics and cosmology, and to the dynamics, thermodynamics and gravitational effects of black holes" (Editorial 1982:71). Hawking has achieved advances in physics that parallel the great achievements of physicists like Faraday and Einstein. He has shown how microphysics and quantum theory are related to the large-scale structure of the universe (Mitton 1979:28).

In the early 1960s, it was determined that Hawking was suffering from a degenerative disease, amyotrophic lateral sclerosis, that renders the voluntary muscles useless and is usually fatal (Boslough 1984:76). His condition continued to deteriorate, and by the 1970s he was confined to a wheelchair. As the ravages of disease have diminished his physical powers, Hawking has still managed to carry on his work at the Department of Applied Mathematical and Theoretical Physics at Cambridge.

This man's life is an extraordinary example of the courage to carry on with very demanding scholarship in the face of formidable physical hardships. Mathematical work is a difficult job under the best physical conditions and with few distractions. To lose muscular control because of a debilitating disease would be an overwhelming obstacle, both to morale and to the ability to remain functionally capable to get work done. It is therefore extraordinary that this man has achieved so much with the resources he has. It is an example to those of us in scholarly work who often find distractions and worries of one sort or another as an excuse for not trying harder to keep going.

I do not want to detract from Hawking's superb courage in any way, but I would suggest that here is a case where altruism enters the picture only obliquely. Here is a case where a person has overcome formidable difficulties and obstacles to achieve great good by contributing in a distinguished way to our attempts to understand the structure and workings of the universe. This form of scientific achievement, of course, characteristically does benefit mankind. Therefore, there is an altruistic element present in dedicated scientific research. But the effort to seek out truth through scientific research is a good objective in itself, apart from the particular applications and benefits that may accrue from it. The altruistic benefit is not strictly necessary for the good of the scientific research as a quest for truth in its own right.

Hence I think we should say that the efforts of a dedicated scientific researcher to persist in making great discoveries despite formidable obstacles and difficulties should be called courageous, whether altruistic benefits happen to be forthcoming or not. I can see, however, where some might disagree with this conclusion. It could be argued that scientific research can have harmful effects, and therefore that scientists must take social responsibilities for their discoveries. By these lights, pure scientific research need not be called "good" unless it is meant to benefit mankind in a socially positive way.

Once again, I do not wish to argue against altruism as a worthy goal—but merely to claim that there can be some cases of courageous actions that were not necessarily meant to be altruistic by their protagonist. I think that such cases are rare, and I do not want to claim that Hawking's motives are not altruistic, or anything of that sort. I cite his case as one of courage by a determined and distinguished scientist. And I submit that to pursue a worthwhile goal, like discovering scientific truth, should be called courageous whether it happens to be altruistic or not.

The point is sure to be subject to further debate, however, and should remain an open problem. I have not required that an act be altruistic in order for it to be called courageous, but I can see why Heyd has required that an act be done for someone else's good to qualify as supererogatory. And I can well appreciate why many people feel that courageous acts always essentially have an element of altruistic risk or self-sacrifice implicitly contained in them. I could perhaps be convinced to add a clause requiring an act to be altruistic to the basic definition of 'courageous act'. But given my arguments above, I propose to leave altruism as an overtone of courage, present in many instances of courageous acts though not necessarily in all.

CHAPTER 6

Moral Deliberation and Conduct

THE THESIS HAS now been advanced that courage is a matter of practical deliberation in a crisis, as opposed to a thoughtless or blind act of emotional elation. It is now time to look at some positive cases that will confirm the reasonableness of preferring the former account as morally and practically the better. These cases will also throw some light on the complex nature of practical deliberation itself.

A crisis in practical reasoning characteristically occurs where a person can bring about something highly worthwhile, but only by means of bringing about something bad (difficult, let's say) and at the risk of bringing about something else bad (dangerous). Courageous actions typically take place in a crisis.

6.1 Reasoning in Practical Ethics

It is helpful in studying the qualities of courage and cowardice to distinguish between two branches of ethics. Ethical theory as the study of general principles to help us classify which types of acts are obligatory, permitted, right, or wrong is one branch of ethical studies. The other, the study of responsibility for how actions are carried out, requires a more practical approach. Here we start with an act, once done, that has a network of consequences. One primary question is whether or not a was in control of the act, whether a "could have done otherwise." If so, and if some of these consequences are of ethical significance, we may raise questions about the motive or intention of the act, and how the act was brought about. Of course, we typically have no very direct access to a determination of motives or intentions, so we try to construct plausible hypotheses about them by making presumptions about what a reasonable person in like circumstances would foresee as likely consequences of this sort of action. Such a retrospective reconstruction of plausible motives or intentions and their connections with external consequences of lines of action is the characteristic task of the assessment of responsibility for actions. We call this a practical inquiry because it involves constructing a plausible scenario of what the agent might have had in mind in relation to how a particular act was carried out. It is a kind of plausible reasoning that shifts the burden of proof in evaluating claims and counterclaims of responsibility, but does not normally yield decisive judgments in particular cases.

An excellent illustration of practical reasoning on how an action was carried out takes place in the historian's explanation of momentous acts in history.[1] When a famous act is called courageous by a historian, a judgment is being made about practical ethics. Sometimes the proper evaluation of such acts is very difficult to reconstruct and may involve virtually a whole biographical saga, taking into account the moral beliefs and deliberations of the agent. The accounts and justifications of actions in history may go into the deliberative moral reasoning of the historical figure in very subtle ways.

Some instances offered by Allan Nevins in his foreword to John Kennedy's *Profiles in Courage* suggest how historical judgments of a person's moral courage depends on the network of moral reasoning that went into his or her actions and stands taken. The precise evaluation of the quality of this moral deliberation may, however, be difficult to assess. Some wished Lincoln to be more "courageous" about emancipation, he observes, "when such intrepidity would have been decidedly premature" (Kennedy 1956:xii). Contrasting with the profiles given by Kennedy of heroes of moral courage who acted "in a noble way for large ends," Nevins gives some instances of acts falling short of truly courageous: (1) the fanatic, who does not act from moral reasoning, but from his own one-sided, dogmatic, and unyielding perspective; (2) the person of erratic temperament, who may show great bravery, but his reasoning is wrongheaded, fretful, or abusive rather than clear-minded; (3) the inveterate objector, who may show great pluck and fire, but little consistency, integrity of principle, or constructive reasoning. Thus, according to Nevins, the instances given by J. F. Kennedy of true moral courage are intelligent, farsighted, and reasonable men with well-developed moral principles and goals. Moral courage, then, occurs at a juncture when such a man, on the basis of his own moral reasoning, is forced to proclaim independence in acting contrary to his erring constituency.

One initially strange and forbidding fact about any sort of inquiry in matters of practical ethics is that all claims are essentially disputable.[2] One reason this is so is that there is a deep pluralism of ethical theories and foundational principles that serve as the basic premises of moral reasoning and argumentation. Thus ethical reasoning about responsibility for actions is more like legal disputation in a criminal case than it is like scientific reasoning in mathematics. In criminal law, the two attorneys dispute each others' claims in an adversarial system, and a judge or jury must arrive at a finding on the basis of "reasonable doubt." Thus what governs the logic of the argument is called "burden of proof."[3]

A similar type of reasoning is characteristic of practical reasoning even outside the more officially structured setting of the criminal court, except that the better sort of practical reasoning is less adversarial than its courtroom analogue. It is this sort of dialogue we enter into when we attempt to classify actions as courageous or cowardly. First, descriptions of the agent's behavior and circumstances will be used as evidence to establish what the act was, who carried it out, what its outcomes were, and whether the agent had other avenues of action open to him or not. These judgments concern the practical reasoning base. More highly disputable statements will then be put forward and tested in argument. These statements will concern proposed estimations of the difficulty or danger of the act, and the worth of the outcome contributed to by the act. In clear cases, there will be agreement "beyond reasonable doubt" and an act will be clearly agreed on as courageous. Often, however, as we have seen, there can be considerable scope for extended argument.

According to Audi (1982:31), the simplest basic schema for practical reasoning is the following. Here G is some end or goal of an action, A.

> Major Premise: I want G.
>
> Minor Premise: My A'ing would contribute to bring about G.
>
> Conclusion: I should A.

By this view, every piece of practical reasoning has these three components: a motivational (major) premise, a (minor) connecting premise that relates the desired state of affairs to the action, and a conclusion that forms a practical judgment to favor the action.[4]

The literature suggests, however, that there is considerable variation in how this basic schema is to be interpreted. Some exponents think that G need not be a desire or want of the reasoner, but merely some possible objective or outcome he is considering in an exploratory way. Some commentators like von Wright take the minor premise to express that doing A is a necessary condition for bringing about G. Others, like Anscombe, interpret this premise as stipulating that doing A would be sufficient to bring about G. Some authors interpret the conclusion as a decision to act, others interpret the "should" of the conclusion as a normative expression, and still others interpret the conclusion as a statement of action, practical resolution, or preference with no ethical force.

The fundamental notion behind this basic conception is that two states of affairs are linked both in reality and in the deliberator's mind by a possible sequence of actions.[5] It is well to emphasize again, however, that this basic conception of practical reasoning is just that, very basic and minimal. Realistic judgments of the courageousness of an act will overlay this basic structure with rich networks of narrative argumentation that explore the inner mental life of an agent. In some cases we need a very full discourse of the deliberations that motivated an agent before we can adequately explain why the act was courageous, or properly defend the act as deeply courageous in nature. This "mental element" explored in deeper evaluations of historical acts, for example, should go far beyond the basic structure of practical reasoning into the reasons and arguments the agent was thought to have formulated as a basis for his or her action in the circumstances in question.

Such deeper evaluations are sometimes so existentially rich that they go into the life purposes of a person, the fundamental goals that this particular person stood for and defended as matters of moral principle. What we see in such cases is that the ethical worth of the action is partly a function of the agent's own arguments that he used to justify the act. In a feedback-loop type of process, we justify the courage of an act partly by reference to the arguments that went into the agent's own motivations in producing the act. To a certain extent, the agent of the courageous act may be his own advocate of the act's courageousness. Of course, as we have seen, not all courageous acts are so deliberatively rich. But sometimes the difference between an act that is heroically courageous or morally trivial lies precisely in the depth of deliberation that went into its execution.

6.2 *Attitudes and Life Purposes*

A thesis of Gray's (1967) is that in order to understand courage in battle, it is necessary to understand the different attitudes different soldiers have toward death. For the constitutional coward, death is the annihilation of the ego, and therefore something to be avoided even at the cost of losing respect of one's comrades. For the forceful leader in battle, who capitalizes on others' fear of death, death is real but not something deeply understood or pondered. Gray observes that other soldiers seek fulfillment in death. The one who follows a glorious ideal, like fascism or communism, sacrifices his life willingly, for death is a mere incident "in comparison with the reality that fills his being" (Gray 1967:116). Other soldiers will die to incur the approval of an influential leader. Again, the motive seems to be a submerging of the individual ego into the enthusiasm for a more highly valued ideal or person. The religious motive is another of this sort Gray mentions, and he thinks that some motive of "otherworldly consciousness" is much more common than many commentators in a supposedly secular age would have us believe. Death, for these individuals, is an obstacle to be overcome toward some ultimate goal. Gray calls this man the "otherworldly" soldier, and observes that his religious conviction may be strengthened in combat.

Yet another type of soldier Gray identifies is the man who learns to regard death as one experience among others that he will face, and is therefore able to take risks with greater calmness than other soldiers who do not have this attitude. For this man, death is something recognized and respected, but it is not regarded as an absolute. Such a man does not want to live forever, and therefore values the transient experiences of this life very highly. An analogy that illuminates the attitude of this person to life and death is the enhancement of erotic love by a recognition of its transience. Death is not something desired or feared, just another possibility of experience.

This lighthearted soldier's attitude toward death evokes our admiration of his courage, according to Gray (ibid., p. 125), but on reflection we may find him not completely admirable. Gray suggests that this sort of person is not reflective or analytical, and his irresponsibility toward all values other than personal experience not only might perpetuate traditional evils but also might encourage the institution of war.

Yet another courageous type of soldier is the professional, for whom duty and discipline are the highest values. This soldier is not reckless about death, but treats it soberly as a normal hazard, and performs as usual to the end. This type of dedication, because it stems from a regard for duty, may be highly regarded as a mainspring of courageous action. However, if this type of soldier's commitment is to a questionable moral order, his courage may likewise be called into question. The German soldier who went to his death rather than execute political prisoners is so stunningly courageous by his act precisely because he found the moral and physical courage to sharply deviate from "duty and discipline."

Commitment pertains to long-term goals (life goals) in practical reasoning. As we will see in chapter 8, commitments are propositions, statements of policies or objectives, that define a person's position in reasonable dialogue. In the next section, we will see how moral reasoning takes the form of a dialogue whereby an act is justified as courageous, or refuted as being noncourageous. The basic structure of this form of moral reasoning is that of question-answer dialogue. In dialogue, the participants accept certain commitments, and these commitment-sets as a collectivity define what may be called a *position*, defended in the dialogue. Commitment can be a long-term aspect of practical reasoning. Therefore it is relevant to questions of whether courage can be a long-term property of persons, as opposed to being a short-term property of actions. These questions of courage as an attribute of character are very controversial (and are taken up in chap. 10).

Examples of commitment are best brought out in cases where an action reflects a commitment to certain moral goals or values. Moral courage provides many interesting cases of this sort. Altruism as a goal reflected in actions also provides a case of moral position reflected in action.

We have often remarked on the "don't want to get involved" syndrome of many bystanders in cases where others are in trouble. This passivity reflects a lack of moral commitment to altruistic goals. On the morning of December 18, 1980, a taxi driver, Keith Woleston, was engaged in a struggle with an armed man who had already killed one person. During their struggle, a shot was fired as the man opened the cab door. A passing pedestrian, Doreen Hewitt, went to the aid of the taxi driver and tried to push the man back into the taxi. Suddenly he jumped from the car and stabbed Hewitt in the stomach, inflicting a severe wound. But the man's murderous rampage came to an end when he was apprehended by the police who had just arrived. Hewitt and Woleston were awarded the Star of Courage (Honors Secretariat 1983).

Citizens taking personal risks and incurring personal sacrifice to aid in the apprehension of violent criminals is an area where personal judgment is called for. It is clear, however, that many individuals are less willing to incur personal risks for altruistic reasons. There may be many reasons for this. But when somebody, like Hewitt, does respond by trying to help another person in grave danger, despite the clear danger to self, it is the mark of a moral commitment expressed by action. It is this position as expressed by free and intentional, knowing action that is the real underlying basis of all judgments that an act should be called courageous. Because these types of acts can reflect a long-term reasoned commitment to moral policies and values, we can sometimes justifiably make plausible conjectures about courage as a personal quality.

However, long-term assertions that so-and-so is a "courageous person" are always inherently fallible and defeasible, and open to many pitfalls and fallacies. Judgments about individual acts of courage should always be treated as evidentially prior to, and more secure than, long-term conjectures about character. Even so, long-term commitments may be involved in judgments of individual acts of courage. Slote (1983) argues that certain personal goals are relative to time-of-life goals, and therefore that not all reasons for actions can extend over the agent's lifetime. In chapter 10, we will study some detailed qualifications that need to be made on the subject of long-term moral judgments of a person's character.

6.3 Historical Judgments of Courage

A very interesting case of a courageous act, chronicled by J. F. Kennedy (1956, chap. 6), shows the importance of moral reasoning and is a situation where an act that conformed to duty could only be described as heroically courageous. Edmund G. Ross was an obscure Republican senator. When President Andrew Johnson had been impeached by every Republican vote in the House in 1868, a frenzied trial for his conviction or acquittal began in the Senate. In their fervor to depose the Democratic president, the Republicans pressed ahead, not marshalling good evidence for a fair trial on the formal issues on which the impeachment was based. It became apparent through the exclusion of evidence, and various forms of pressure, even including attempted bribery (ibid., p. 113), that their interest was not so much in making a good case as simply getting the votes required for conviction, by any means possible. The Republicans nearly got their majority, but in the end the whole outcome depended on one remaining uncommitted senator, Ross.

At that point, Ross was subjected to an enormous barrage of pressure to conform. All the details of his background and life were investigated and publicized. He was hounded, warned, and threatened by party sympathizers. Committees of congressmen and people from all walks of life sent him telegrams and constantly lobbied to see him. Ross responded that he would vote for the highest good of the country according to the dictates of his judgment (ibid., p. 117). In a packed Senate, he voted "Not guilty" and, as a result, President Johnson was acquitted.

Ross knew this would mean the end of his political career. Frequently called a traitor, he served out his term and was never reelected. Nobody would listen to his justification of his action when he wrote later that it was, in his mind, a question of an attempt at partisan rule based on "insufficient proofs" (ibid., p. 120). History, however, has vindicated Ross's act, which according to Kennedy (ibid., p. 107), "as a result may well have preserved . . . constitutional government in the United States." If in retrospect it seems that Ross was right, it is quite remarkable that he should have acted against the majority of his party at such a crucial juncture and under such enormous pressure.

Ross was doing his duty as he saw it, as a member of the Senate. Hence it is unusual that his act was a heroic one under the circumstances—even though it was not "above and beyond the call of duty." Here is a case where doing an act of duty was made extraordinarily difficult by the pressure of external forces, which were so formidable that it is hard to think of Ross's act as anything but heroic.

A second interesting aspect of this case is the integrity of Ross's intrepid moral reasoning, coolly thinking out the issue—rightly, as it turned out—against the massive *ad populum* assaults. He refused to be distracted, fully knowing the consequences of acting in accordance with his judgment. His act of dissent is thought to be courageous just to the extent that his evaluation of the case against Johnson is justifiable. Should history have it that the case against Andrew Johnson showed good evidence for a legitimate impeachment, Ross's dissent would become not courageous at all, but at best a misguided act.

Thus this act was heroically courageous because the obstacles to making a clear and dutiful judgment were, as Kennedy describes the case, of a truly formidable order. But it was also courageous because of a second ingredient, the clear and justifiable reasoning that formed the basis of the act, which was subsequently evaluated as morally defensible by the historical judgment of those who now stand in evaluation of the act.

What about the skillful, brave, and dedicated soldier who happens to be fighting on the wrong side? Since the goodness of the ultimate end he fights for is questionable, we may be reluctant to call his acts "courageous," even if the soldier himself thinks he does his duty at the time. The career of Field-Marshal Erwin Rommel has been much discussed in this regard. Rommel's conduct as an officer was exemplary. He was a serious professional soldier, much respected by his own troops and fellow officers, and, remarkably, even enjoyed the respect of his enemies, who universally thought him a tough but fair opponent. His courage as a leader in the mountain fighting in Rumania and Italy in World War I is legendary. As Desmond Young puts it, the records of his feats would be almost incredible if they were not carefully verified by the testimony of other participants in these battles.[6] His method was to infiltrate the enemy lines with a few men and attack the enemy from the rear with his small force. Dangerous tactics, but Rommel again and again seemed to use them successfully by taking advantage of surprise. He never hesitated to attack, even despite his own wounds, illness, lack of sleep, or bad weather conditions. His campaigns show a characteristic pattern of boldness, initiative, determination, and skill—a soldier's soldier.

Rommel is also much admired by military experts for displaying these same qualities in the African campaign and other battles of World War II. Whether or not these acts should truly be called "courageous," however, has to be argued in light of the fact that their ultimate end was to support a government that organized massive concentration camps for the extermination of millions of innocent victims. Of course, Rommel was not himself a Nazi, and in the later stages of the war came to be associated with a plot to kill Hitler. For this he was executed by Hitler, or at least forced to kill himself.

All this poses a problem of practical ethics. Was Rommel's intrepid soldiering during the African campaign truly courageous conduct, given that the real impact of it was to prolong the existence of a totalitarian regime during a time when many atrocities were committed by it? A utilitarian might wish to argue, for example, that the net consequences of Rommel's soldierly activities during this period were more bad than good. Therefore, would it not be better to say that his acts were not truly courageous, seen in a broad moral perspective? Surely this is the sort of ethical question that biographers and historians often ask and then answer.

I think that what one has to ask to approach this sort of question correctly is: What was Rommel's purpose or end in conducting the African campaign in the way he did? The question is not what the actual consequences of his conduct were, but how he perceived the possible consequences at the time. If he thought himself to be merely doing the "soldier's duty" of following orders without heed to possible consequences, we might think that somewhat culpable by present standards, but not as bad as if we thought he was a dedicated Nazi.

There is a question here as well of relatively long-term or short-term ends. If we ask why Rommel acted in a particular way during a particular engagement, his end may have been to seize the initiative, to shorten his supply lines, or whatever. But in attempting to evaluate the real worth of the end he had in view, that information is not directly helpful. We need to know whether, in pursuing all these limited ends, he was still thinking that his efforts were helping his country in a worthy struggle or if he had begun to realize the corruption and evil that had taken hold in Germany.

If I am right that this is the sort of question we should be asking in evaluating the courage of this man's acts, one consequence is that a soldier runs a great risk to himself in simply following orders that flow from politicians without formulating some overall purpose in acquiescing to them. We have seen, however, that there is always an element of moral luck and riskiness in taking a stand. Despite your best efforts to take the most plausible moral position, it could become clearer later that your position cannot be justified. It may even take moral courage to retract that previous position and subsequently take up a diametrically opposed moral stance. In such cases, judgments of the agent's practical reasoning over a longer period can be complex, and open to dispute. In the case of Rommel, it may be possible to argue that there was an element of "moral bad luck." In his defense, it should be remembered that he reversed his earlier position by acting against Hitler, and died in this attempt.

6.4 *Courageous Compromise: A Contradiction?*

J. F. Kennedy (1956) proposed the subtle and interesting thesis that sometimes it may be the compromiser who is more morally coura- geous than the one who always does what he thinks is right, ignoring popular pressure. This thesis seems paradoxical in light of the Aris- totelian conception of courage as doing the right thing or acting for the good end in a difficult situation. But one can see the sense in it by reflecting that what is politically best is often tempered by the fires of compromise. The deepest and most acute moral reasoning does not always operate in a moral solitude but in the dialectic of sifting intelligently over the pros and cons of conflicting interests. The basic problem of political decision making is that it is rarely simple to de- termine what is in fact the best course of action for the group, or the fairest course of action where the aspirations, needs, and interests of many groups conflict.

Kennedy points out that in political life there are many pressures and pressure groups—constituents, party, comradeship of one's col- leagues, pride in office, the importance of remaining in office, and so forth. It is easy, but hardly courageous, for example, for a senator to survive and be popular by representing local or popular interests exclusively. But to acquiesce altogether in such pressures is to lose the freedom of conscience that ultimately is the real justification of holding the office.

Some would say the answer to the problem is simple: always do what is right, and ignore popularity. But, Kennedy questions, does that mean that an elected official has the right to ignore the demands of his constituents when his primary responsibility of office is to represent their views? Or can we say, to pose another problem, that one's individual view of what is right can never conflict with national interests? Would not a senator who altogether dismisses his respon- sibility to the national interest or to his constituents be in violation of a public trust?

These pointed questions suggest that the politician who truly acts responsibly and for the best ends will attempt by intelligence and foresight to balance the commands of his own conscience against his obligations of office to arrive at a decision. According to Kennedy (1956:17),

> Compromise need not mean cowardice. Indeed it is frequently the compromisers and conciliators who are faced with the severest tests of political courage as they oppose the extremist views of their constituents. It was because Daniel Webster conscientiously favored compromise in 1850 that he earned a condemnation unsurpassed in the annals of political history.

Kennedy's thesis about political courage can be extrapolated to moral courage generally. For moral reasoning in a pluralistic society, lacking a single well-established moral theory or clearly identified and fixed set of values, must always take place as reasonable dialogue rather than as algorithm. Not only can there be disagreement about how to determine what constitutes in general the 'good' end of a "courageous" act but in a particular case there may be disagreement about whether the act is courageous. However, conflict of ethical theories and principles is not too surprising in a democratic country where there is no official state philosophy.

The reaction to this pluralism should not be a moral relativism and consequent thoroughgoing psychologism or sociologism in defining courage, that is, a "courageous" act is one this society currently approves of. Nor should it be a hard stance of dogmatic authoritarianism. Rather, the reflective and honest person must attempt to negotiate a reasonable definition based on truthful and clear-minded dialogue. Thus, when we require an act of courage to be good in order for it to qualify as truly courageous, goodness need not be strictly defined in terms of some authoritarian code that covers all possible acts. The courageous person must engage in moral deliberation in seeking to act courageously, and the onlookers who put themselves in the precarious position of judging his act courageous or not must retrace the steps of his reasoning in making an argument for their own conclusion.

If moral principles are disputable, the person who wants to act rightly must also think rightly. Practical reasoning requires an assessment of the facts of a situation, a grasp of the probable consequences of the various possible alternatives, and an understanding of moral principles or generalizations that can be appealed to in argumentation. While it is true that moral courage is sticking to one's principles in the face of opposition and pressure from others to persuade one to go along with them, sticking to one's principles too stubbornly or dogmatically may be fanaticism rather than courage. The person of moral courage is open to persuasion and reasonable discussion, but will not give in to pressures until convinced the path is right. Compromise is therefore not intrinsically a sign of weakness or cowardice—it could in some cases actually be a mark of courage.

6.5 Finding Advantages in the Circumstances

Although it may be unusual for a professor of academic philosophy to venture this suggestion, I feel that practical arts and skills should be accorded more credit as valuable accomplishments in themselves. The practical person who is alert to grasp the advantages of a difficult situation and coolly overcome aggravating obstacles and problems should be more a proper focus of our admiration than he or she customarily is. In scientific developments, too often the technician who made a breakthrough possible is not given adequate credit for the part he or she played.

Similarly, in ethics, very little attention has been given to how an action is brought about, as opposed to the ultimate end realized. For courage, properly conceived, has to do with the practical question of how some advantage is wrought from the circumstances.

On the morning of September 26, 1981, a fishing boat capsized after colliding with a freighter, and two men were trapped inside. Two members of the Surrey Detachment Diving Team of the Royal Canadian Mounted Police arrived on the scene to find that only one man at a time could enter the inverted hull. Corporal Robert Teather decided to go ahead, aware that the boat was sinking and that help was miles away. Although he was not experienced in this type of dive, and was uncertain of the dangers inside, he made his way into the engine room, finding the two men. Having calmed the first man and instructed him in the use of the breathing apparatus, Teather took him on his back. However, the seaman panicked, knocking off Teather's mask. Despite this, Teather managed to force the man to the surface. He then repeated the process, saving both men. For accomplishing this dangerous rescue he was awarded the Cross of Valor (Honors Secretariat 1983).

Socrates used a hypothetical argument quite similar to this real case (see 3.1). Socrates argued that the skillful diver who descends into a well may be less courageous than the man who performs a similar act but has less skill in diving. Teather must certainly have been a qualified diver, but was not experienced in this particular type of situation. Because he was unsure of the precise risk, but knew full well the possible dangers, we feel that his act was one of great courage.

Courage is more than simple daring. It is often the ability to persist effectively and inventively in a disastrous situation, perhaps even the result of the person's initial blunder. Often there is a continuous aspect to excellence of practical reasoning as a situation unfolds. Perhaps the expression "roll with the punches" captures the idea of someone striving creatively to respond as effectively as possible to an ongoing, adverse set of circumstances not altogether in one's control. What better incident to reflect the creative response to disaster than the act of Alan A. McLeod, who won the Victoria Cross at the age of eighteen in an air battle over the Somme on March 27, 1918. McLeod was piloting a slow reconnaissance bomber when he and his observer, Lieutenant Hammond, were attacked by seven German fighters. As McLeod put it, they gained altitude and "foolishly stayed to scrap" with the enemy planes (Swettenham 1973:97). During the fight, the floor of the aircraft fell out, and McLeod had to control the aircraft while standing on the wing. At the same time, Hammond, firing while perched on the edge of the rear cockpit, shot down a third enemy Fokker. Coming down in flames, both having sustained multiple wounds, McLeod managed to crash land the aircraft and drag his companion clear of the exploding wreck before collapsing from loss of blood.

Here the two men's situation was so precarious it verged on the ridiculous. The magnificent aspect of it is the advantage they ultimately extracted from the impossible circumstances by their cool tenacity. It is like the parable where one soldier flees, dropping his broken sword, and another in a desperate situation quickly picks up the discarded weapon and uses it to beat back his enemy. What served as an excuse for the one to give up was perceived by the other as a valuable tool to reverse a seemingly hopeless situation.

A combination of boldness or promptness to seize an initiative, along with a methodical calculation to secure an objective, are characteristic of acts of courage. Perhaps central to both ideas is the notion of *taking advantage of the circumstances*, which could be a mark of practical reasoning. The gist of this skill lies both in the quick perception or sizing up of a situation and the ability to exploit quickly changing circumstances without losing one's head. This particular combination of qualities is noted in the description of the act for which Christopher P. J. O'Kelly was awarded the Victoria Cross. On October 26, 1917, Captain O'Kelly took part in an assault at Passchendaele. He advanced his men under heavy fire with no artillery support, sweeping over a hill and routing the German position. He then personally organized and led a number of attacks on strong points, capturing six "pill-boxes," one hundred prisoners, and ten machine guns. According to the description with his citation, "O'Kelly led his men with wonderful judgment, selecting the point and method of attack with cool precision, and never losing sight of this main object—to gain ground and consolidate the ridge" (Swettenham 1973:79). Both elements are clearly emphasized in this description. This attack was boldly conceived and executed, certainly taking the defenders by surprise and catching them off balance. But more than merely bold, the action was especially cited as showing "wonderful judgment" and "cool precision." It is the skillfulness with which the circumstances were exploited by deliberate judgment which makes the act remarkable.

Courage is reflected in the very human situation of man confronted by a capricious web of circumstances that, despite his efforts and technical innovations, he can never fully control. It is in the tangled web of events and actions that lead up to some end that courage is found, and in the deliberations and qualities that have to do with the process whereby that end was achieved.

Courage and cowardice are adverbial in their deepest semantical structure. They are properties that have to do with the process of how an act is executed. Except for some recent analyses by philosophers of linguistics, adverbs have never received the continued attention that has been given in philosophy to nouns and verbs of action. There has been a linguistic favoritism parallel to the neglect in ethics of practical questions pertaining to how actions are brought about. I hope, then, that this study will show that the practical and the adverbial are worthy of serious thought.

6.6 Justified Belief and Commitment

We remember that in formulating the practical reasoning base of our definition of a courageous act, we used the expression "the agent considers that it is necessary to bring about one state of affairs in order to bring about another state of affairs." In so describing the agent's judgment, mere belief was not enough, we argued. The agent must have a justified belief that one thing is necessary for another. However, this requirement of justified belief, as we found in this chapter, is far from a matter of certain knowledge. It is a matter of reasonable argument and foresight, of taking a position that is arguably reasonable in the present circumstances, but that could turn out later to be wrong. The reasonable position at the time may not turn out to be the position that can afterward be justified with the advantages of hindsight. In all practical judgments, the element of moral luck must never be entirely ruled out.

Perhaps, then, it is worth stressing again the point brought out earlier (chap. 3), that the best definition of courage should be phrased not merely in terms of the agent's actual beliefs about the situation but rather in terms of his arguably justified beliefs in light of the situation as he saw it at the time of his action. The following case is a good illustration of this point.

Lieutenant Colonel Leon R. Vance was leading a bomb attack over Wimereaux, France, in June 1944 when his plane was hit by fire that killed the pilot.[7] Several crew members were injured, and Vance's right foot was almost severed. Having applied a tourniquet to his leg, Vance took over control of the ship and, although only one of the four engines of his plane was still running, he led the formation over the bombing run. On the return flight to England, however, he realized they would not make it and ordered the crew to bail out. But, believing that one crew member was unable to jump, he decided to ditch the plane in the water to give this man a chance, even though a bomb was stuck in the bomb bay. His foot, hanging onto his leg by a few tendons, had become lodged behind the copilot's seat, so he could only land by operating the aileron and elevators while lying on the floor and looking out the side window. After the plane landed and started to sink, it exploded and blew Vance clear, and he was subsequently rescued.

We don't have any trouble here recognizing that Vance's actions in this situation were highly courageous. He was awarded the Congressional Medal of Honor for "his gallant and valorous decision to ditch the aircraft in order to give the crew member he believed to be aboard a chance for life."[8] Clearly, not only this gallant decision but Vance's entire conduct in coolly and skillfully piloting the ship under the most excruciating and trying conditions was an inspiring act of courage.

One aspect of this case will turn out to be especially interesting in light of the discussion of practical reasoning in chapter 8. Vance believed, on the basis of what we may take to be good evidence, that another man remained on the stricken aircraft. However, his belief turned out to be false. We still think his act courageous, even though it was premised on a false belief. Yet other cases where a person acts on a false belief could be perceived as careless or foolish rather than courageous. What is the difference? The basis of such distinctions seems to turn on the question of whether the agent's judgment of the situation was based on a justified belief or a belief that was reasonable on the evidence at the time, even if it turned out to be false.

The important lesson of cases like this one, I believe, is that when we make evaluations of whether an act was courageous we should do so on the basis of what we judge to be the agent's reasonable position, based on his reasonable estimate of the situation. Hence we refer to the agent's "justified belief" even if this belief about the situation later turns out to be false. But I think that in using the phrase "justified belief," the emphasis should be on the term 'justified'. We should speak not so much of the agent's actual beliefs, but of his commitments, his position as formulated in light of the situation as he saw it.

If the agent's beliefs are wildly erroneous—far out of line with the judgment of a reasonable person—we tend, rightly, to think of the act as not courageous but foolish or injudicious. However, if these beliefs turn out to be false but justified by the evidence available at the time, the act can still be considered courageous.

CHAPTER 7

Deliberation in
Particular Circumstances

IT IS NOW time to review and summarize our analysis of courage to
this point. We have defined a courageous action as one where an
agent contributes to some highly worthwhile outcome by bringing
about something very difficult or dangerous. The danger or difficulty
of the act and the worth of the outcome together constitute the ethical
matrix of the definition; the sequence of actions and outcomes is called
the practical reasoning base. If we drop the part about the worth of
the outcome and define 'difficulty' or 'danger' nonnormatively, we
get a nonnormative alternative account, which I argue corresponds
more correctly to 'bravery' rather than 'courage'. Courage, I have
argued in support of Aristotle, is essentially a normative concept. I
have also argued, however, that it is important, in theory, to be able
to separate the practical reasoning base and the ethical matrix.

A cowardly action is defined as one where the agent fails to bring
about something that would contribute to something he should do,
because of his fear. So defined, courage and cowardice, I have argued,
are not (contradictory) opposites. Of course, we have to remember
that these two definitions are merely basic structures and need to be
supplemented by some peripheral meanings if our analysis is to be
more semantically and normatively adequate to the way courage and
cowardice are used as terms to evaluate actions. These overtones
particularly come into play if we attempt to define courage and cowardice as general qualities of persons or traits of character displayed
over a prolonged period. That is a project we do not attempt here,
however.

The overtones include the following aspects of courage. First, in
some cases an act is thought particularly courageous or gallant because
of its altruistic character.[1] Second, an act may be called intrepid or

brave, in a sense meaning less than fully courageous, if it has all the characteristics of courage but lacks a clearly worthy end or outcome. Third, a positive mental element of determination, grit, resolve, or persistence is often a mark of outstanding courage. Fourth, courageous acts are often characterized by a quality of presence of mind— an ability to think practically and quickly and take advantage of the circumstances. Certainly this overtone is one aspect of Hemingway's expression "grace under pressure." Fifth, what we called constitutional courage refers to an ability to grasp the essentials of a situation and not be distracted by details that we think are morally or practically trivial. Sixth, an act is morally courageous rather than physically courageous if the danger or difficulty is not so much physical as a moral loss, for example, loss of one's good reputation. Each of these overtones supplies an optional fuller dimension of courage that is appropriate in some, but not all, instances of courageous action.

We shall not try to supply a parallel set of overtones to fill out the basic definition of cowardly action, though no doubt this job could be done. However, we will pose the following interesting question: If cowardice is not the opposite of courage, then what is? The answer is that there is no single suitable term to mean 'noncourageous', referring to the simple failure of the basic definition of courage to apply to an act. Because of the overtones of the basic definition, there are many possible different ways in which an act can fail to be courageous. Thus, an act may be not courageous because it is not brave, or because it did not show presence of mind, and so forth. The precise relationships between the overtones and the basic meaning of courage are complex, however, and we will not study them further here.

More urgently required is a theory of practical reasoning, for that has been the vehicle of our definitions and provides their theoretical structure and setting. Before turning to that job (which will be undertaken in chap. 8), let's defend and consolidate the analysis of courage and cowardice a bit further.

7.1 Relationship of Fear and Courage

Von Wright (1963) adopts the hypothesis that it is necessary for an act to overcome fear in order for it to be a truly courageous act. By contrast, I am committed to the hypothesis that an act can be courageous even if the agent does not fear doing it. Here then are two different points of view on the subject of courage. Each of them has its pros and cons.

We could sum up the opposition between von Wright's approach and my own by means of introducing the following square suggested by John Bishop (discussion in Auckland, June 3, 1983). Von Wright's view is represented by the diagram below.

By von Wright's view, true courage must be an overcoming of fear. Hence only the top cell of the dark rectangle represents courageous action. If there is no fear involved, as in the bottom cell of the dark rectangle, then the act cannot be strictly described as courageous. Instead, it should come under the heading of a fearless act.

We could contrast von Wright's view with the approach to courage which allows an act to be courageous even if it is not done by over-coming fear. Take an example of a soldier who throws himself on a grenade without hesitation or time for forethought, saving several of his platoon in a trench but losing his own life. It seems we want to say his act is truly courageous even if we do not think there was time for him to exhibit or experience fear before he acted. Looking at Bishop's square, it would seem that the alternative to von Wright's approach is to define courage as the whole of the darkened rectangle on the left. We might call this the *inclusive* view of courage.

By the inclusive view, courage and cowardice are clearly oppo-sites—courage falls into the darkened rectangle on the left and cow-ardice encompasses the remaining rectangle on the right. They are mutually exclusive and exhaustive classes. In contrast, by von Wright's view, the courageous acts are restricted to the top square of the dark-ened rectangle. But also by von Wright's view, it would seem appro-priate that the cowardly acts fall into the nondarkened rectangle on

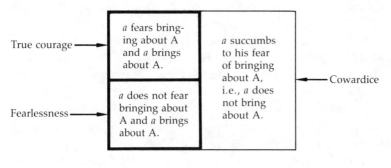

the right. These are the acts where fear was involved but the agent failed to bring about the outcome in question because of the fear. Hence, on this view, cowardice is not the opposite of courage but rather the opposite of courage-or-fearlessness. On what we take, then, to be at least one permissible interpretation of the von Wright type of account, courage and cowardice are not opposites.

Perhaps it may be a good thing to take a real example to indicate the real import of the problem for any view that, like von Wright's, requires a courageous act to be an overcoming of fear.

Sometimes a bold and prompt action before there is time to think turns out to be the most successful course in a rapidly changing or uncertain situation. When his tank was hit by a rocket, forcing the crew to abandon it, Private Herbert H. Burr, a U.S. Army gunner, climbed into the driver's seat and entered a town in Germany in 1945. Rounding a corner, he was confronted by an 88 mm antitank gun, the astonished crew of which had only to pull the lanyard to destroy the tank. However, Burr steered straight for the gun at speed. By this unexpected action he ran right over the gun, demolishing it and causing the gun crew to flee in confusion. After sideswiping and overturning a truck, he drove the tank to his company's position. For this feat, and other acts to aid his wounded sergeant, Burr was awarded the Congressional Medal of Honor.[2]

In this situation, deliberation would have been disastrous. In a changing and uncertain situation, it may be that indecisiveness can be very effectively exploited by a bold and sudden move by one party. This idea is of course well known to military strategists, who often stress that bold aggressiveness is a good policy in warfare.

It is fair to add that not only is this sort of example a problem for von Wright's sort of view but it is also a difficulty for views—like my own—that take courage to be a form of practical reasoning or cool deliberation in a bad situation. Burr had no time for deliberation or fear, yet his act was courageous.[3]

Now for another important reservation. While Bishop's square does indeed represent two possible views of courage and cowardice, I must point out that it does not fairly model my own view as one of these two alternatives.

We remember that Aristotle is careful to distinguish between courage and fearlessness.[4] And of course I want to agree with von Wright, and most other commentators it would seem, in taking the position that not all fearless acts are courageous. Some fearless acts, for example, may be simply reckless or foolish. If we want to fairly represent my own view on the Bishop square, we need to recognize that it is different from the inclusive view.

On my view, it is true that some fearless acts are courageous, but not true that all fearless acts are courageous. By this view, the soldier who threw himself on the grenade could have acted courageously even if he felt no fear. His act would have been courageous if it involved a dangerous or difficult means to accomplish a highly worthwhile end. Yet another fearless act, like senselessly rushing into danger with no highly worthwhile objective in mind, could not be called courageous. Hence, on my view, the courageous acts only include some of the fearless acts.

On my view, then, the class of courageous acts does not include all the acts in the dark rectangle of the Bishop square. It includes all the acts in the top square of the dark rectangle, and *some* of the acts in the bottom square of the dark rectangle. Hence my view is not the inclusive view of courage.

The Bishop square does a good job of representing von Wright's sort of view. It expresses the idea that no fearless acts are courageous. But the Bishop square inadequately represents what seems the reasonable alternative—namely, my own sort of view—that allows fearless acts to be courageous. The reason is that on my view, of course, not all fearless acts are courageous. Only some of them are. Hence my view and von Wright's are not as strongly opposed as they might seem at first.

Despite this important reservation, the Bishop square should be acknowledged as a good way to bring out differing philosophical approaches to the relationship between courage and cowardice. Those, like von Wright, who feel that the overcoming of fear is essential to the truly courageous act, surely claim as an advantage of their approach that it clearly distinguishes between fearlessness and courage as distinctive opposites of cowardice. And the Bishop square represents this view of the relationships in a graphic manner.

On my view, courage consists in overcoming some dangerous or difficult means to obtain a valuable or noble objective. Of course, sometimes fear is just such an obstacle to be overcome to achieve something worthwhile. If the fear itself is significant enough an obstacle, an act that overcomes it can be courageous. But fear is not the only difficult obstacle to achieving good. Hence fear is not essential to courage.

Courage, therefore, is clearly not just fearlessness. Some courageous acts are done despite fear, and in some courageous acts, the agent does not experience fear at all. In fact, it may be in the case of some acts of courage that the act is motivated to some extent by fear or even desperation.

I am quite willing to concede that both von Wright's view and my own are subject to argument, but I am convinced that, on balance, the view I have chosen to defend is the better one. No doubt further arguments will turn up more defenses and objections to both viewpoints.

It is not the psychological factor of fear that is an essential or defining characteristic of courage. Rather, what is essential is that the situation is truly dangerous, and that the courageous person has the experience or knowledge of the situation to correctly realize the danger. No doubt, in a truly dangerous situation, the experienced person will in some sense have a fearful attitude toward the situation. But that is not what counts in rightly determining whether his or her response to that situation is courageous. Awareness of the danger of the situation does count.

In extreme danger there must be an element of chance and risk, a situation running out of control. When the experienced person sets out to save the situation, he must appreciate the nature of the risk involved in intervening. Yet even if he fails, losing his own life in the attempt, the act may be courageous, provided only that the courageous person recognized correctly that there was some hope of successful intervention. Indeed, in the end it is not the failure or success of the action that counts in how we view it as courageous. Rather, it is the agent's deliberation and judgment in striving to carry out his noble objective despite his perception of the real possibility of failure and even loss of his own life as well as that of the other.

On the June 3, 1918, Arthur Hamilton Ambury heard a call for help while climbing on Mount Egmont in New Zealand. During the rescue attempt, one of the less experienced climbers slipped and slid down a steep ice slope toward Ambury, who braced himself and reached out to catch the other man. Both men were precipitated off the mountain and fell to their deaths. In the account of the *London Gazette* on January 3, 1919, it is noted: "[Ambury] was an experienced mountaineer and must have realized how terrible a risk he was running in endeavouring to save the falling man" (reported in O'Shea 1981:62). The Albert Medal was posthumously awarded to Ambury, and an obelisk provided by public subscription was placed on a slope of Mount Egmont. The obelisk bears an inscription including the quotation, "Near to renunciation, very near, dwelleth eternal peace."

Clearly, an important part of our reconstruction of this act as courageous is the awareness of the danger of the situation we reason must be attributable to this man. What matters is not whether he experienced fear or not, but whether the act involved grave danger and whether the agent was aware of the danger, yet willingly took the risk. In this case, our evidence for inferring that all these elements of a courageous act obtained relates to Ambury's known experience as a mountaineer. From such circumstantial evidence, we are able to piece together a reconstruction of the practical judgment that was the basis of the act.

In certain situations it may take experience to judge risk, and we think an act courageous where, although it is a very close thing one way or the other, the agent strives forcefully to make the best of it against the known risk. A case parallel in certain respects to the one above also shows that the success or failure of the attempts may not count at all in our judgment of courage.

On February 13, 1974, Sergeant Murray Ken Hudson was supervising live grenade practice when one of the men in the practice failed to throw an armed grenade. Hudson ordered the man to throw it but there was no reaction. The sergeant then quickly grasped both hands of the man and attempted to force the grenade over the parapet. Although he was within inches of success, the grenade exploded, killing both of them. The *London Gazette* report of October 11, 1974, notes: "As an experienced soldier, Sergeant Hudson would have realized immediately that once the grenade became armed there was less than four seconds to detonation" (reported in O'Shea 1981:32). The report adds that while Hudson "must have been aware of the great risk involved he took no action to safeguard himself" (ibid.). Hudson was awarded the George Cross, which was received by his wife, two children, and other family members at a special ceremony in Wellington in December 1974.

In this situation we can see how close to success the act was. Therefore, the outcome was terribly tragic. But it might not have been, and in our reconstruction of the act, the extensive training and experience of the agent serves as evidence for our conclusion that he must have been very aware of the nature of the risk he took. And that is what makes the act especially courageous.

These two citations show that it is not the psychological aspect of fear that leads us to view an act as courageous in many cases. What is important is the objective factor of danger or risk. But there is a "mental" factor involved as well in the way we judge actions to be courageous. This factor has to do with the agent's awareness of the nature of the risk, his knowing the extent of the danger. It is these two things combined that figure in our judgment of the agent's practical reasoning in the situation. There must be formidable risk, but not so overwhelming that someone experienced in this type of situation would say there was clearly no hope of saving it by intervening at further risk. Yet the risk must be so great that the danger of intervening is truly formidable.

The objective factor of the actual consequences of the intervention, however, may be of little or no importance to our evaluation of the act as courageous or not. This fact may seem paradoxical to some, who might suggest that it shows that virtues like courage are not properly matters of ethics at all. Others might find it hard to square with the consequentialist view that it is the actual outcome of an act which should be the determinant of its moral value.

Perhaps what is really shown is that an act of courage involves a judgment of practical deliberation by the agent. This judgment entails that there should be genuine risk in a situation and that the agent should be aware of the nature of the risk and alternatives involved. What is involved is a balance or comparison between the objective situation and the agent's subjective estimate of it.

7.2 Courage and Rationality

Von Wright's view of courage requires that a courageous act must be an overcoming of fear in order to achieve some worthwhile end. My own view does not require the presence of fear in every case, requiring instead that some danger or difficulty of considerable magnitude must be overcome in order to achieve the good end. Segerberg has formulated an objection to my view of courage, based on the type of situation pictured below.[5] The points (nodes) of the tree represent different actions or outcomes of actions.

Let us suppose that at point A_2, the outcomes B and C are mutually exclusive and exhaustive. That is, in the language of probabilities, that the probability of B occurring is the negation of the probability

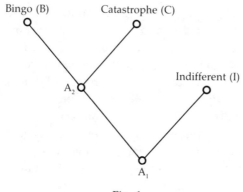

Fig. 1.

of C occurring: $pr(B) = 1 - pr(C)$. This means that at the point A_2, exactly one of B or C must occur. Now look at the whole picture.

At A_1, the agent has a choice. He can make I occur—with no harm, but also no outstanding benefit to anyone—or he can make A_2 occur. But if he makes A_2 occur, then at that point he is confronted with the reality that one of B or C will occur next. Let us assume, as is characteristic of real life, that the agent has partial control over what happens. He can bring about a certain outcome, but there is a certain element of chance involved—Nature does not always fulfill our hopes and expectations.

The situation posed by Segerberg could be illustrated by a gambler. His problem is: should he play it safe and take no risk of great gain or loss? Or should he take a chance of great gain, even where there is also a chance of great loss? Let us assume that the utility of B or C as an event is greater than the utility of the event I. That is, let's suppose for the sake of argument that the utility of B is greater than that of C. And let's assume that the value of I is equal to zero.

According to the viewpoint of maximization, the decision maker should choose to bring about I or A_2 on the basis of which of these outcomes has the greater net utility (the probability of the outcome times the value of the outcome for the decision maker). According to the theory of maximization, then, the rational thing to do is to go for net utility and not worry about the value or disvalue of risk itself versus caution. For example, if B is the gain of a million dollars and C is the loss of a million dollars—and the odds are 60 percent that B will occur versus 40 percent that C will occur—then the rational thing to do would be to choose A_2 rather than I.

At any rate, Segerberg's objection can now be posed. If courage is defined as taking the risk of danger to bring about some great benefit, then the courageous thing to do simply turns out to be the rational thing to do (assuming for the moment that maximization is our theory of rational action). But—continues Segerberg's objection—surely there is a difference between rationality and courage. If so, the view of courage we are discussing must be incorrect.

This objection represents a fundamental problem for the sort of analysis I have supported. Although I have, in effect, taken the position that courage is a kind of rationality, that of practical reasoning, still there must be a difference between courage and rational thought or action generally. Moreover, the kind of rationality represented by practical reasoning may be quite different from the model of rationality represented by maximization. We need to know precisely what the difference is between these two notions.

Von Wright's conception of courage does not incur the same difficulty from Segerberg's problem, or at least not to the same extent. For von Wright can say that courageous action is that special kind of rational action where fear is overcome. I do not have that way out, although I can argue in some instances that courageous actions are those which represent rational action where certain overtones or qualities are present, for example, presence of mind, altruism, or determination. The still leaves me with the basic problem of distinguishing between courage and rationality in a case where none of these optional meanings happens to be present. What is one to say here?

To get at the problem posed by Segerberg's objection, let us try to state our model of a courageous action in a parallel picture. Let us presume the existence of two catastrophic events, C_1 and C_2.

The idea of courageous action we have in mind is as follows. If the agent does nothing at A_1, then some catastrophe C_1 will follow. But if at A_1, the agent commences some arduous or painful sequence of actions $A_2, \ldots, A_3$, then he can possibly bring about the valuable state of affairs B (Bingo) at some future point. There is also risk involved, however, because C_2 could possibly happen if the agent fails. This figure represents courageous action. How is it different from the notion of rationality as represented in Segerberg's picture?

One difference is the order. In figure 2, the agent has to carry out a painful or difficult sequence of actions $A_2, \ldots, A_3$ in order to achieve his objective. Remember the actions of Sergeant Erwin who

142

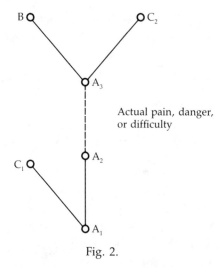

Fig. 2.

saved the aircrew of his plane by picking up a burning phosphoresce bomb in his arms and deliberately and coolly went through a difficult procedure to find a way to get it out of the aircraft.[6] He achieved his objective, and averted disaster, by confronting terrible pain and difficulty in carrying out a procedure in a crisis. He had to carry out this procedure to achieve his intention of saving the crew from destruction. It is a question of the agent's intention and the procedure, the sequence of actions needed to carry out that intention.

Another difference is that the issue is not primarily one of maximization of a set of outcomes. In the case of Erwin's action, we know that C_1 and C_2 are very bad (destruction of the plane and crew), and we know that B (preventing such destruction from taking place) is very good. But Erwin's problem was not one of choosing between these two outcomes on the basis of their numerical value or probability. His problem was to find and carry out some procedure for getting the right outcome, or at least the one he wanted. It is hard to see how any calculation of expected utility or maximization might have been helpful in this task. Nor does it seem that considerations of maximization play any significant role in our evaluation of his act as being courageous. He wanted any sequence of actions that would do the job and he found one. Perhaps there was a better one—but that hardly matters. Hence the problem was not one of maximization but one of practical reasoning.

What, then, is the difference between practical reasoning and maximization? Once we answer this question, we will be further along in responding to Segerberg's objection.

7.3 Satisficing

Maximization is the appropriate method of decision making if every possible outcome of a situation is given. An alternative method, called satisficing by Simon (1977), is the process of looking for a "good enough" outcome where it is not feasible to compare all possible outcomes. Simon (1977:173) discusses the problem of finding the sharpest needle in a haystack with needles in it. The maximizing method is to find all the needles, compare them for sharpness, and then select the sharpest one.

But if the haystack is large, and time and resources for searching are limited, might it not be more practical to stop searching at some earlier point? An economist would tell us to stop searching when the process of searching starts to cost more than likely improvements in sharpness. But Simon notes that, in practice, it may be easier to define "sharp enough" than "marginal value of additional sharpness." He suggests that, in a particular situation, the best method might be to stop when you find a needle sharp enough to sew with.

With the method of satisficing, it is not necessary to look at all the possible outcomes and then select the best one, as in the method of maximizing. Instead, you start the process of searching with a particular job or problem in mind, and stop when a solution is found that is good enough to do the job. And that is characteristic of practical reasoning. The reasoner starts with some specific objective in mind, and then stops searching once some means of carrying out that objective is found.

A simplified outline of the sequence of steps involved in each model of decision making is given below.

Satisficing

1. Is there a particular goal I would like to pursue? If not, stop here. If so, go on to 2.
2. Is this goal consistent with my overall values? If not, stop here. If so, go on to 3.

3. Is there an available procedure that might realize this goal? If so, carry it out. If not, go on to 4.
4. Is there an alternative procedure that might realize this goal? If not, stop here. If so, carry it out and stop.

Optimizing

1. Same as 1., above.
2. Same as 2., above.
3. Is there an available procedure that might realize this goal? If so, keep it in mind and go on to 4. If not, go on to 4.
4. Is there an alternative procedure that might realize this goal? If not, go to step 5. If so, keep it in mind and repeat step 4.
5. Scan over all the alternative procedures in memory and select the best (greatest value). Go on to 6.
6. Carry out the selected procedure and then stop.

Looking at both sequences of reasoning, we can see that step 5 of the optimizing sequence is what especially distinguishes optimizing, as a decision-making process, from satisficing.

Now that we understand the basic idea behind these procedures, we need to see that, in practice, they are more complex. The reason for this complexity is that actions are characteristically linked into longer sequences. In deliberating on how to carry out a goal, an agent will normally reason from both ends of the sequence. The following more lengthy description of the satisficing procedure—while still not perfect in all requirements—serves to indicate in a more realistic way how the process works.

Satisficing Procedure

1. Is there a particular proposition p_n (the goal) I would like to make true? If not, stop. If so, go on to 2.
2. Is making p_n true consistent with my overall values? If not, stop here. If so, go on to 3.
3. Is there some proposition p_m (the means) such that p_n can be brought about by bringing about p_m? If not, go on to 4. If so, go on to 5.
4. Is there some alternative proposition p_m^a such that p_n can be brought about by bringing about p_m^a? If not, stop here. If so, go on to 5.

5. Now I have selected p_m (or some alternative p_m^a, whichever is selected), what other propositions need to be made true in order to make p_n true given that p_m is made true? After listing these other propositions p_l, go on to 6.

6. Is there an available procedure p_o such that p_m will be made true by making p_o true? If so, make p_o true. If not, go on to 7.

7. Is there some proposition p_k such that p_m can be brought about by bringing about p_k? If not, go on to 8. If so, go on to 9.

8. Is there some alternative proposition p_k^a such that p_m can be brought about by bringing about p_k^a? If not, stop here. If so, go on to 9.

9. Now I have selected p_k (or an alternative p_k^a), what other propositions need to be made true in order to make p_m true given that p_k is made true? After listing these propositions, go on to 10.

10. Is there an available procedure p_o such that p_k will be made true by making p_o true? If so, make p_o true. If not, go on to 11.

11. Keep searching, going on to p_j, and so forth. After a designated number of steps, if no p_o is found, go back to step 4.

12. Select another alternative p_m^a at step 4 and go through the sequence again. When all the alternatives are exhausted, stop.

The general strategy of the satisficing procedure outlined above is to find the "missing links," or necessary means. The agent wants to carry out a goal p_n, and finds a means p_m. But his problem is to find a way to carry out p_m. Not finding a way, he reasons that p_m could possibly be carried out by carrying out p_k. And he sees there is a procedure p_o he can directly carry out that could lead to the carrying out of p_k through the step of carrying out p_j.

Now the agent has narrowed the problem down. He needs to find a series of steps that will lead from p_k to p_m. Once he finds these "missing links" his goal p_n can be carried out. For p_o is a procedure that he can directly carry out—it is part of his repertoire of routine actions. And his deliberations have shown him a way to select a p_o that will lead ultimately to the carrying out of p_n, the goal he intended to realize in the first place.

It has long been accepted that optimization is a form of decision making to narrow down the options. Now we can see how satisficing is also a rational model of decision making.

This approach is quite congenial to the model of courageous action proposed above. In searching for some way to bring about a valuable

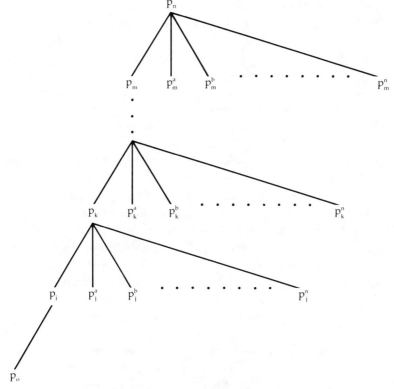

Fig. 3. Satisficing Search Tree

objective, an agent looks for some sequence of actions that would lead to that objective. An act is courageous if the means is found and carried out even if it is very difficult or dangerous for the agent to do it. The courageous act is not necessarily the best possible solution to the problem. For it is characteristic of acts of courage that they take place in a crisis or emergency, where there may be little time for finding the best possible outcome. Instead, the courageous act is a means found good enough to save the situation, by finding an acceptable way to proceed.

When it comes to reconstructing the rationale behind the valor or grace of a courageous action, it is often inappropriate to view the agent as selecting the best possible outcomes among all the possible solutions to the problem. That could, in some cases, model procrastination more than courage. Instead, the agent has an objective or intention in mind, and looks around for some way of carrying it out practically which can be actuated in the circumstances.

Practical reasoning may be defined as the sequence of steps of action undertaken by a deliberating agent who reasons to carry out a generally formulated intention in relation to the given, practical circumstances of a situation. Hence practical reasoning, as we have seen, is involved in both optimization and satisficing. However, satisficing is a simpler, or less refined, form of practical reasoning than optimizing.

In chapter 8, we will explore much more fully what practical reasoning amounts to as a form of reasonable inference. Up to this point, we have seen how practical reasoning underlies the structure of decision making when an agent tries to carry out some intention or goal. But the same practical structure underlies the evaluation when we look, in hindsight, at how an action was carried out. In evaluating whether or not an action may be said to have been courageous or cowardly, we are adopting the point of view of referees who are looking backward to a past action and trying to explain why and how the agent did what he did. In historical judgments, we may be looking back very far; in cases of military or civilian commendations for valor, the act in question may have taken place in the recent past. In making such judgments, we are engaging in a form of practical reasoning. We are trying to reconstruct the alternatives considered by the agent at that past time, and trying to figure out which consequences he might have been taking into account in deliberating on how to act. However, the agent who acted in the past was himself also engaging in practical reasoning when he deliberated on what to do by examining the various lines of action. We might make a useful distinction here between first-person or first-order practical reasoning by the agent prior to his action and second-order or reconstructive practical reasoning by those who set themselves to explain or evaluate his action.

Not all actions are the result of highly rational deliberation or thoughtful choice. As we saw, some actions properly called courageous are impulsive, or at least not evidently characterized by careful planning. Conversely, although many cowardly actions are impulsive or thoughtless, some persons such as the constitutional coward may be very calculating in pursuing their cowardly strategies for avoiding danger. In explicit deliberation, one can take into account the beliefs and desires of the agent at the time. However, according to Føllesdal (1980:240), some practical decisions depend on beliefs that were not consciously entertained by the agent. In some cases, an agent might even deny that certain beliefs or desires influenced him at all. Føllesdal cites one of Suppes's examples where a young boy might deny that his zeal for asking schoolwork questions after class has anything to do with the fact that the teacher is a very attractive female. Where we have reason to think that a person's action may spring from unconscious motives rather than deliberate reasoning, psychological or physiological explanations can be used to supplement or fill out explanations on the basis of practical reasoning alone.

However, we have seen many cases of courage and cowardice where a process of deliberation among alternative and manipulating circumstances to consciously work toward a certain outcome is the characteristic framework of action. To evaluate such cases, we may have to go deeply into the beliefs and objectives of the agent at the time, his beliefs about what avenues of action are open to him, and his ways of contending with the situation as he sees it.[7]

Often there is not much direct evidence still available to help us reconstruct the scenario we need to explain the action. Therefore, the arguments of the referees should be carefully supported by what evidence there is that the agent had certain beliefs or desires. The agent himself may even have been operating with incomplete knowledge of the situation at the time, and being aware of such lack of knowledge may be an important factor in explaining why he acted as he did. Føllesdal (1980:240) points out that if the agent knew something but forgot, or overlooked an important alternative, evidence of such a lapse—perhaps by pointing out that some information never reached him—could be an important basis for a plausible explanation.

In a particular, real instance of courageous or cowardly action, there is the evidential problem of documenting and proving one's allegation. Particularly in the case of cowardice, proving that someone's action was cowardly is no trivial affair. The consequences can be devastating. Anyone should have a right to defend his acts against such an allegation. The ultimate board of arbitration may be a legal proceeding, or in the case of agents long dead, it may take the form of a historical inquiry.

It is well to review an actual case of this sort to help us fully grasp what is at stake.

7.4 *An Allegation of Cowardice*

Lord George Sackville is best known as the British secretary of state for the American colonies, the minister in charge of conducting the war against American independence. Most historians have portrayed Sackville as an incompetent and disastrous minister, but his poor reputation could stem from an earlier incident. He had been court-martialed for disobedience as an officer at the Battle of Minden in 1759. According to Fortescue's *History of the British Army,* "It is possible that on the day of Minden Sackville's courage failed him."[8] Although this statement falls just short of calling Sackville's failure to act cowardly, the suggestion was often made by Sackville's contemporaries and subsequent commentators.

In a careful piece of historical research, Mackesy (1979) investigates the complex story of what happened in relation to Sackville's conduct and decisions on August 1, 1759, the day of the battle. What happened during the battle is far from clear, but Mackesy's account of it suggests that the allegation of cowardice is not consistent with the known facts and what can be reconstructed of Sackville's intentions. Mackesy's historical inquiry is an excellent case study of the type of evidence and arguments used to substantiate or rebut an allegation of cowardly conduct.

Sackville was a member of parliament and a very able speaker and advocate for his case. Eventually, he was able to get a trial to defend himself against the charges that led to his dismissal. He even printed his own version of the trial proceedings. The court's verdict was that Sackville was guilty of disobedience and judged unfit to serve the king in any military capacity.

Although the court's verdict sounds severe, the judgment was in fact quite lenient in that there was no sentence or penalty other than loss of military rank and privileges. No motive for disobedience was established by the trial, and no allegation of cowardice was made because there was very little evidence of physical fear as a possible explanation.

According to Mackesy (1979:228), however, one witness did speak of Sackville's "condition" at the time of the battle as "alarmed to a very great degree" and of "in the utmost confusion." Some took this to mean that Sackville was afraid, but Sackville himself interpreted it as meaning that he was anxious because he was perplexed about the situation and his orders. In fact, he had received three conflicting orders from different messengers from his commander, and could not tell which was the latest order. He was ignorant of the terrain because he had not been able to properly reconnoiter it before the battle. And he did not have reliable information on enemy troop dispositions. So it is not unreasonable that he might have been confused.

Mackesy concludes that although Sackville's planning of his troop dispositions did leave him open to some criticisms of misjudgment, there was no good evidence for allegations of fear or intentional disobedience of orders. The charges against him seem to have arisen out of a network of personal intrigues and animosities. It seems that Sackville became something of a scapegoat in court politics. It seems fair to conclude that allegations of cowardice, and courage for that matter, can be highly controversial and difficult to prove or rebut in particular cases. Historical inquiries or legal proceedings would seem to be the methods used to conduct such inquiries. These methods basically involve the asking and answering of questions about the acts and intentions of some person at some past time.

Sackville and his accusers were each arguing for a different reconstruction of his deliberations as implemented in his actions. Each tried to draw on the resources of the eyewitness evidence of the facts of the battle to support his case. Sackville asked and answered questions that contributed to his reconstruction of his practical reasoning at the time he issued orders during the battle. His goal was presumably to win the battle by correctly interpreting the orders given to him and by carrying them out. However, the question of how he judged the situation in finding the right means to carry out these intentions was a matter of dispute. Sackville claimed that his orders were unclear, and that the situation was unclear. Consequently, he claimed, he had to use his best discretion in interpreting the orders, and in finding practical procedures to carry them out on the basis of how he reasonably estimated the situation. The context of the legal cross-examination and historical reconstruction detailed in Mackesy (1979) is an illustration of the structure of a satisficing procedure representing a plausible analysis of Sackville's practical reasoning.

The possibility of viewing a realistic historical case of this type as an instance of satisficing, however, involves a problem formulated by MacIntyre (1981). Analytical theory of action and practical inference singles out one isolated action at a time, but fails to tell us how a network of related actions are woven into a narrative discourse.

7.5 MacIntyre on the Virtues

Of the so-called virtues, some, like prudence or piety, are antiquated and now lack much force of intuitive moral impact; others, such as justice and truthfulness, have been extensively treated by philosophers but little is made of their status as virtues. Courage seems to have somehow fallen unnoticed between these two extremes. Although still a term of commendation in wide use and with an extraordinarily powerful moral impact, it seems to have fallen into neglect as a significant topic of study in ethics.

Now the concept of a virtue has been resurrected by MacIntyre (1981), who defines virtue as an acquired human quality that enables us to achieve goods internal to practices. It is too soon to tell whether the resurrection will be entirely successful in achieving a reorientation of moral philosophy. For, indeed, the notion of an acquired human quality is a difficult and complex one to clearly articulate and defend as a methodological tool for ethical studies.

Rather than confront the notion of a "human quality" directly, I have chosen the approach of defining courage as a property of single human actions. The further project of extrapolating from the courage of an act to the characteristic of courageous disposition of a person is, I think, better thought of as a second—and difficult—stage in the analysis of courage. I will leave this second step for chapter ten, though, to be sure, the work of MacIntyre offers many guideposts to one who would undertake the project. Because of many analytical problems we have formulated in connection with courage and cowardice, it has become apparent that at this stage of developing precise definitions and consequences, it is best to make our basic structure as clear and elementary as possible. For my intent in studying courage has been somewhat more analytical in nature than historical or speculative.

Where MacIntyre's account of virtue makes tremendous gains is in his notion of an excellence achieved in a practice. A practice may be portrait painting or playing chess—it is a socially established cooperative human activity that can realize standards of excellence. There are different kinds of excellence achieved in practice—the excellence of the result and the excellence of the performance itself, for example. However, there are also internal excellences that involve the skills and competence acquired in competition and the quest for excellence. These internal goods or virtues are worth having for their own sake and, far from taking away goods from others in their achievement, they enrich and contribute to the whole community and are also contributed to by the community. These values are the goods that back the goodness of the intentions of the one who acts truly courageously.

Although we have been addressing ourselves to a practical inquiry in this book, it now begins to seem that here we have become somewhat more theoretical. How can we readjust this seeming misorientation? Throughout, we have been making sense of the most commonplace conversational accounts and judgments of courageous actions, and in many cases we were able to see reasonably well why a particular act can reasonably be thought to be courageous, but we have in fact been using a (highly informal) conception of practical reasoning. If our interests are purely narrative and conversational, such evaluations do make a good deal of sense in themselves as to what might be called a narrative level of discourse.

But it is natural to ask whether practical reasoning can also be justified and explicated so that we can give a simple but more precise model of the basic structures underlying the arguments in particular cases. Some critics would say that one or the other of these levels of analysis, the practical or the theoretical, is useless or beside the point. Many action theorists seem to suggest, for example, by their concentration on logical structures and simple acts like moving one's finger, that pragmatic implementations of these structures are not necessary or enlightening.

On the other side, MacIntyre (1981:194) criticizes those analytical philosophers who have constructed accounts of human actions around a single action. He feels that such accounts already presuppose complex sequences of human actions as embedded in our practical discourse. At this practical level, an action cannot be understood except as part of a sequence, a line of action, that flows from a human agent's deliberations, motives, and intentions.

Now, of course, our study in cases of courageous acts has borne out MacIntyre's thesis fully, particularly in our individual cases of moral courage and historical judgments about courageous and cowardly acts. To really understand why an act is justifiably thought courageous or cowardly, we have seen that the particular episode must indeed be placed in the context of what MacIntyre calls a set of narrative histories. Yet if we do not have some precise account of the forms of argument and definitions of the key terms underlying pragmatic discourse about courage and cowardice, then my narrative history is just as good as yours, and we are in no position to understand the concept of virtue as practical excellence. To fill this gap, we need to put the concept of a virtue in a broader teleological perspective.

If the narrative context of the practical discourse on complex sequences of human actions can be understood as practical reasoning, then perhaps a setting may be found for the concept of a virtue in ethics.

7.6 *Virtue Ethics and Personal Consistency*

The concept of virtue seems alien in the context of modern ethics precisely because the dominance of duty-based ethical theories has made universalizability seem to be the mark of moral judgments. But virtue ethics, traditionally, has always been a personal standard of morality. By comparison, virtue ethics can easily be dismissed as a subjective or personalistic part of ethics, perhaps too individualistic to be trusted as a principled source of guidance of one's conduct as it affects others.

This contrast can be seen when we reflect that the test of any ethical principle or reason as a guide for action ultimately comes down to a question of consistency. For an ethics of duty, the test of any proposed action comes down to the question of whether I could say that someone else, in the same circumstances, who is unlike me personally in any way, should, as a moral agent, carry out this action. This is a question of interpersonal consistency. The problem to be addressed by the moral reasoner is whether his carrying out this act is consistent with the judgment that anyone should be allowed to do it.

This kind of consistency is an external one that relates one's own proposed conduct to the possible conduct of other moral agents. But the test for a judgment in the ethics of virtue is a "personal" one that relates to the agent's own internal consistency of conduct. The question here is whether my proposed action is consistent with my own intentions and actions in relation to my present circumstances.

The distinction between virtue ethics and what might be called social ethics or universal ethics is between maxims valid for the position of one person and maxims valid for all persons as moral agents. In the first case, consistency is relative to the narrative content and individual aims and qualities of the person who is to decide how to proceed. In the second case, consistency is a question of abstracting from the individual qualities of the person who is to make the decision, treating him as being equal to any moral agent who could be in the same situation. One is a personal judgment in the sense that the other should be impersonal.

I am not sure whether "social ethics" or "duty-based" ethics are exactly the right terms here. At any rate, the kind of impersonality of judgment required by dominant approaches to recent ethical theory can be illustrated by the theory of Rawls (1974). According to Rawls's moral philosophy, neutral procedures for choosing rightly among alternative courses of action are based on a principle of each moral agent taking a viewpoint that everyone can adopt on an equal footing. Rational choice, according to Rawls's view, is exclusively constrained by the formal value of universalizing the choice that is selected. This means that the choice should not be constrained by the individual's commitments to his own personal goals or intentions. The principle is that all like cases must be treated alike, and individual or personal aspirations must be abstracted out. Rawls requires that each member of a morally well-ordered society must negotiate from an "original position" that abstracts from each agent's personal position. By this abstraction, Rawls can argue that all moral agents should enter into an agreement to be bound by truly universal maxims.

By contrast, the personal position of the agent is all-important for an ethic of virtue. As we have seen in evaluating acts of courage, the primary questions for moral judgment in such cases are what this individual agent's intentions are and how he has implemented these intentions in his personal conduct. It is the agent's personal position as the basis of his action that matters, not the "original" position of the agent as in social ethics.

Sullivan (1982) brings out this contrast between virtue ethics and what I have called social ethics very clearly. According to Sullivan, Rawls's device of the original position is meant to demonstrate why all rational beings would choose a social union with principles of distribution of goods (1982:109). The original position makes social cooperation a rational morality for all moral agents who enter into a social contract. Sullivan (ibid., p. 110) contrasts this framework with an ethics of virtue: "For an ethics of virtue, character or the intentionality of the agent provides the connecting syntax through which the various acts and projects of the agent attain consistency." Sullivan adds that this form of consistency is rational in that it can be described through the intentions of the agent which guide his actions and reflections. The kind of rationality he alludes to, however, is one that "unfolds and can be displayed only through the narrative of an intentional project" (ibid., p. 110). What needs to be analyzed, then, to support an ethics of virtue, is the concept of the consistency of a person's position where consistency here is a relation between the actions and intentions of an agent.

This analysis is the object of the next chapter, on practical reasoning. Our analysis of practical reasoning will yield a model of action—theoretic personal inconsistency. The kind of inconsistency at issue here is the basis of ad hominem (or *ad personam*) criticisms as they occur in moral disputations.[9]

To give a realistic example of the sort of allegation of personal inconsistency we are after, consider the case of some Catholic politicians who have recently said that they personally oppose abortion but support freedom of choice. Recently, a Catholic bishop criticized this stance as being no more logically tenable than that of an office seeker who advocated personal views but made no practical proposals to implement them.[10] The problem posed by this type of dispute is the relationship between one's personal position and one's recommendation meant to apply equally to all moral agents. Can one personally committed to Catholicism consistently argue that as a matter of public policy abortion is generally acceptable? We will take up this problem in the next chapter.

If we are right that there is a distinction between the ethics of virtue and social ethics, then perhaps a case can be made for saying there is an important moral difference between the following two types of cases: (a) the person who adopts a personal position, but does not act consistently with that position, and (b) the person whose conduct is consistent with the personal position he advocates, but who does not recommend that this position be imposed on the conduct of all moral agents. If there is room for argument between (a) and (b), then our distinction between the personal ethics of virtue and the universal ethics of duty can be defended as morally significant.

The best way to approach this moral problem is to try to gain a better understanding of the logically binding nature of the consistency that binds the actions and projects of an agent into a personal position. This means gaining a general grasp of the norms of practical rationality which guide an agent's personal conduct. Once we gain some understanding of how personal consistency guides rational action, we may be able to test the limits of this binding in evaluating conduct.

The problem is that the ethics of virtue is personal and therefore is often said to be an ethics of character. But if so, there is a danger of a drift into personal subjectivity and moral relativism. Yet we have seen that the question of whether an action is courageous or cowardly is not simply a matter of character or personality. It is the individual action itself that should be evaluated as courageous or not. To be sure, in the evaluation we need to take the agent's intentions and his personal assessment of the situation into account. But his character, in a broader sense, may very often be rightly excluded as entering into the evaluation in any highly significant way, for example, in the case of Leading Seaman Triggs (chap. 1).

In the next chapter, we turn to the study of practical reasoning as a model of consistency of one's personal position in action. Later, in the last chapter, we will return to a discussion of character. Our particular studies of actions we have found to be courageous have been morally revealing. But hard disputes about whether an act is truly courageous can only be refereed rationally if there is some clear conception of practical reasoning underlying them to which we can appeal.

CHAPTER 8

Practical Reasoning

IT IS CHARACTERISTIC of any deliberate human action that the agent first forms an intention and then searches for some procedure to carry it out. Searching for the right procedure may involve a series of steps to link one's general intention to some specific procedure that one can begin to carry out in present circumstances. For example, I may form an intention to tidy up some of my back correspondence. I look through the pile of letters in my "in" basket and select one that seems to have priority. I then think about the appropriate response and pull out a sheet of letterhead paper. I pick up a pen and begin to write the letter. In this ordinary example of human action, we started with a general intention and eventually came down to a specific action, a procedure that could actually be initiated in a given situation. In between were a number of steps or subactions.

Sometimes the sequence of steps is much more obvious and direct. I form the intention to open my office door. The procedure for carrying out that action is so immediate and routine that it needs no further deliberation or planning. I simply get up and, in the usual way, open the door.

An excellent example is given by Aristotle in *Metaphysica* (Z.7–1031b25–1032b29). A physician is confronted with a patient who has a certain disorder. The doctor's intention is to produce a healthy patient. Suppose the physician reasons that if the patient is to be healthy, there must be a uniform state of the body. Next, he reasons that if this is to be produced, there must be heat. He casts around for a way to make the patient warm. He can do this by rubbing the patient's body, and he then proceeds to do this. The physician's sequence of inferences forms a chain: *health → uniform state → heat → rub patient*.[1] He started out with a general intention, set by the nature of his profession, and in a particular case he needed to search for some procedure available in the circumstances which would lead toward his formed objective.

It is this sort of sequence that practical reasoning is all about. Many of the examples of courageous acts we have looked at share this characteristic sequence of actions involved in the carrying out of some intention by some procedure.[2] Let us go back to the example of Staff Sergeant Henry Erwin's removal of the burning phosphoresce bomb from the aircraft (described in chap. 1).

Erwin found himself in a plane loaded with phosphoresce bombs, one of which had exploded in the launching chute and shot back into the aircraft. The burning bomb struck him in the face, blinding him and burning off his nose. If the burning bomb stayed in the plane, both plane and crew would be destroyed. Realizing this, Erwin, intending to save the crew, set about trying to eject the bomb while blinded. Knowing that the copilot's window was the only available opening, he picked up the burning bomb and crawled in what he thought was the right direction.

Finding the navigator's table preventing his passage, he had to carry out a procedure to raise the table by releasing a spring lock. To carry out the required action, it was necessary for him to grasp the burning bomb between his body and his other arm. After a number of other actions, he was able to gain access to the window and throw the bomb out. By this complex procedure, he was able to carry out his intention to save the crew.

The problem of practical reasoning is what to do in a particular situation. Judgment is needed to assess the given circumstances and then to act accordingly and carry out the required steps and deliberations. In a desperate and distracting crisis, that task becomes much more difficult and demanding for most of us. Erwin's judgment was not impaired by his being injured and blinded, or by the desperation of the unfamiliar, confusing, and unstable situation. His resolve to carry out his intention was not deterred by the reality of the terrible cost to himself. He succeeded in carrying out his objective where most of us would surely fail. It is difficult and perhaps unprofitable to generalize, however, for the problem was one of doing something in a unique, particular set of circumstances that would not likely be anticipated. Erwin reacted in the best way one could imagine.

8.1 Practical Inferences

Each step in a sequence of actions to carry out an intention is an instance of what has been traditionally called practical inference.

However, philosophers disagree about the precise form of such an inference, and we do not know what it means to call such a step of judgment an inference.[3] Using the term 'inference' suggests that such a step is sometimes correct and sometimes incorrect or faulty. What general standards for correctness or validity are appropriate, if any are, is an unsolved problem. The best we can do is to review the conceptions of it in the literature and try to offer guidance on how to proceed in better understanding practical inferences.

One view of practical inference is that the agent has some goal or intention and contemplates undertaking some action necessary to bring about that goal. Foremost among the exponents of this approach is von Wright ([1972] 1978:48) who proposes the following schema for practical inference. E is an end, A an action, and X an agent.

> X intends to make it true that E.
>
> Unless he does A, he will not achieve this.
>
> Therefore, X will do A.

The sort of example von Wright (1963) has in mind is the following. X intends to meet his fiancée in London. Unless he takes the next train, he will not meet her. Therefore, X will take the next train. This example is quite plausible as an instance of an inference we commonly make. But it has many puzzling aspects. If the conclusion is an action, as von Wright's schema suggests, then the inference is not deductively valid.[4] For even if X truly intends to meet his fiancée, and taking the train is necessary to achieve this, there might be any number of reasons why X might in fact fail to take the train. Accordingly, von Wright considers various modifications of this basic schema.

Whatever precise form the ultimate expression of this schema might take, let us call it the *necessary condition schema* of practical inference. By contrast, other philosophers have concentrated on what we might call the *sufficient condition schema*.[5] Anscombe (1957) was one of the first in recent times to draw our attention to the existence of this form of argument in several interesting passages of Aristotle.

The type of example Anscombe and Aristotle thought most important is one like this: this medication is effective to cure condition C; this patient has condition C; therefore this medication is indicated for this patient. One wonders here whether the conclusion of this practical inference should be an action or some form of policy or recommendation to carry out a certain type of action. As with the necessary condition schema, it remains unclear with the sufficient condition schema what sort of inference is involved. At any rate, parallel to von Wright's initial schema, the following tentative form of the sufficient condition schema seems appropriate.

> X intends to make it true that E.
>
> If he does A, he will achieve this.
>
> Therefore, X will do A.

Again, whether the conclusion should state that X will do A or that X should do A remains unclear. And what it means to say that such an inference is "valid" or "correct" appears elusive. But the hunt is on. We can all easily appreciate that some kind of inference like the ones represented above is quite an important basic building block of the structure of human action and deliberation.

8.2 Binding Nature of Practical Inference

Although von Wright in an earlier work (1963) seemed inclined to think of practical inference as valid, he later (1971) came to the views that the premises of a practical inference do not entail behavior[6] and that the demonstration is a practical rather than a logical one. In another article (1972), he wrote: "Its [the practical inference's] nature stems from the fact that its conclusion declares the intention which an agent is logically bound to have within the teleological frame which in the premises he acknowledges for his prospective action." This approach might suggest recasting the forms of practical inference as follows.

Necessary Condition Schema

> X intends to bring about E.
>
> X realizes that E cannot be brought about unless A is.
>
> Therefore, X intends to bring about A.

Sufficient Condition Schema

> X intends to bring about E.
>
> X realizes that if A is brought about, E will be too.
>
> Therefore, X intends to bring about A.

Presumably, what it means to say one of these inferences is "valid" is this: if the two premises are true of X, then if X's intentions are to be consistent with his other intentions and beliefs about the circumstances, the conclusion must be true of X. What is meant by "consistent" is that X's plan of action—his intentions and his beliefs about the situation and how to proceed—should be internally coherent as a sequence. Here we refer again to Aristotle's and Simon's idea of the sequence of acts and intentions in a productive action.

The problem is that the pair of schemata above, as stated, do not bear out this notion of act-consistency, for three reasons. First, there may be more than one way to bring something about. Suppose I intend to satisfy my appetite, and am presented with a basket of apples. Let us say that, from my point of view, any apple would do, and all of those presented to me look equally appetizing. For example, I realize that if I eat *this* apple, my appetite will be satisfied. But I also realize that if I eat *that* apple, my appetite will be satisfied, and so forth. The practical inference applies equally to each apple. But it does not tell me of any particular apple: If you are to be consistent, intend to eat *this* apple.

This means we have to modify the second premise of the practical inference. If there are a number of equally acceptable ways to bring about E, the agent should choose one. If one is the best way, the practical reasoner should choose that.

The second problem is that there may be something intrinsically objectionable to X in bringing about A. Suppose I intend to ventilate the room. I realize that the windows do not open in this room and that the only way I can ventilate the room is to smash the window. By the necessary condition schema, I reason that I should intend to smash the window. But surely that conclusion is not necessarily the best or even proper inference to draw. On the contrary, I should refrain from smashing the window if I am just a little warm and merely feel the need for a cooling breeze. I should form the intention to smash it only if the situation is so urgent that it outweighs the damage that would be caused by breaking the window.

This also means that we have to modify the second premise of the current version of the practical inference. If the action A is in itself not acceptable for X to bring about, then the conclusion does not necessarily follow for X. We need to add the premise that A is in itself an acceptable act for X to carry out.

The third problem is that there may be foreseen consequences of an action which may not be intended. This is the problem of side effects. For example, a doctor may know that in order to cure his patient of cancer, it is necessary to bring about certain painful side effects, for example, the patient being nauseous or his hair falling out. Now, it is quite incorrect to say of the doctor that he intends these side effects to take place, even if he knows full well they will occur as consequences of the treatment.

Hence both the necessary and sufficient schemata are shown to be invalid. The doctor intends to cure his patient. He knows that these unpleasant side effects are necessary. Or, alternatively, he may know that what he does will have certain unpleasant consequences. But he does not intend the unpleasant side effects to occur. Or, at any rate, a majority of moral philosophers have held that he need not be forcibly accorded such an intention. The premises are true, but the conclusion is false, in such a case. Hence both schemata are invalid as practical inferences.

To contend with this problem we need to change the conclusion of each schema to say something less than X fully intends to bring about A. Some philosophers would make a distinction between "directly intends" and "obliquely (indirectly) intends." They would claim that although the physician does not directly intend to bring about the unpleasant side effects, nevertheless they are part of the "whole package" he intends to bring about, therefore he obliquely intends to bring them about when he applies treatment. This distinction is a controversial one, however, and some still contend that the doctor does not intend the painful side effects at all.[7]

The problem of side effects is quite a general one because all actions are complex in the real world. Suppose a man wants to kill a bird that is on a branch, but there is another bird sitting beside it. If he throws the stone he is holding, he will kill both birds. Hence killing the second bird is an unintentional side effect of his intentionally killing the first bird.[8] The problem arises because the act he carries out is complex. Characteristically, Nature allows us to do one thing only at the cost of creating additional consequences in a ripple effect. This complexity is the source of many moral problems.

Ultimately, I think the best way to contend with this third problem is to rewrite the conclusion of the practical inference, removing the term 'intends'. Consequently, I will follow the approach of von Wright and phrase the conclusion as 'X sets himself to bring about A'. This means roughly that the agent embarks on the road to carry out his end, even if he is prevented or cannot accomplish the action despite his attempt (see the discussion of von Wright 1972:52–56). Thus the conclusion of a practical inference states that the agent will embark on the action in question if his actions are consistent with his intentions and appreciation of the situation as reported in the premises.

Whether these forms of inference have a general logical structure depends on whether there is a logic of deliberation and action. It is too soon to tell, but recent work of Segerberg (1981, 1982) is very encouraging, and points the way to an intentional language for deliberation in action.

At any rate, the various qualifications and emendations of the schemata for practical inference suggest the following more careful statements of these forms of practical reasoning. The set $\{A_o, A_1, \ldots, A_n\}$ is a set of actions, for finite n.

Necessary Condition Schema

(N1) X intends to bring about E.

(N2) X realizes that doing at least one of the set $\{A_o, A_1, \ldots, A_n\}$ is necessary to bring about E.

(N3) X has decided on one member A_i as an acceptable, or as the most acceptable necessary condition for E.

(N4) Nothing prevents X from doing A_i.

(N5) Bringing about E is more acceptable to X than not doing A_i.

Therefore, X sets himself to do A_i.

Sufficient Condition Schema

(S1) X intends to bring about E.

(S2) X realizes that one of $\{A_o, A_1, \ldots, A_n\}$ is sufficient to bring about E.

(S3) X has decided on one member A_i as an acceptable, or as the most acceptable sufficient condition for E.

(S4) Nothing prevents X from doing A_i.

(S5) Bringing about E is more acceptable to X than not doing A_i.

Therefore, X sets himself to do A_i.

I shall not try to say further what is meant by the term 'acceptable' in these premises. Suffice it to say that the conclusion expresses the idea that the agent's setting himself to do A_i is acceptable relative to the premises.

Are the above schemata for practical inference in some sense "valid" or "complete" as stated above? I am not sure whether further loopholes may be found, but it could be that further work on the logic of action will show them to be valid inferences. Both schemata express forms of deliberation taken by an agent who sets out to produce an end or carry out some intention. Practical reasoning is the linkage of practical inferences into chainlike sequences. The previous example of Aristotle's physician suggests how a sequence of actions is made up of steps that correspond to practical inferences of the two types shown above.

When a long sequence of practical inferences is set out in a particular case, we come to understand how the agent's actions and intentions fit together in his deliberations. This pattern of implemented intentions, once it is fitted into the particular circumstances of the case, yields a narrative discourse and sets out the position of the agent. Further actions can be evaluated in relation to an existing position.

A sequence of actions that translates an intention into specific actions available to an agent in a particular situation is the thread of practical reasoning that underlies satisficing and optimizing procedures. Simple examples of such procedures can be found in instruction manuals for practical tasks like assembling an item of furniture or installing an appliance in a kitchen.

A good example is found in the booklet for cleaning a coffeemaker (*Operating Instructions for Mr. Coffee Model* CM and CMX *Series*, North American Systems, Inc., Bedford Heights, Ohio).

CLEANING INSTRUCTIONS

1. Pour 1 quart of white household vinegar into top of coffeemaker.
2. Place empty decanter and brew funnel with filter in place on coffeemaker.
3. Plug power cord into electrical outlet and turn switch ON.
4. After vinegar has been pumped through coffeemaker into decanter, turn switch OFF and pour the vinegar into the top of the coffeemaker.
5. Allow vinegar to remain in the unit for approximately 1/2 hour.
6. Then turn switch ON and allow all the vinegar to be pumped out into decanter. Save solution for future coffeemaker cleaning or discard.
7. Flush the system by cycling through 10 cups of clear tap water.

8. Repeat flushing procedure. If your coffeemaker's pumping action still stops in the middle of the brew cycle, then it requires an additional cleaning cycle. By removing the latch, the cross over and the riser tube assembly from the coffeemaker, these parts may be cleaned separately. Be sure the coffeemaker is first unplugged before performing these operations. Reassemble and then your coffeemaker is ready to brew coffee again.

Each of the first seven steps involves one or more actions to be carried out in the sequence indicated. The last step calls for repeating the procedure, and also offers several conditional steps, alternatives, and precautions.

This is the sort of procedure we mean when we have talked about satisficing and practical reasoning. The intention of the agent is to clean his coffeemaker. To carry out this objective, he must first undertake various preparatory actions, all of which are necessary conditions. Having done these things, the agent must then start at step 1 of the instructions. To do that he must pick up the quart of vinegar. He must remove the flap on top of the coffeemaker, and so forth. It is this whole sequence of actions we refer to by the phrase "cleaning the coffeemaker."

In this example, we can see how each step in the sequence of actions represents a single practical inference of the agent. Putting the whole sequence together in the right order, we can see how the list of cleaning instructions above could be expanded into a narrative discourse that would explain how the agent cleaned the coffeemaker in a particular instance. To be sure, cleaning a coffeemaker might not be all that exciting or ethically contentious in most cases. But the same kind of teleological explanation of an action is at work when we evaluate some exciting or controversial instance of human action as courageous or cowardly.

Practical inference is such an important analytical tool in ethics and philosophy of mind because the concepts of a necessary condition and sufficient condition can be seen as steps of practical inference which are linked together in the teleological framework[9] of narrative discourse. The extended sequence of steps represents the agent's position, his commitments, and actions. Therefore, satisficing is a personal ethic because it relates to the plan and actions of a particular agent.

The agent's reasoning at each step can be "logical," however, because necessary and sufficient conditions are involved. But necessary (sufficient) conditions must mean, in practical inference, 'necessary (sufficent) *in the circumstances*'.[10] More than purely logical necessity or sufficiency is meant.

Provided that we can have some provisional yet clear and reasonable grasp of the nature of practical inference, we can get on with the job of showing how courageous action presupposes the concept of practical reasoning.

8.3 Consistency of Statements and Actions

The notion of practical reasoning derives from the work of Aristotle. The basic form of practical reasoning, the type of inference schematized in the previous section, has sometimes been called the *practical syllogism*. The conclusion of this form of argument is an action, or at least a recommendation that a certain action should practically be brought about. But as MacIntyre (1981:151) points out, the idea that an argument can terminate in an action is one that some philosophers have found puzzling or repugnant. For, they would ask, how can actions enter into the relationships of consistency, inconsistency, and logical consequence which characterize deductive reasoning? According to MacIntyre, actions can enter into these relationships because they often serve to express beliefs.

As an example, MacIntyre (ibid.) asks us to consider the case of a man who goes outdoors in winter without his overcoat. Suppose this man has expressed a wish to stay healthy as well as a belief that it is necessary to keep warm in winter to remain healthy. Let us suppose in addition that this man justifiably believes that the only way to keep warm in winter outdoors is to wear an overcoat. Is such a man inconsistent? Yes, MacIntyre would reply—his action expresses a belief inconsistent with his other expressed beliefs. Therefore, such a person is illogical in the sense that his reasoning contains an inconsistency. Thus the practical syllogism serves as a requirement for the logical consistency of a person's statements and actions.

The word *hypocrisy* stems from the Greek word for 'pretend' or 'play a part' and is often used to refer to one who pretends to have a virtue that he or she does not in fact practice. To be shown hypocritical is such a serious and deadly form of refutation in disputational exchange that the argument directed to showing such a practical inconsistency of word and deed even has a traditional name, the *cir-*

cumstantial ad hominem (against the man) argument. For example, suppose your doctor argues that smoking is unhealthy and that since health is valuable, you should give up smoking. But suppose your doctor smokes and you point this out by replying, "What about you, doctor? Aren't you being inconsistent by not following your own advice?" This form of rejoinder is sometimes called the *tu quoque* (you too) argument.[11] The question of interest here is whether the tu quoque is a correct form of refutation of someone's argument. Often, the circumstantial ad hominem has been known as a logical fallacy, an incorrect type of argument.

But perhaps the incorrectness of this form of argument is only partial, and may be brought out as follows. Suppose the patient who replies tu quoque to the doctor's practical argument is really proposing the following refutation: "You, my dear doctor, have cited all sorts of statistics and medical findings that tend to indicate that smoking is very bad for one's health. But you yourself smoke! Therefore, your argument is inconsistent. You are quite mistaken, and for all your argument shows, smoking may not be bad for one's health at all." In this response, something seems wrong. What is it?

The best explanation of what has gone wrong in this attempted refutation of the doctor's argument is that two things are confused. First, there is the issue of whether the statistics and other medical findings cited do, in themselves, constitute good or reasonable evidence for the conclusion that smoking is bad for your health. Second, there is the question of whether the doctor's own personal practice is or is not consistent with her own statement of what ought to be done, given that the doctor herself also presumably wants to be healthy. The fallacy, if there is one, could consist in arguing incorrectly from the second issue to the first. That is, the refuter seems to be arguing that because the doctor's own actions are practically inconsistent with the argument she herself proposes, therefore the argument put forward by the doctor is *in itself* internally inconsistent or incorrect. But surely this is a fallacy. The doctor's argument that smoking is unhealthy may be, in itself, perfectly sound, even though her own failure to follow the argument's recommendation seriously impugns the doctor's personal advocacy of that argument. There is a difference between the two questions of (1) whether the argument is in itself internally or logically correct, and (2) whether the advocacy of the argument as a recommendation is practically consistent or sound.

Hence there is an important difference between logical inconsistency of propositions (statements) and practical inconsistency between someone's statements and actions. We say that two propositions A and B are *logically inconsistent* if, and only if, it is not possible for A and B to both be true. To use another word for the same thing, we can say that A and B are contraries if both cannot be jointly true. However, let us now say that A and B are *practically inconsistent* for some person if and only if (i) that person brings about one of these, say A, and at the same time asserts the other one, B, and (ii) A and B are logically inconsistent. In the second definition, A and B are still propositions, except we introduce the idea that some agent can make a proposition true (bring about a state of affairs) by something he or she does. Thus practical inconsistency, or pragmatic inconsistency as it is called in Walton (1985), is quite different from logical inconsistency, although the two kinds of inconsistency are of course related. Unfortunately, as the ad hominem fallacy illustrates, they are often mischievously confused in disputation.

To paraphrase Archbishop Whately, in the ad hominem argument, the conclusion actually established is not the absolute and general one, but the relative and particular one that *this man* is bound to admit such-and-such a proposition if he is to be consistent with his own conduct.[12] Whately also observed that the effect of an ad hominem refutation, if it is successful, is not to show that a certain proposition is definitely proven to be false. Instead such a refutation shifts the burden of proof against the disputant who is shown to be practically inconsistent. It is not that his assertion is by itself shown to be false, but that the position he advocates is, as a whole, weakened by his failure to follow his own advice. Thus in the dispute he must try to resolve the practical inconsistency. For example, when the governor of the Bank of Canada, Gerald Bouey, urged salary freezes and other measures to control inflationary wage demands, many critics pointed out that he himself then had a salary in excess of a hundred thousand dollars a year. This criticism was really an ad hominem attack against Bouey's advocacy of his own argument.[13] The effect of it was not to disprove the reasonableness of Bouey's recommendation in itself, but to question his own advocacy of that recommendation at the practical level. Thereby, the burden of proof was shifted onto Bouey to clear up the apparent practical conflict in his position if it was to be vindicated.

The reason the ad hominem is such a dangerous ploy in argument is that it tends to shift the focus off the issue of whether propositions are true or arguments are logically valid and onto questions of personal advocacy of arguments or positions. From there, the step to personal quarrel and defamation of character may represent a speedy degeneration of the argument into chaos.[14] The ad hominem is therefore quite rightly regarded as a suspicious character in arguments. It is well to be clear, however, that ad hominem argumentation need not always be intrinsically fallacious. In some instances it serves a legitimate function of shifting the burden of proof in dialogue.

8.4 Why-Questions in Dialogue

Practical inferences reflect the Kantian dictum that whoever wills the end also wills the necessary means that are in his power. But as we have seen, "wills" is not quite the right word. The physician who wills the cure of his patient does not necessarily "will" the painful treatment needed to effect that cure. However, by electing to carry out that treatment with full knowledge of its painful side effects, we can say that he deliberately set that treatment, with its painful side effects, into motion. Practical reasoning may commit the physician to using the means he thinks necessary to carry out his intended goal. It is fair to say that a man's intentions can commit him to an action in certain circumstances that dictate necessary or sufficient conditions.[15] Practical inference is valid insofar as it may commit one who accepts the premises to carrying out the action described by the conclusion.

If there turns out to be a logic of practical inference, no doubt it will prove to be useful in designing robots and systems of industrial production and in showing us how computers "act" to carry out ends (programs). Such mathematical models of practical reasoning will no doubt have other scientific uses, not least in the social sciences. The methodology appropriate to study the ethics of courageous actions needs, however, to be more humanistically oriented. Its methods must be more like the processes of explanation and justification used in history and the law. We have already seen that history is concerned with the evaluation of actions as courageous or cowardly in some cases. Insofar as they are supererogatory, however, these kinds of acts are not of primary interest in criminal law, that area of law which is usually such an interesting source of material on the mental element (*mens rea*) in actions.

Philosophers have occasionally suggested that the proper method of explanation and justification of actions in the law and history, and humanistic inquiries generally, is that of the question-answer dialogue.[16] I will suggest that the method of logical dialogue—what Aristotle called *dialectic*—is the best method for evaluating allegations of courage and cowardice. Although dialectical methods are more useful in science than has been traditionally recognized, they may be contrasted with cumulative methods of scientific verification which strive for convergence of well-established hypotheses by mathematical modeling and experimental confirmation. The paradigm of such a cumulative model would be the axiomatic presentation of a theory.

By the dialectical approach, however, the reenactment of a historical action is not a process of interpretation which yields a final answer. When the process of questioning and answering has come to a provisional end, it is because the commitments of all parties to the dialogue have become articulated in public. This process need not always lead to agreement. But it does often lead to a shift of position by one or more participants in the dialogue. It always remains possible, however, that a better question could be asked or that the process of dialogue could start again.

We saw in the case of Lord Sackville that the ultimate board of arbitration for an allegation of cowardice may have to be a court case. In that instance, Sackville wanted to bring his critics' allegations out in the open so he could respond to them. By his skillful conduct of the dialogue, he was able to gain a measure of justice in vindicating his actions as not cowardly. That was the best he could have hoped for. So it is with dialectic—it shifts the burden of proof, but rarely provides a highly conclusive proof of a man's intentions, actions, and deliberations where courage or cowardice are at issue. For all its open-endedness, such dialogues often make it very clear that an act was courageous or cowardly.

In the case of some historical actions, the agent has not attempted to justify or defend his act by arguments or statements of his intentions. In the case of citations and decorations for valor, we often only have the official recommendation and description of the act to go by. In such a case, the action must speak for itself. By empathy and reasonable presumption, we supply the intentions that seem plausible and generous in the circumstances. To be fair, we assume that the intentions and perceptions of the situation accorded to the agent are the expected and favorable ones suggested by the circumstances.[17] If a man falls on a grenade and saves several comrades, we presume that his intention was to save his comrades. There is no opportunity to ask him afterward, or engage in dialogue with him regarding his intentions and his perceptions of what he thought necessary. But, as in law, we presume that a man knows the usual and expected consequences of his actions if we have no evidence to the contrary. The charitable interpretation, in such a case, is the fair one. The burden of proof is on the critic to give evidence if he thinks that such an act might not have been courageous. It is as if the agent adopts or expresses a certain position, a certain moral stance, by acting the way he did in the circumstances. This position can then be challenged or defended afterward by historians, legal inquiries, or biographers.

In discussing practical reasoning, we thought of the practical inference as a step made by an agent in acting to produce a certain goal or end. Such calculations take place before the action is undertaken. However, there is also a retrospective use of practical reasoning. Once the action has taken place, those of us who want to understand it need to place it in a sequence of actions and intentions. We ask: Why did he do that? The answer: In order to do this other thing. Again we ask: Why did he want to do this other thing? The answer: Because he intended to realize such-and-such a goal. The dialogue takes the form of a question-answer series that reconstructs the sequence of actions and intentions.

Collingwood (1946) was one of the first to develop the question-answer method as a system of handling testimonial historical evidence to explain human actions in history. My retrospective use of practical reasoning to help us understand courageous acts is in the tradition of Collingwood's view of history as the reenactment of past experience. As Collingwood puts it (1946:282), the historian is not an eyewitness to the facts he wants to know. His knowledge of the past is inferential. It is the retrospective use of practical reasoning that yields the required type of inference.

It does not matter that many deliberate actions are not undertaken with a plan consciously preformulated in any elaborate way. For we can still reconstruct the action as bearing out the intention we can reasonably take the agent to have had. As Dray (1957:123) puts it, "there is a calculation which could be constructed for it: the one the agent would have gone through if he had had time, if he had not seen what to do in a flash, if he had been called upon to account for what he did after the event, etc." While this reconstruction is based on factual evidence given by the testimony of witnesses, it is the subsequent dialogue that establishes the sequence of intentions and actions that we impose on the agent's conduct as expressing our interpretation of the matter.

By taking the view that courageous and cowardly actions can be evaluated by a question-answer process of practical reasoning, we have now raised the question of how such reconstructions can express truth. Are they "explanations" or "justifications" of actions? The stance I will take is that courageous actions put forward a certain position, and the reconstructive dialogue refines, articulates, challenges, or criticizes that position.

8.5 Position in Dialogue

According to MacIntyre, actions can be inconsistent with statements of a person because actions often express beliefs. This assertion is quite true, but we have already seen the pitfalls inherent in offering an analysis of discourse about courage in terms of one's psychological beliefs. Instead, I would like to propose that we explicate the logical relationships between actions and propositions in terms of the commitments of a participant in a game of dialogue. A commitment does not necessarily represent the belief of a participant in an argument. Rather it is a proposition that belongs to a set—the commitment-store of the arguer—where membership is defined by the rules of a game of disputation. The type of game we have in mind is a question-answer dialogue game of the sort recently investigated by Hamblin,[18] Hintikka,[19] Rescher,[20] Carlson,[21] and Barth and Krabbe.[22] In these games, a player can indicate propositions he is committed to by making certain moves in the game. For example, if he answers a question "Do you accept proposition A?" in the affirmative, his response would commit him to A. In some types of games, such a response would also commit him to some set of propositions that are logical consequences of A, where "logical consequence" is defined by the language of the game.[23] These games are a valuable tool for discourse analysis in linguistics and the study of logical disputation and fallacies. But they can also be of some use to the moral philosopher, as we will see.

A *position* of a player in a game of dialogue is defined as the whole set of commitments of that player at a given stage of the game.[24] The game is defined as a sequence of questions and answers where one participant is the questioner and the other the answerer. The rules may allow that the players can switch roles from time to time. A stage of the game is defined as a given point in the sequence of moves (questions and answers).

There is also another quite distinct way of defining the notion of a person's position: as a set of propositions that form a basis for acting when one is formulating a plan of action. By this conception a person's position is a *code* or *policy*, a body of propositions which represent outcomes the person plans to bring about through his deliberation and action. A position in this sense may consist of a personal statement, but it can also represent the collective resolve of a group of individuals, say, to support nuclear disarmament. It may be a professional code of behavior or collective policy, for example, on politics or religion.

The reason we can analyze the type of inconsistency we previously found between actions and statements (characteristic of ad hominem reasoning) is that the two definitions coincide in certain cases. In an action game, if some proposition A is brought about (made true) by a player at some stage in the game, as permitted by the rules, then A, and all logical consequences of A as defined by the practical syllogism, become commitments of that player. The set of all commitments of that player, now defined as his position, represents a pool of propositions against which he may be charged with inconsistency. That is, if at any move a player commits himself to some proposition A by something he says or does, that player may be refuted by an ad hominem charge of inconsistency. Thus the type of action-theoretic inconsistency appropriate for practical reasoning may now be quite clearly given an underlying logical structure as positional inconsistency in an action game of dialogue.

I argue that the most favorable method and structure for the study of practical reasoning—and hence courage and cowardice as practical excellences and lapses of action—is not exclusively the empirical (experimental) method of the social sciences. The method of rational disputation captured by the question-answer logic of dialogue can be helpful and informative. In evaluating whether or not an act is courageous, we are undertaking a normative and conceptual inquiry. But the evaluation is by no means purely subjective or "disputational" in the sense of an unregulated quarrel; it is partly normative by virtue of the ethical matrix of courage, but also partly objective because of the underlying structure of logical dialogues. Conversational disputations about whether an act is courageous do reflect practical reasoning and therefore the sequence of such reasoning may be modeled by action games of dialogue.

The value of dialogue is that it articulates the position of a participant by subjecting it to reasoned questioning and criticism. By this process, propositions that were part of one's deeply held position, but were not clearly known or articulated, come to the surface—they become a part of one's public commitments. Commitments move from the dark side of one's store of commitments to the light side. Clarification of one's position is new knowledge of a sort.

How the concept of a moral position functions in disputed moral issues concerning actions is nicely brought out by Dworkin (1966). Dworkin considers the case of a man who tells someone that he is going to vote against another man running for public office. The reason he offers is that he believes homosexuality is immoral, and he knows the man running for office to be a homosexual. Suppose, Dworkin continues, that the man who is told about this accuses the first man of acting on prejudice or on the basis of an unreasonable personal repugnance of homosexuals. The two men may then enter into an argument on this issue, each trying to win over or convert the other to his stand. Each tries to convince the other that his vote is based on a morally defensible position. If both men are reasonable, then each one's act of voting should be based on a position he can defend or argue for. The subsequent argument may lead to each of these men changing his position, even if, at the end of the argument, they still disagree on their basic positions.

Interestingly, Dworkin (1966:995) notes that the attempts of each of these men to persuade the other is likely to alter the judgment of character each has for the other. If one, for example, defends his position reasonably and fairly but without basically changing it, the other might think him somewhat eccentric (e.g., puritanical), while still recognizing his right to act on his convictions. If his convictions were ably defended in the argument, the one man could respect a person who can reasonably defend his convictions, even if he still disagrees with the point of view defended.

Ad hominem criticisms of an arguer's position are very common and powerful forms of argument in political and moral argumentation. Consider the case of the woman who decides to have an abortion and is then criticized as follows: "You of all people should agree that abortion is wrong. After all, you're a Catholic." If the woman accepts that she is a Catholic, the criticism seems very powerful. The position she appears to be committed to seems internally inconsistent. On the one hand, she is Catholic, but on the other hand, her action and decision was to have an abortion in her own personal case.

But is the apparent inconsistency necessarily a good refutation? For the refutation to be tighter, it would be necessary to spell out the Catholic position or at least enough of this position to imply that abortion is wrong. But the critic has not done this. Moreover, although Catholicism may be in some respects a well-defined position, Catholics may disagree on some issues, and there may be legitimate room for argument. And even in some cases, for example, where the life of the mother is threatened, Catholics might agree that an abortion is permissible. Thus perhaps the woman who is criticized could defend her position as a Catholic in relation to the particulars of her own case. Yet the criticism puts her on the defensive—it tilts the burden of proof.

Another factor is that probably neither the woman nor her critic are Catholic theologians. They both probably have some idea of the Catholic position on abortion, but what this position comes down to in specific instances, where exceptions may or may not be permissible, is not likely to be known by either of them. A position that plays a role in an ad hominem criticism very often has a "dark side"—we might plausibly conjecture the gist of the position, but the specific details may be unknown to the arguers. More dialogue may be needed to see whether the position is truly defensible or not. Often, one's position may only begin to emerge as the argument unfolds. Many arguments are revealing precisely because they serve to more sharply articulate one's own dimly held commitments.

In light of these remarks, what can we say about the case of the Catholic politician who says that he personally opposes abortion but supports freedom of choice as a matter of public policy? Here the case seems to be quite different because the opposition to abortion is a matter of virtue, a question of one's personal stance, not a matter of policy which applies to everyone. Or so the politician claims. The analogy is to the courageous soldier who throws himself on a grenade to save his platoon at the cost of his own life. His act is courageous— a virtuous act—yet it does not imply that everyone in a similar situation has a duty to act the same way. By analogy, the politician may be claiming that his personal position against abortion is above and beyond duty—a matter of personal virtue.

This is a good argument, as far as it goes. But there is a fatal flaw in it if the politician is truly a Catholic, and if—as seems a correct interpretation—the Catholic stricture against abortion is meant as a matter of universal duty and not simply as a personal or individual matter of virtue.

In other words, it could be quite consistent for the politician to argue: "I am personally against abortion as a matter of my own ideals, but I do not wish to impose my personal standards on everyone else. If someone else wants to have an abortion, then they have a right to choose, based on their own personal position, and I will not condemn their action." But if that politician is committed to being a Catholic, it becomes much more dubious that the same argument can go through. For Catholics should be opposed to the direct taking of innocent human life, according to their moral position. And it seems that they view this opposition as a matter of duty as applied to all moral agents.

At any rate, the study of contentious arguments, like those on abortion and other public controversies, shows how dialogue can refine or articulate a position. A position may be purely personal, but in some cases it may express the commitments of a group of agents and may have rules meant to apply to all moral agents.

Our reasoned discussion of courageous acts has refined our intuitions by looking at particular examples or cases. In some cases it has challenged and questioned the interpretations that seem customary and expected, but in other cases it has defended those intuitions.

This closes our discussion of practical reasoning. Our treatment of this topic, which deserves closer attention in moral philosophy, is by no means the final word. Perhaps, however, it may have afforded some insight into the humanistic disciplines as a worthwhile study and helped us to explore courage and cowardice as properties of actions.

As a technical postscript to this chapter, let us consider the disputed question of whether courage and cowardice are opposites. I will show that, given certain assumptions about practical reasoning, courage and cowardice are not strict opposites on the analysis proposed earlier.

8.6 Are Courage and Cowardice Opposites?

It is time to refine our contention that courage and cowardice are not strictly opposites. It is necessary first of all to clarify what we mean by "opposites."

Let us say that two propositions are *contrary* if both cannot be jointly true. We shall also say that two propositions are *contradictory* if both cannot be jointly true, and both cannot be jointly false. For example, '*a* is red' and '*a* is green' are contraries in the sense that both propositions cannot be jointly true (for the same individual *a* over its whole surface, at the same time). Yet both can be jointly false, for example, if *a* is black. Consider, however, the pair of propositions, '*a* is red' and '*a* is not red'. These two propositions are contradictory. They cannot be jointly true, but in addition they cannot be jointly false. For any individual object *a*, at least one must be true.

Now the propositions '*a*'s act is courageous' and '*a*'s act is cowardly' are opposites in the weaker sense that they are contrary to each other. This claim can be proven upon the following two assumptions. First, we need to presume that (E1), the statement that B is (highly) worth *a*'s bringing about, is equivalent to this disjunction: either it is *a*'s duty to bring about B, or B is worth *a*'s bringing about but it is not *a*'s duty to bring about B. The second part of the disjunction means that bringing about B is a supererogatory act beyond the call of duty for *a*. Given this presumption, we can now show why courageous action and cowardly action must be contrary by the proposed definitions.

Second, we need to presume the general principle of practical reasoning that if A is necessary for B or C, then A is necessary for B and A is necessary for C. For example, if this pen's being colored is necessary for this pen to be red or yellow, it follows that this pen's being colored is necessary for it to be red, and this pen's being colored is necessary for it to be yellow. And, in general, if A is necessary for either of B or C to obtain, then A is necessary for B and A is necessary for C.

Given these two presumptions '*a*'s act is courageous' and '*a*'s act is cowardly' are contrary opposites. By the definition of the latter expression, it follows that *a* failed to bring about something that is necessary for bringing about something that is his duty. By the definition of '*a*'s act is courageous' and the first assumption it follows that *a* brought about something that is necessary for bringing about something that is either his duty or is beyond his duty. It follows by the second assumption that *a* brought about something that is necessary for bringing about something that is his duty. But we have arrived at a contradiction. Failing to bring about something necessary for duty is the direct opposite of bringing about something necessary for duty. Thus 'courageous act' and 'cowardly act' are contrary opposites, according to our definitions.

But as we have shown by examples earlier, courage and cowardice are not contradictory opposites. If an act is not courageous, it does not follow that it need be cowardly. If an act fails to be necessary for something beyond duty, that does not mean that failure to carry it out would be a failure to do something necessary for duty. For example, my writing these words on the page is not courageous, but it is not cowardly just because it is not courageous. Similarly, an act may not be cowardly, but it need not follow that it is courageous.

These properties also follow from our earlier definitions. For example, assume that an act is not courageous. Then, by the definition, the agent fails to bring about something necessary for bringing about something that is either his duty or beyond duty. It does not follow that he fails to bring about something necessary for bringing about something that is his duty. Hence it does not follow that his act is cowardly. Moreover, of course, it need not follow that his failure to act was by reason of fear. If an act is not courageous, it does not follow that it is cowardly. Hence an act can be neither courageous nor cowardly. Hence 'courageous action' and 'cowardly action' are not contradictories.

If we ignored the fact that courage is defined in terms of danger or difficulty whereas cowardice is defined in terms of fear, then courage and cowardice would be contradictories if we restricted courageous acts to those done strictly in the line of duty. No doubt that is why it may seem plausible to think that courage and cowardice are contradictory opposites. But even disregarding the difference between danger and fear, courage and cowardice fail to be contradictories in the case where the act is heroic.

The soldier who holds a position he has been ordered to hold, even at great risk, may act courageously even if he is only doing his duty. However, the soldier who throws himself on a grenade to protect his comrades shows heroic courage beyond his duty. As Urmson noted (1958:203), in such a case his superior could not have decently ordered him to do this. Had he not done it, his failure to act would not have been cowardly, nor could anyone have said to him "You ought to have thrown yourself on that grenade." Nor could anyone have justifiably said to him "Your failure to throw yourself on that grenade was cowardly." Thus his act was courageous, in fact heroically courageous, because it was supererogatory, and his not so acting would not have been a cowardly failure. However, in the case of the soldier ordered to hold his dangerous post, failure to hold it without justifiable reason would be cowardly, if fear was the motive.

CHAPTER 9

Ethical Theory and
Justification of
Courageous Acts

WHEN WE COME to investigate the ethics of courage and cowardice, we appear to be bereft of intellectual resources and cast into a theoretical vacuum, as MacIntyre (1981) has documented. We are either given over to the social scientists, who are not well equipped methodologically to pursue questions of ethics, or we are—perhaps by the same route—thrown back onto a nonmethodology of moral relativism. By this now-dominant perspective, emotions and feelings are their own justifications—"If it feels all right, then it must be morally acceptable or justifiable as a course of action." Small surprise then that topics like courage and cowardice have for the most part (with few welcome exceptions previously noted) been neglected and, as a result, sequestered in a hinterland of ethical curios.

Yet we have seen that courage is often a supererogatory property, not a matter of duty so much as a matter of personal ideals and aspirations. Accordingly, there is a double challenge to courage as a moral quality of actions. If courage is a matter of personal ideals, what is to stop us from presuming that judgments of courage are purely personal and subjective (beyond ethics)? The theory of practical reasoning (discussed in chap. 8) is, I propose, the only sound defense against such an attack. The other challenge, also previously encountered, is that courage could be a morally negative quality, more macho swagger than moral virtue.

We have already pointed out that traditional ethical theory has not only neglected the study of courage and acts of moral heroism but has also taken, in some instances, a negative moral stance. Kant, for example, in the *Critique of Practical Reason* ([1788] 1956:87) warns of the moral fanaticism of exhortation to actions expected of people not because of duty but because of their own bare merit: "The mind is disposed to nothing but blatant moral fanaticism and exaggerated self-conceit by exhortations to actions as noble, sublime, and magnanimous." This sort of attack on supererogatory acts of heroism as acts of moral aspiration or merit requires some reply if courageous actions are to be justified as truly morally commendable.

Heyd (1982) has already countered this negative Kantian argument by his rebuttals justifying the intrinsic worth of supererogatory acts beyond the morality of duty. Heyd's justification of supererogatory acts turns on their discretionary nature. He takes a Strawsonian view of ethics that distinguishes between social morality and individual ideals.[1] In the latter category are morally good acts whose omission is not wrong. The moral goodness of these supererogatory acts is justified, according to Heyd (1982:172–178), by individual autonomy— an individual is justified in pursuing his personal ideals because he has a good reason for fulfilling his own needs even before getting involved in the needs of others. Heyd's argument is that the general good presupposes individual good: "If everyone worked for the promotion of the *general* good, *whose* good would be promoted?" Hence, according to Heyd, the morality of duty and public welfare must find room for the integrity of personal life plans.

The disputed issue between Heyd and Kant turns on the fine but vague line between personal aspirations and public duties. This is a perennial issue for ethics, but one we do not need to resolve here, for in fact most acts of courage, as we have defined courage, turn out to be acts of personal sacrifice for the welfare or safety of others. But in this dispute, we certainly side with Heyd in supporting the view that there are meritorious acts of courage that exceed the requirements of duty. Hence a problem remains. If such acts are especially good or meritorious even beyond conformity to duty, then what is so good about them other than their conformity to duty or to the public welfare in general? Can our intuitive feeling that acts of conspicuous valor are highly commendable be justified by appeal to ethical principles or theories of conduct?

To some extent we have already given justifications of the value of courage as a moral notion, but it remains to do so in a more systematic way. Of course, we have also shown that whether or how courage can be justified depends on how it is defined. Now to the question: As defined here, how is courage to be justified as a commendable quality? That is, wherein as a matter of ethical theory does the merit of an act of courage lie?

9.1 *Personal Excellence of Actions*

What does the merit of courageous conduct consist in, if it is not a matter of utility or duty? One common answer is that courageous acts reflect the excellent character of the agent. One serious problem with this view is that sometimes courageous acts are carried out by persons who are not wise or courageous in their behavior generally. C. S. Forester's story of Ordinary Seaman Triggs brought out this point quite forcefully.[2]

Could it be, then, that there is something intrinsically meritorious about an act of courage apart from the question of the general or usual disposition of the agent? I have argued that the real merit of an act of courage is that it shows the good intentions of the agent at the time and his commitment to those intentions. What is shown is the high personal standards and ideals of this person as reflected in his action.

This does not mean that the person who acted courageously need be an excellent or noble person in every respect—indeed, such an attitude may reflect the false idolatry of uncritical hero worship.[3] Rather, it means that the single action, or course of actions, shows the strength of commitment of a person to good ends through particular episodes of conduct. It is true that some, like Sister Theresa, go on exemplifying this excellence of conduct beyond duty in difficult circumstances over a lifetime of dedicated service. Others, however, may not be striving toward a life plan of commitment to noble ideals and self-sacrifice. They may be quite ordinary people, perhaps even tending to be selfish or cowardly, who in one magnificent act of courage, show their deeply buried commitment to an ideal of conduct.

I think it is a remarkable and wonderful thing that perfectly ordinary and unexceptional people can reveal their depth of commitment to the good, their aspiration to ideals of excellence, in an emergency or other difficult situation where they are called upon by circumstances to act. In some ways, I think that by unselfishly and nonpremeditatively responding to the urgent needs of a situation into which they have been thrown, such people show the clearest of all cases of courageous action. For there can be little doubt or suspicion of their motives in wanting fame or personal attention in so acting.

The courageous act in itself thus can be an object of merit and commendation apart from the question of the character of the agent as a general disposition.[4] What we mean when we say that an action was good, as opposed to right, is that it was carried out with a good intention in mind. But more than that, we mean that the agent deliberately acted in accord with his appreciation of the circumstances to carry out good intentions by the means at his disposal or that he could create. We mean that he acted for discernible reasons, and that these reasons are reflected in the deliberative structure of the act-sequence as we can reconstruct it afterward. The sequence of actions, the intentions, and the circumstances of the action all need to be combined into an evidential picture in our dialogical reconstruction of the act and the agent's frame of mind at the time.

The more familiar application of practical reasoning in the evaluation of conduct is in criminal law, where the mental element (*mens rea*) clearly plays a key role in our understanding of actions.[5] But there the blameworthiness or culpability of the act is at issue—the focus is on responsibility and excusability for acts thought to be wrong or misdirected. There is no like emphasis in the law on studying the conditions for the moral praiseworthiness of actions or on giving credit for meritorious acts. Legal tradition provides plenty of resources for helping us to understand criminal responsibility for bad or wrong actions, but not for guiding our understanding of how we evaluate meritorious or heroic acts. Perhaps, then, the neglect of such topics in moral philosophy is understandable.

So we need to become reaccustomed to the idea that morally superb and excellent actions are not only good but are very good. This seems a simple idea, but it is remarkable how ethical theory seems to have strayed from it and even denied it.

Of course, the definition of courageous action previously proposed requires that a courageous act be undertaken with reasonably justified good intentions. So our defense of courage as a moral quality is really also a defense of the possibility of this sort of definition of the quality.

9.2 *Value and Valor*

The moral value of acts of courage, according to the definition I have proposed, is to be found in the value of the act itself as a reflection of both the good intentions of the agent and his resolution and sacrifice in order to carry out these intentions. The moral value of an act of courage is personal merit insofar as it represents the intention and the sacrifice of that agent as an individual. But the moral value of an act of courage is not purely a matter of personal merit—the act is of intrinsic moral value in itself. The reason for this is twofold. First, the intention of the act must be intrinsically good for the act to be truly courageous. Second, the difficult or dangerous circumstances of the act mean that the carrying out of the act is an attempt to overcome something intrinsically bad (or of negative value in itself). This means again that in relation to its intention, the act represents some end that is intrinsically good in itself.

The value of courage is not exclusively a matter of personal merit. A man may, in his lifetime, perform only one courageous act, and many cowardly actions. It does not follow that he is a courageous man. It is the act that is courageous, most fundamentally, and it is courageous because of the values that are expressed by its intentions.

The act of courage is a valuable thing in itself. Regardless of the character or past of the person who committed it, the act is complete in itself as a noble and excellent thing. It stands as a reminder that everyone should strive for excellence of personal conduct. Excellence of conduct is good in itself and needs no apology. Outstanding excellence in acts of heroic courage is, fortunately, fairly rare, and like any rare thing is more highly valued. Fortunately, circumstances are not always so bad as to require heroic efforts to accomplish something good.

The foregoing vindication of the value of courage, of course, stems from our way of defining its basic structure as a species of practical reasoning. But we have also seen that courage has a number of overtones or optional meanings. The value of the overtones—determination, presence of mind, altruism, and so forth—would appear to require little, if any, argument or justification. And, anyway, what value these overtones have as properties of an action seems strongly tied to the basic notion of courageous action as practical reasoning in a bad situation.

One might wonder how the overtones of courage are combined with the central definition in a particular action. For example, how can altruism be combined with practical reasoning? The answer lies in the two-part nature of the basic definition of courageous action. Altruism has to do with the intention of the act. Practical reasoning has to do with how the act to achieve that intention was carried out.

An example may be helpful. Sergeant James Ward was the copilot of a Wellington bomber returning from an attack on Muenster on the night of July 7, 1941.[6] Attacked by German fighters, the Wellington showed flames from the near-starboard engine. Fed by gasoline from a split pipe, the fire threatened to burn up the wing. The crew forced a hole in the fuselage and tried to deploy fire extinguishers but could not solve the problem and prepared to abandon the plane. As a last resort, Ward volunteered to try to crawl out onto the wing. He was persuaded to wear his parachute and tie a rope to himself, but the rope might have been more danger than help if he were blown off the wing.

The *London Gazette* (August 5, 1941) describes his actions as follows (Army Headquarters 1969:11). Putting on his parachute, Ward climbed out the hatch and onto the wing, despite the difficulty posed by the wind pressure.

> Breaking the fabric to make hand and feet holes where necessary and also taking advantage of existing holes in the fabric, Sergeant Ward succeeded in descending three feet to the wing and proceeding another three feet to a position behind the engine, despite the slipstream from the airscrew which nearly blew him off the wing. Lying in this precarious position he smothered the fire in the wing fabric and tried to push the engine cover into the hole in the wing and on the leaking pipe from which the fire came. As soon as he had removed his hand, however, the terrific wind blew the cover off and when he tried again it was lost. Tired as he was, he was able with the navigator's assistance to make a successful but perilous journey back into the aircraft.

Eventually, the fire burned itself out because there was no fabric left near it to continue burning. Despite the damage to the aircraft, a safe landing was made. By extinguishing the fire, Ward had made the flight home possible. For this act, he was decorated with the Victoria Cross.

Ward's action was an altruistic one in that he volunteered to undertake this dangerous attempt to save the plane and get the aircrew home safely. But in undertaking the task, he showed considerable ingenuity and attention to a tricky job under very dangerous circumstances. So the means of carrying out this altruistic act involved practical reasoning under pressure.

We can see how the overtones of courage can be combined with the core notion. Although altruistic actions are good in their own right, the special value of a courageous action when it is altruistic— as good acts so often and almost characteristically are—lies in the moral reasoning that went into the act of sacrifice and the practical reasoning in the carrying out of the act.

9.3 Ethics of Ideals and Aspirations

Heyd (1982:167 f.) is very concerned to argue for what he calls un-qualified supererogationism, the view that supererogatory action is altogether optional. He wants to argue that even though a supererog-atory act is good, it is permissible for the agent to forbear doing it. The moral position of his critics is that 'good' entails 'ought' in a prescriptive and personal sense. That is, the antisupererogationist argues that all good acts are matters of duty and their performance is mandatory, not optional. Therefore Heyd rejects what he calls the "good-ought tie-up" (ibid., p. 171).

According to Heyd, 'good' may be used impersonally, whereas 'ought' involves human agency. Moral reasons for prescribing an 'ought', he argues, arise from a special relationship between the agent and the beneficiary of the action, for example, family relationships or jobs. However, according to Dent (1983:66), Heyd's argument is weak here because he leaves unclear why such special relationships should make the difference between 'good' and 'ought'.

This is very difficult and controversial territory in current ethical theory, but surely it must be said that Heyd is right to argue an act can be good yet morally optional. It is very unclear just where, in general, the border between public duty and personal conscience is to be drawn. But surely many acts are thought discretionary even if they must be acknowledged as achieving great good.

There may be several reasons for the optional nature of supererog-atory acts of courage, but certainly one is an unwillingness to dictate as expected duties courses of action that may have costs most would be unwilling to bear.

Let us go back to the case of Sergeant Ward. Why would it be improper or unreasonable for a superior officer to order one of the crew to have done such an act? Why would we think it morally acceptable for a crew member not to have undertaken this act?

There seem to be several reasons. One is the uncertainty of the outcome. The nature of the problem was not clear at the outset, and it was not clear that somebody getting out on the wing to try to smother the fire would surely solve the problem. Another reason is the extreme danger. Struggling out onto the wing of a burning plane in flight is such a preposterously dangerous kind of act that making it general policy to deal with fires in an engine would hardly be realistic or successful. Clearly Ward was very lucky that he wasn't killed in this attempt. (Sadly, he was killed in action on a later mission.)

Another reason is the difficulty of the act. Although many men might be capable of getting out on the wing and attempting to do something, probably most of us would be so terrified that our attempts to put out the fire would be futile anyway.

Another reason is that even though all of us might recognize some objective as a good end, carrying out some method of achieving that end may be a complex and highly individual matter, requiring ingenuity and finesse. Perhaps Sergeant Ward had a good idea that getting out on the wing was the best way to deal with the fire, and he felt confident that doing it would solve the problem. The actions of another man who was less confident that this course of action was the best solution might bungle it, or act with less effect. Individual initiative is not to be underrated in getting something done.

Another reason is the personal sacrifice involved. Some men might justifiably feel that the risk of their loss of life, and the loss to their families, might be too likely in this instance to justify the possible benefits of such a perilous act. Given the risks involved in this particular act, it seems appropriate that this attitude should be respected.

It seems then that Heyd is right. Not all good actions should be expected as matters of duty—some should properly be regarded as discretionary. Failure to personally carry out an act that has a balance of good consequences is not always culpable.

But why Heyd's position is the right one seems to be more elusive. I think several factors are involved. One is that a person's intentions are fashioned partly by his personal life plan, and this should be a matter of one's individual philosophy or aspirations to goodness. Our ideas differ, and it is proper that it should be so in a morally pluralistic society and in a democracy.

Another factor is that one's conceptions of how to carry out an action in particular circumstances vary from person to person, especially in an emergency. Where life is at risk, naturally one hesitates to impose one's view of the situation on somebody else, if only for fear of responsibility for the consequences should disaster occur.

Another is the problem of side effects.[7] While good intentions may be clear, the costs of carrying out those general intentions in particular circumstances may be less clear. At some point, the costs and efforts required may make an action optional. Even if we all agreed on what, in general, is "good," no doubt we could still disagree on how to translate these intentions into operational plans. Indeed, presumably much of our moral disagreements precisely concern the best way to carry out objectives we generally agree on. All may want peace. But while some think disarmament is the best way to achieve that goal, others think that a balance of power, which may mean armament, is the best way to achieve it. Thus our disagreements about means, as opposed to ends purely considered, are by no means morally trivial.

Where I would criticize Heyd's position, or suggest a way to improve it, is in his statement (1982:172) that moral reasons for action arise "not from desirability of states of affairs, but from a certain *relationship* between the agent and the beneficiary of the action." The relationship is not between the agent and beneficiary, but between the agent's plan of action and the state of affairs he thinks desirable, better described as his intention in acting. For even if we agree on what, in general, is to be considered good, there may remain plenty of room for individual conceptions of how to implement good ideals.

Nevertheless, I would still want to agree with Heyd's argument that room should be given for personal autonomy in formulating intentions as well as in questions of how hard those intentions are worth struggling to achieve. This means that in many cases the individual has the right to pursue his own ideals even at the cost of his noninvolvement in the fulfillment of other people's needs. It is precisely because we can legitimately differ on the priority placed on values and on how to implement those values that the individual life plans of persons can count in our evaluation of acts as commendable or good. Hence a courageous supererogatory act of heroism can be commendable and good even if its commission is discretionary rather than a matter of strict duty.

What is needed is a recognition of the place of personal values and aspirations—over and above rights and duties—in ethical theory. Just as the best discipline is self-discipline, it is a good thing that some morally commendable acts are not universalizable and are imposed autonomously from within, from the inner voice of a person's own values.

The notion of treating a person as an end in himself is supported and enhanced by the dignity of individual purposes and life plans. Too much of an insistence on the letter of rights and duties overlooks the special individuality of morally heroic and courageous actions. An act that reflects the inner integrity and special goodness of one person may be inappropriate to make mandatory as an obligation for another. Personal ideals can lay a special value on certain prized goals, even while tempering the actions to carry out these goals against the requirements of duty and a sense of what is fitting in the circumstances.

It is the personal nature of the ethics of some conduct that makes the ad hominem such a telling refutation in dialogue. It is a self-rebuttal of a person's plans and ideals if that person expounds and stresses certain personal goals on some occasions while acting to contravene or undermine those goals on other occasions. We may well suspect that such a person is not consistent. It is as if such a person has no integrity, no serious commitment to personal ideals. This is a severe form of moral condemnation.

Thus Kant is wrong, or at least omitting something, in defining autonomy as conformity to the law of duty.[8] Contrary to Kantian ethics, the best analysis of acts of courage requires that there should be morally commendable and good actions that are not universally obligatory for all moral agents. We need room in ethics for personal aspirations and ideals, within a framework of good intentions carried out by practical reasoning and deliberation. Ethics should make room for excellence of conduct.

9.4 Difficulty, Danger, and Commitment

On our account, a courageous act is morally commendable for two basic reasons: (1) a courageous act is always directed toward a good end, and (2) a courageous act overcomes great difficulty or danger. Let us discuss each of these separate aspects of courage.

On our account, an act of courage is justified primarily by its intentions. This means that any ethical theory compatible with our account of courage will have to stress the importance of intentions in the moral evaluation of actions. The theory of practical reasoning outlined above (chap. 8) defines an intention as something created, stipulated, or set down by an agent when he plans a deliberate course of actions. It is up to the agent what sort of intentions he or she chooses to adopt, and therefore one is morally responsible for one's intentions. Intentions can be good or bad.

The notion of good intention in an act of courage is perhaps easy to appreciate as a source of the commendability of the act. But let us turn to our second reason. To rephrase a question asked previously: If two acts A and B are equally good in all other respects, why should bringing about one of them be more commendable because it is more difficult or dangerous? This is a perplexing question because there seems to be no obvious resource in traditional or recent ethical theories to turn to in attempting to answer it.[9] By utilitarianism, the Kantian approach, or other current theories, it would seem that there could be no moral difference between A and B. The utility of an act would seem to be decreased by the danger or difficulty of carrying it out. And if an act is one's duty, it would seem to remain one's duty even if it is dangerous or difficult to carry out—unless perhaps one has a duty to be careful, but that would not make the act more commendable. If anything, it would make it less obligatory. How then could the more difficult or dangerous act be thought better or more meritorious?

The answer I will offer to this question involves something, to my knowledge, virtually overlooked in ethical theory: good intentions are not enough. The answer is that it takes effort, ingenuity, and sometimes even risk and sacrifice to carry out good intentions. The fact is that Nature and other agencies often frustrate a person's good intentions by providing obstacles and contrary forces. Many good things that can be brought about are only obtainable, in their given circumstances, through confronting dangers and grappling with difficulties and problems. The overcoming of such problems is necessary to achieve good and therefore contributes to the bringing about of good. Consequently such an action is itself an instrumental good.

We have already seen the bias of ethical theory against instrumental goods in the doctrines of Moore and Prichard that it is only the end of an action that is good in itself. By these lights, no means to carry out some good end can themselves have any real moral value. The particular circumstances in which the act was carried out in order to achieve a certain end are irrelevant, on such a view, to the moral worth of the act.

But this is a view that is hopelessly at odds with our moral intuitions about courage and cowardice. Let us compare two simple cases. In the first, Mr. Brown, on the way home from work, sees a small child who has fallen into the shallow duck pond in the Auckland Domain. He reaches over, and with very little effort, lifts the child to safety. In the second case, Mr. Black sees a small child in a burning auto crash. A number of onlookers are milling about worriedly but are afraid, or not clear about what should be done. It is clear that the gas tank of the car may explode at any second. Mr. Black leaps from his car and races to the burning vehicle, clawing his way through the wreckage and wresting the child to safety. As a result, he is severely burned and sustains several contusions and cuts.

In both cases the outcome is the same—one saved child. In both cases the intention is the same—to save a child in danger. Yet one act is courageous and the other is not. Both acts are highly commendable, but the second one is highly meritorious and gallant in a way that the other is not conspicuous or outstanding.

In some respects, the one act is no better than the other. Both are equally good in outcome, and both are highly commendable as actions. Yet in the way in which we morally evaluate the courageousness or cowardliness of actions, Black's act is the more courageous. It is more courageous because Black overcame greater dangers from obstacles in carrying out his intention. From this point of view, then, there is a morally significant difference here over and above matters of intentions or consequences.

What is of moral import in evaluating actions over and above the goodness of an intention in itself is the commitment of the agent to carrying out that intention. The depth of that commitment is indicated by the time, effort, ingenuity, and sacrifice the agent is willing to put into the carrying out of his good intention. Hence factors like altruism, determination, and persistence in the face of painful consequences are all characteristics (overtonal meanings) of truly courageous acts. The greater the sacrifice, risk, and danger of carrying out a good objective, the more meritorious is the course of action directed to that end.

Courage, then, is more than a matter of having the best intentions. It is a matter of the agent's depth of commitment to carrying out these intentions, as expressed by his actions.

Courageous acts take place at the nexus between the natural flow of events and the human will to express normatively formulated commitments through action. Action is the junction point between the mind of the agent and the forces of external circumstances. To see the value of courage, the force of circumstances must be taken into account.

Any action is swept up in the tide of natural circumstances and events, and thereby enhanced or diminished. Consequently, in retrospect it is difficult, if not impossible, to evaluate the action apart from the subsequent flow of events that carried it along. When Mitchell designed the Spitfire before the Second World War, who could have foreseen the ultimate impact of his creation on the fate of his country in its time of peril? Yet the greatness of his achievement stems in no small measure from the tide of events that locked the world in a desperate struggle after Mitchell himself had died.

Our evaluation of an act of courage has to do with the agent's plan of action and how he justifiably sees and judges the particular situations and events that are likely to flow from it. In retrospect, therefore, our evaluation of the courage of an action will not be entirely independent of factors outside the control of the agent. Our evaluation is in fact highly conditioned by our perception of the situation at the time, the problem that faced the agent. The more difficult the problem, the greater the merit of the act of solving it. The tougher the circumstances, the more we can be justified in claiming that the act of contending with them was courageous.

This perception is morally correct and right because good intentions by themselves should never be thought morally sufficient for the goodness of actions. Depth of commitment to those intentions expressed in the manner of their being instrumentalized is a matter of ethics as well.

9.5 Courage and Inspiration

Any worthwhile and civilized society should be proud of its acts of heroic valor, should carefully record them, and should rank them with artistic and scientific achievements as ideals of human excellence. Moral excellence should be a source of inspiration because the ability to persist under the worst conditions in purposive action, directed toward one's commitment to the good, is a tribute to the human species. Acts of courage show moral excellence not exclusively in some lofty or high-flown purposes but in the most modest attempts to carry on in a helpful and well-intentioned way even under the absurd buffetings and hard circumstances that characterize emergencies and crises.

Technical Sergeant Forrest L. Vosler of the U.S. Army Air Corps was serving as a radio operator on a bombing mission over Bremen, Germany, in December 1943. A cannon shell from an enemy fighter exploded in the radio compartment, painfully wounding Vosler in the legs and thighs. A direct hit under sustained attacks by fighters badly wounded the tail gunner as well. Responding to the need to protect the vulnerable tail section, Vosler took over the tail gun. While firing, he was hit by another cannon shell in the chest and face.

Pieces of metal lodged in both eyes, impairing his vision to such an extent that he could only distinguish blurred shapes. Displaying remarkable tenacity and courage, he kept firing his guns and declined to take first-aid treatment. The radio equipment had been rendered inoperative during the battle, and when the pilot announced that he would have to ditch, although unable to see and working entirely by touch, Sergeant Vosler finally got the set operating and sent out distress signals despite several lapses into unconsciousness. When the ship ditched, Sergeant Vosler managed to get out on the wing by himself and hold the wounded tail gunner from slipping off until the other crew members could help them into the dinghy. Sergeant Vosler's actions on this occasion were an inspiration to all serving with him. The extraordinary courage, coolness, and skill he displayed in the face of great odds, when handicapped by injuries that would have incapacitated the average crewmember, were outstanding. (COVA 1973:710)

For his actions on that day, Sergeant Vosler was awarded the Congressional Medal of Honor.

These actions were truly heroic and courageous not especially because of some special ideological nobility of purpose or lofty sentiments inherent in them. Vosler no doubt was merely trying to do the best he could in the circumstances to carry on with his job and to help the others in his crew. It is the fact that he did so, with calm and skill, under the most disconcerting conditions and appalling disabilities, that is even now inspiring to recall and relate.

It is a tribute to the human spirit that there are such individuals who do act purposefully, coolly, and practically in situations that would be disheartening and incapacitating to an earnest and well-intentioned person. These difficult actions are excellent in themselves. The very fact that they are inspiring is the ultimate basis of justification for their moral merit as acts of excellence.

To say someone has acted courageously, then, is not to claim that he or she is a better person than you or I in every way. Rather, it is to say that on this occasion the person exhibited that special excellence of conduct that is in itself a special mark of moral commitment and practical judgment. It is a worthy mark of achievement, and in some ways, I think, even more admirable than scientific achievement or artistic excellence.

The ethics of duties and obligations are marked by universalizability, the requirement that everyone in such-and-such a situation should fulfill certain norms.[10] But the ethics of ideals is marked by its very lack of universalizability. If one of us were in Sergeant Vosler's situation, it is not to be expected that we would act the same way. If we did not, it is no moral failure, nor is criticism of our conduct appropriate. Nor should a sensible person wish to be placed in Sergeant Vosler's situation, or one like it, in the hope of thereby achieving excellence or merit. Ideals are personal and should be individual, based on one's own life plan and moral reasoning, one's own estimate of what is possible and worthwhile. But without personal ideals, life would be insipid and less satisfying—some would even say meaningless.

Uncritical emulation or worship of what is taken to be heroic can, however, lead to a good deal of mischief. But the fact that we are so greatly influenced by models of conduct we take to represent ideals means that we neglect the study of this branch of moral philosophy at our peril. Propaganda all too often successfully exploits and perverts our perceptions of the heroic ideal of conduct.

Acts of conspicuous gallantry, like that of Sergeant Vosler, should be recorded and decorated as expressions of an ideal conduct, the highest one might aspire to. Our proper attitude should be one of gratitude and respect, remembering the sacrifice of acts of valor and the well-meaning intentions of truly courageous conduct. The act of courage is individual—it is unique to the particular circumstances of the situation and unique to the skills, the intentions, and the ideals of the agent. Its educative function is that we can each be made firmer in our resolve to seek to make a contribution in our own way and to strive to carry out this contribution without being disheartened or distracted by the difficult obstacles and dangers that are an inevitable part of everyone's ordinary life.

If life were a peaceful and unproblematic utopia with no worries, dangers, or calamities, there would be no need for courage. Courage is a concomitant of the nasty, the awful, and the annoying. As such, we don't like to be reminded about that too much, and a sensible person hopes to get through life and be lucky enough not to be courageous. The wish to be courageous is somehow absurd. Indeed, an "intention to act courageously" can be an indication of the wish for fame or applause, an intention that may serve to defeat an act's claim to being truly courageous.

Ideals of conduct are not acts to be mimicked in every detail, but reminders that each of us can strive for excellence in his own appropriate way and that good conduct and action in the service of others is a worthwhile and commendable thing in itself—satisfying to one's sense of individual correctness and the fittingness of conduct to the situation in which one finds oneself.

9.6 *Personal Integrity and Conscience*

Courage as a virtue represents an ideal of conduct that is highly personal in nature. However, personal reasons for acting or refraining from acting are sometimes felt to be moral reasons, even if they are not justified by rules of conduct that apply to all moral agents. A good example is the stance of the physician who refuses to participate in an abortion or blood transfusion, even though such participation could be justified as consistent with medical ethics as it applies to professional conduct for all physicians. This particular doctor could argue that although participation in a particular act may be allowed by hospital policy, and may be acceptable for other physicians, he does not feel that it is right for him. And we may rightly respect his position, even though it is based on his own personal morality rather than on rules that apply to all doctors. This suggests that personal ideals of conduct may be accorded legitimate status as a morally justified basis for acting, even if they are individual and personal. Such personal reasons are often justified using the language of conscience. The doctor may say "I thought it out, and decided that my conscience could not permit me personally to participate in this particular act." And if his stance is justified by a good argument, we may be morally right in respecting his decision as the right course of action *for him.* This suggests that moral justification of an act based on personal ideals of conduct is sometimes justifiably accepted as morally reasonable.

By such reasoning, actions or positions can be justified on the basis of personal integrity rather than universal rules of conduct. A person may reflect, "I couldn't live with myself if I failed to carry out this act (or refrain from carrying it out)." Beauchamp and Childress (1983:270) suggest that many common expressions reflect this moral notion of personal commitment: "I couldn't live with myself if I did that" or "I could not look at myself in the mirror." These expressions suggest the idea that although a certain line of conduct might be morally permissible in principle, it may not be found consistent with one's personal moral commitments.

We could define "personal integrity" as the consistency that obtains when a person acts in accord with his personal commitments, his own moral position as defined by his practical reasoning in a particular situation. The negation of personal integrity, as we have seen, is personal inconsistency that can amount to a kind of hypocrisy where the agent's actions clash with his position. In this type of case, as we have seen, our reconstruction of the agent's position can be shown to exhibit an ad hominem inconsistency.

We have seen that a referee's evaluation of an agent's past conduct is characteristically the basis of judgments of personal morality. Here again there is a common language of such judgments in terms of "conscience." We may say that a person has a "bad conscience" or feels "morally troubled" about his past actions. This feeling of dissonance could have its moral basis in the notion that there is a personal inconsistency in the agent's position as defined by his actions and commitments. A fundamental idea here is called by Beauchamp and Childress (ibid., p. 272) a "conflict of conscience." When a person examines his moral convictions, he may reconsider his commitments in relation to a present situation requiring a personal decision. Conflicting moral demands may make for a moral problem that can only be resolved by a process of dialogue and consequent adjustment of one's position. If such a process of argument can be reasonably conducted and evaluated—as I have argued—then the personal morality of integrity can be defended as a reasonable form of moral judgment, even if it is personal and therefore, in a sense, "subjective."

Of course, appeals to conscience, like appeals to personal models of heroism, are open to abuse and inadequate or bad justification. But does the concept of justification bear enough rational weight to support the morality of virtue as a truly "morally justified" form of evaluation? Once again, I think that the best defense of virtue ethics must come back to the model of practical reasoning we have defended through this book.

CHAPTER 10

Courage as a
Quality of Character

COURAGE IS COMMONLY thought to be an attribute of character, a property of persons rather than their specific acts. Take the examples of moral courage we studied where a politician persists with unflagging integrity in a lonely course of action to fight for a moral ideal of conduct against tremendous group pressures and popular persuasions. The courage of such conduct seems to stem from a rock-solid integrity of character that can firmly but reasonably withstand external pressures to give in.[1] Probably, then, most of us who have not had the occasion to think of courage very deeply as a philosophical notion are inclined to think of it as a property of character in general rather than as a property of an individual action.

The argument of this book so far has been directly against that common conception of courage. Remember the fictional case of Ordinary Seaman Triggs (1.1). He was not a particularly moral or deeply thoughtful person. His general character was, on the contrary, not consistent with the reasoned formulation of moral principles, or with integrity of character or habit. He was a person who had to be constantly supported by his crewmates because he was unstable, given to drunken sprees and disorderly, thoughtless conduct on the least provocation. His character was quite the opposite of what one would consider the thoughtful integrity of the morally courageous person. Yet his marvellous act of courage—opening the red-hot door and saving many men while burning his hands to the bone—should undoubtedly be conceived of as a courageous action. Its very unexpectedness somehow even adds to the grace of the act as deeply courageous. Here was an act that transcended the usual and expected, and its courage, perhaps for that reason, stands out as remarkable and extraordinary.

Here, then, is a noteworthy basic conflict: Is courage best thought of as a property of individual actions or of long-term qualities of character? It is well to be reminded here that a person who acts courageously in one situation may not act courageously in another. A person who is courageous one time may be morally insensitive, perhaps even a liar or a cheat, on another occasion. Hence conjectures about long-term dispositions or qualities of character are hazardous at best. Moreover, the notion of a "moral character" is plagued with many traditional philosophical disputes and problems. If one's character is formed by heredity, or by habit induced by early training and family life, how can one take credit for traits of character that one did not freely choose to adopt? In fact, there are many reasons to doubt that the qualities of a person's character are subject to much individual control in many cases. Perhaps it is only in rare cases that a person freely chooses to adopt certain attributes of character by moral reasoning or thoughtfully decides to follow certain role models or examples of good conduct. So how are we to judge when a quality of character like courage is morally praiseworthy rather than merely the product of reflexive conditioning? It could be agreed that even habitual behavior may justifiably be called "courageous"—meaning morally meritorious and creditable. But it would seem to be so only by virtue of the fact that the habitual behavior could be based on or tied to antecedent moral reasoning or justification somewhere along the line. Acts based purely on habit reflect no moral merit or supererogatory credit to the agent—only to his or her training. At any rate, if this sort of thesis is arguable, grave doubts are cast on the justifiability of judgments based exclusively on claims of having a courageous character. To say that so-and-so is a "courageous person" may be so full of undermining qualifications and pitfalls that it may scarcely, if ever, make sense to put forward such a judgment with reasonable justification.

So far, the argument of this book for a specific analysis of the courageous action has been quite positive. That much seems relatively clear. But what about courage as a personal quality of character? Is it so unclear that it should be rejected entirely as a sort of popular myth? At the present stage of the argument, I have been largely inclined to think so. Yet the notion is so widespread and deeply embedded in moral thinking that it bears further exploration, if possible. Hence this chapter will focus on the exploration of the problems and difficulties inherent in the project of trying to make sense of courage as a quality of character. The result will be to some extent more negative and problematic. So this chapter is best seen as a tentative study of some problems for further research and discussion. For all its tentativeness, some interesting questions are raised and discussed.

10.1 *Courage Based on Integrity: A Case Study*

Courage as a general property of character could be based on something deeper than habit or disposition to respond in a certain way. It could be based on a reasoned moral position or set of principles thoughtfully adopted or held by a person. For example, Socrates has been widely held up as a model of courage not only because he faced death calmly and was a fearless and dutiful soldier in battle. We think him especially courageous because we know that these actions were based on his well-argued and well-defended, deeply held general moral principles of conduct. We also feel he was a courageous man par excellence because he cleaved in his personal conduct to principles that he argued for cogently. He stood against the hard pressures of social and legal censure while defending a stance that might have appeared merely idiosyncratic except that he offered arguments that one can follow and thereby come to recognize the reasonableness of his stand, at least as he saw the issues. It was not merely that he acted fearlessly, or was unafraid of controversy or social pressures. Over and above that, his actions can be understood as principled ones, based on a personal code, that were defended in reasonable dialogue. We can perceive his actions as based on a nondogmatic, defensible position.

Of course, the cases of moral courage we have studied are based on well-articulated moral positions. In other cases, a long-term commitment to a courageous stand may be based on an underlying integrity based on tough, moral responses to a bad situation. Cases of this sort sometimes occur where a person may face both moral pressure and physical danger in taking a long-term stand against corruption. Repeated courageous reactions to strong pressure do quite plausibly offer evidence of a long-term moral stand expressed in actions.

Frank Serpico came from an immigrant family where thrift and hard work were proudly held values. He grew up in New York to idolize the police in his neighborhood as models of all that is noble and heroic in selfless service.[2] As a highly motivated young police officer, time and time again he came into contact with situations in which it was clear that policemen were continually getting free meals, "fringe benefits," and all kinds of smaller or larger unethical payoffs and bribes in the course of their duties. Serpico always managed to avoid accepting these payments, cleaving to an ideal of conduct he found to be more and more unusual in his line of work. Gradually, Serpico came to see that there was a widespread inconsistency of practice between the regulations set by the police department and the real practices of the police officers. Practices like taking free food, goods, or meals from local merchants were widely accepted by policemen as a matter of course.

As Serpico was transferred to different precincts, he became aware of these bribes and corrupt practices but always managed to personally avoid them, saying that he did not want to "get involved." The other police officers accepted this stance, but were often very suspicious of it. In this job, Serpico found, it is a matter of life and death to depend on your brother police officers. Therefore, anyone who was perceived as being dangerously different or unusual could be at high risk. Serpico found himself gradually drawn into a situation where he was forced to make a choice.

Finally, he was transferred to a precinct where payoffs from professional gamblers were virtually universal among the policemen. Even officers who did not like the idea were forced to go along with it, for the others were not about to give up this lucrative source of regular income. Their standard of living from these bribes was very high, and nobody seemed to question the practice of accepting this money.

Serpico was caught in a dilemma. Should he follow his personal moral beliefs, or the relentless organizational pressures to conform? Serpico finally made the decision to report the corruption. He went to a senior officer he felt was sympathetic and trustworthy, through whom he hoped to contact the assistant chief, a man who was perceived as being outspokenly against police corruption. However, these attempts ultimately amounted to nothing. After many attempts, over several years, to report the practices of corruption to high officials of the police department and the city, Serpico got no results. By this time, his fellow officers ridiculed and ostracized him, and often threatened reprisals as their suspicions of him grew.

Serpico came to realize that such widespread police corruption could not exist unless it was tolerated at the higher levels of the police department. Finally, in desperation, he persuaded a senior officer to go with him and tell the whole story to the *New York Times*. After the mayor's office had taken a public stand against corruption, the story was allowed to be released. A wave of publicity followed, and in subsequent trials, Serpico was several times asked to testify against fellow officers who were charged and convicted.

On February 3, 1971, Serpico was shot in the head and severely wounded during a drug raid. He always wondered whether he had been set up. A year later, the police department awarded him the Medal of Honor for this incident. Serpico felt it was absurd that he should be given an award for that reason and not for his courage in reporting corruption.[3] In spring 1972, he left the force with a disability pension.

This man's lonely odyssey is a revealing story of high moral courage. Not once, but many times over a period of years, he defied terrible risks and crushing pressures to persist in his attempts to set things right. According to his own statement, "a policeman's first obligation is to be responsible to the needs of the community he serves."[4] He felt that this relationship is destroyed if the patrolman loses the respect of the public through corrupt practices. One of the things that Serpico especially despised was the feeling of degradation when he observed a police officer getting a small bribe, like a "tip," from a known criminal.

It is every police officer's duty to speak out against corruption. Therefore one might say that Serpico only did his duty. But where there is widespread and deeply rooted corruption as the accepted practice, it may be terribly difficult and dangerous for one person in a group or profession to come forth and speak out against the practice.[5] Where doing a duty is so difficult and hazardous, its performance can come to involve great personal sacrifice that makes it seem to transcend duty. Whether Serpico's actions were beyond duty or not, they bear the mark of moral courage and physical courage combined. His history of efforts to act against corruption were not only done in the face of grave danger to himself, but against constant and tremendous pressures to conform.

What kind of character could lie behind a history of acts of this sort which stands out as so unusual and uncompromising? It seems the biography of a man who clearly thought out his own position on an issue on many occasions rather than be influenced or coerced by what was expected as the conventional standard or norm. However, it was my impression, from his various personal remarks, that Serpico is a man who holds high personal standards of morality but who is not fanatical or dogmatic about them. He seems from the biography to be a forgiving and caring sort of man, not inflexible yet insistent in some circumstances on certain firm principles and standards of behavior. My impression is that this sort of moral courage stems from a deep and thoughtful integrity of character—a judicious moral position that is arguable, but refuses to compromise or bend before clear transgressions of honest conduct.

Whitman Knapp, the chairman of the committee that heard Serpico's testimony, spoke of Serpico's "almost fanatical sense of truth."[6] Some of Serpico's supporters have said that "his integrity was too fiercely uncompromising to allow him much peace of mind."[7] Serpico himself felt that he had only done his duty, and that things have not changed much, that the police mentality is still much the same today: "It's OK to be corrupt; just don't get caught."[8] Others have said that the New York Police Department is much better as a result of the revelations that came out of Serpico's testimony.

We have before us a case where it is not just one single act of courage that is at issue, but a lengthy history of courageous acts that seem to stem from a basic integrity of character. Caught in a dilemma where his integrity and his view of his duty as a police officer were flatly contradicted by the practices he saw around him and the pressures to become corrupt, he was finally driven to a decision to blow the whistle. He persisted in acting toward this end, even when such a course of action became increasingly difficult and dangerous.

Here it is strongly tempting to conclude that not only were the actions courageous, according to the biographical statement of Maas (1973), but the person himself was courageous. For the courageous acts stemmed from an underlying integrity of character expressed in many connected actions over a prolonged period.

In talking of the various overtones of courage—altruism, determination, moral courage, and so forth—surely there is a similar presumption that courage can be an underlying character trait as expressed in actions. To some extent, at any rate, we are committed to the notion of courage as a trait of character. How can we understand this idea as a meaningful ethical judgment?

10.2 Dispositions

In explaining acts of courage, one approach is to say that the courageous person has a certain kind of disposition that inclines toward action in a courageous manner. To say that a person has a disposition to carry out a type of act is to say that he is likely to carry out that type of act in the right circumstances.[9] Disposition is a matter of habit or probably expectation to act in a certain manner. One who takes this approach of dispositions will then propose that where there is a courageous action, there must have been an underlying disposition on the part of some person to act in a courageous manner.

The problem with this sort of explanation of courageous acts is that it fails to tell us why an act of courage is of moral value or has merit as an act of moral excellence. We may be responsible for our habits or we may not—it is hard to tell in many cases. But if we are not, it is not clear that we should receive moral credit for a worthwhile act that was produced exclusively as a function of a habit or habitual disposition.

Moreover, I think that saying an act of courage is a result of a courageous disposition is an easy way out of accepting moral responsibility for conduct. One can always say, "True, this person stepped forward to help a policeman, and risked his life to do it. I could have stepped forward, but didn't. But then, he had a 'courageous disposition' and it so happens that I don't." The approach of dispositions makes this sort of excuse too readily available to cover every case without further questions.

In Cambridge, Nova Scotia, in December 1979, M. Brian Toney learned that there was a person inside a blazing house. Entering, he saw a man lying on the floor and began dragging him to safety, but the smoke forced him to leave. Against the pleas of others at the scene, Toney plunged in again, but was again forced out by the smoke before he could drag the victim out (Honors Secretariat 1983). Toney attempted to enter a third time, but was restrained by onlookers. When he got free, he rushed in again, but this time was forced out by the heat, and so he ultimately failed to rescue the person inside, who died in the fire.[10]

How do you explain an action like this? One person courageously put his life on the line to try to save another, while others present do not act the same way, and even tried to restrain him. It is too easy to say that some people have a "courageous disposition" and are therefore habituated to act where others fear to. This explanation, it seems to me, does not give sufficient credit to Toney's moral commitment. Surely, it is better to presume that the most appropriate explanation for Toney's gallant action was his goal of wanting to help the person in the burning house.

But how do we explain the act of someone who pursues this goal even at great risk to himself? It should surely be by presuming that such a person has a moral commitment to the objective of helping someone else in trouble. This person must have based his action on a position of caring and consideration for others—a position of altruistic caring held strongly enough even to express itself in action at great personal risk. Having a moral position or stand, a kind of commitment, is best thought of as a policy freely adopted by a person. But there are many real cases where habit or disposition may also have had a role in the action. In such cases, we can make a leap to conclude that it was "as if" the person had freely adopted this set of values. We can at least give such persons the benefit of the doubt, provided they sincerely acted at risk for an objective that they rightly considered to be good and valuable. Hence, in the end, moral commitment is normally a preferable explanation of acts of courage, over any attempt to explain such acts through dispositions.

Even if the agent has not articulated a moral position as the ethical matrix of his or her action undertaken in the face of danger or difficulty, it can be justified as courageous if, in retrospect, we and the agent can agree that the goal was morally good. This kind of retrospective or hypothetical plausible reasoning can be applied where the courageous person is more likely to have acted from habit, reflex, or teaching rather than as a result of his own independent moral reasoning.

The case of courageous acts by children is a good example where moral competence may not be assured, but goodness of goals may be presumed and then afterward confirmed by further questioning. On November 19, 1976, a house was set on fire when some young children, alone in the house, tried to light a Coleman lamp. Glenda Meshake, aged thirteen, led two of the children out of the house. Then she returned to the burning house to bring out the other two. When the police arrived, she had all four children wrapped in a sleeping bag at a safe distance from the house, which burned to the ground. She was awarded the Medal of Bravery (Honors Secretariat 1983).

Can a thirteen-year-old make competent and responsible moral decisions based on a reasoned moral position? Each case must be judged on its merits, but if we agree that the goal of saving the children was highly commendable, we rightly presume that this young woman acted courageously to undertake that goal, and knew what she did. Hence, even in the case of children, who may be acting on the basis of moral habits rather than practical reasoning of a more well-articulated sort, we make a presumption of practical reasoning. Dispositions or habits are not necessarily the best explanation.

There is yet another reason that dispositions can be a misleading way of explaining the merit of acts of courage. The "halo effect" of putting heroic personalities on a pedestal has already been remarked on as a source of mischief. Heroes who are larger than life have all too often been projected for purposes of propaganda. The notion may be that certain persons are singled out as heroes because of some "courageous disposition" that makes them exceptional. This may or may not be true in some cases. But it overlooks the fact that many courageous acts are done by people who are perfectly average and unexceptional in every noticeable way, yet care enough to take risks or make an exceptional effort because of moral convictions and a wish to help even at the cost of personal sacrifice.

Of course we have already seen in the case of Lord Sackville[11] that evaluating acts of courage or cowardice can involve much highly complex practical reasoning. It comes down to trying to determine the moral position that the individual was acting on. To sort this out we need to go into many details of the entire sequence of actions and consequences.

In many cases, it is not easy to make uncontestable presumptions. To simply assert that the individual whose conduct is at issue acted out of some reflexive "courageous disposition" or "cowardly disposition" begs the question. We need to know the position that the individual took as expressed by the sequence of actions. In arriving at such judgments, it seems that questions of character may often be involved.

Norman Bethune was a Canadian surgeon who left a comfortable practice in Montreal to volunteer his medical services on the battle-fields of the Spanish Civil War. Some years later, he went to China and directed the medical services for the army of Mao Tse Tung during the revolution. He was remarkably dedicated as a battlefield surgeon and saved many lives.[12] He eventually died of infection incurred while operating in the field. He is now revered as a hero of the People's Republic of China. For many years he was not known in Canada, no doubt because of his outspoken Communist political sympathies.

A provocative kind of moral inquiry can be raised about the lifetime conduct of Bethune. One can see his career as an expression of a deep love for humanity and a quest to help people in need through concrete action, at great personal sacrifice, in a way that unselfishly tran-scended boundaries of race, culture, and nationality. So perceived, he is a hero.[13] In contrast, those who have had reservations about the moral disinterestedness of Bethune's character and career have no doubt perceived his position as being ideologically motivated. Anti-Communists see Bethune's activities in the Spanish Civil War, and later in China, as being an expression of Bethune's passionate advocacy of communism and a political philosophy. This ideological coloration puts an entirely different perspective on Bethune's moral stature as a courageous hero. Hence a deep ambivalence runs through historical appreciations of his career. He has always been idolized as a national hero in China, yet strangely neglected in Canada until recent years, and even now in Canada he remains a controversial figure.

He is often held up by Communists as an ideological hero. By those suspicious of ideological motivations and political affiliations—especially Communist ones—Bethune could no doubt appear to be a misguided fanatic. This kind of ambivalence of interpretation is to some extent a function of the endless disputability of political affiliations and arguments, but it contains the kernel of a genuine philosophical problem.

If we perceive Bethune's conduct as the expression of a thoughtless or reflex commitment to a political dogma that we think irrational or indefensible, it follows that our perception of his character and career is not accorded the merit of "courageous." However, if we feel that Bethune's moral position was truly a well-thought-out and reasonable one, based on his own sincerely held and justified moral principles (even if they might have been open to question), surely his character comes into bold relief as outstandingly and extraordinarily courageous. It depends on whether Bethune's personal moral position stands up to reason and was articulated and reasonably defended by the man himself, or by historians who undertake to defend him. Hence the dispute about the heroic stature of Bethune the man, political disagreements aside, turns not just on what he did but on the nature of the moral position from which his actions stemmed.

It is no good simply saying that he had a disposition to be an unpatriotic Communist, or that he had a disposition to be a caring person and man of humanity. We have to look at his own account of his reasons for what he did and evaluate them on their merits. What was he committed to? What was his position? Even if we do not agree with his position in every way, we could still respect him as a man who acted consistently with a position that he could defend as morally tenable.

I conclude that thinking of courage as a trait of character in terms of dispositions does nothing to solve the problems of courage and cowardice posed in previous cases. However, I feel constrained to concede that talking of courage as a trait of character is sometimes necessary if we are to understand and justify certain actions as courageous or cowardly. So we cannot dispense with traits of character altogether, despite the serious problems involved in making sense of them in moral discussions of courage and cowardice.

We must also revert to another knotty problem that turns out to be connected to the concept of character. The reader will remember that we were very perplexed by actions such as famous feats of mountaineering and the Terry Fox marathon run.[14] The reason these actions tend to be perplexing is that they are ubiquitously said to be highly courageous, yet one is hard pressed to articulate what their morally worthwhile goal is in precise terms. Fox's marathon was to raise funds for cancer research. And it was certainly a difficult undertaking. But one feels that there is more to it than that. Why was this act felt to be such a conspicuously courageous one? There might be many reasons, but surely it had something to do with a heroic odyssey—undertaking a difficult quest for his own private needs to build or test his own character.

This type of quest is typified by feats of mountaineering. Such individuals freely set out to undertake dangerous and difficult feats at their own risk, and evidently for their own private reasons. Are these feats truly courageous by my definition of courage? So far, it would seem not. Or if so, it would seem hard to say why. Advocates of rock climbing are likely to reply that this activity builds character. That could be justification of the courageousness of many risky acts. It bears further investigation.

10.3 Mountain Climbing and Self-Knowledge

Mountain climbing would seem to be an activity that requires courage. It would also seem that many particular acts of courage take place in the ascent of a dangerous slope. Let us take the example of the final ascent of Everest by Tenzing and Hillary in 1953.

When these two finally came to the sweep of snow that led to the summit, Hillary decided to go straight up the snow and ice instead of trying to climb the unstable ridge of rock used in the attempt of his predecessors. However, this snow slope was steep, powdery, and unstable. A slip might mean an unrecoverable fall or starting an avalanche. Hillary later commented, "My solar plexis was tight with fear," and Tenzing later recalled that it was one of the most dangerous places he had ever been on a mountain.[15] However, they decided to go up the snowy slope and were successful in climbing to the summit of Everest by that route.

Here, it seems, we have the classic instance of a courageous act—a dangerous and difficult obstacle successfully overcome by the climbers' sound judgment and skilled actions. But we must remember that by our definition another element is needed. Their goal was to achieve the summit, but can we say categorically that this goal is good, or that it was justifiably considered to be good by these two men? It certainly led to fame and attention but presumably that was not their motive, nor is it a particularly honorable goal in itself. Hence we need to ask: What sort of goal did these men have in mind?

After reading Hillary's biography, *Nothing Venture, Nothing Win*,[16] I still did not feel that I understood precisely what his goal was in climbing dangerous mountains as an avocation. One gets the impression that he was an extremely energetic person who found this sort of activity satisfying and gradually became more involved in it once he had, more or less by accident, become introduced to it. But I do not find a place in the book where he formulates some general goal as the rationale for the activity. Perhaps it is absurd to expect mountain climbers to formulate such a goal. Or perhaps it cannot be done. Possibly the activity is an end in itself, and satisfying as such, without any "ulterior motive." But the problem remains that unless the goal of the action can be justified as good, the action to undertake it is not truly courageous—at least by my definition. And if we do not know what the goal of an action is, we can hardly justify the action as courageous on the grounds that it has a worthwhile goal.

Of course the obvious suggestion, one often made by climbers, is that achieving the ascent of the summit of the mountain is the goal. This goal is no doubt uppermost in the climber's mind as he struggles and strives to move ahead, up the side of the mountain. But we still need to ask: What is the point of standing on a particularly high or inaccessible piece of rock? The answer "Because it's there," suggests either that the task is truly pointless, or that somehow difficult things are worth doing in themselves and need no further justification.

There is a curious phenomenon in mountain climbing that once a peak is climbed, the goal to be achieved shifts to a different way of climbing it. First comes the attempt to climb to the summit by any means. This usually means that the easiest or most convenient route is taken, and any tools may be used. Once that has been done, however, climbers seem to turn their attention to gaining the summit by a more difficult route. Or they may try to do it without certain mechanical aids, like oxygen tanks. The phenomenon is a curious one, and seems to suggest something about the goals of climbing. But it is sometimes also an object of puzzlement. Unsworth (1981:343) comments:

> Non-climbers frequently cannot understand this [phenomenon]. To them the summit is the obvious goal—and in one way it is, which is why it is always the first challenge to be overcome. But it isn't the real goal; the real goal is the outcome of the struggle between Man and mountain, with the latter always presenting fresh challenges and the former wondering whether he dare accept them. It is an endless, fascinating, titanic struggle.

Somewhat paradoxically, Unsworth (1981) adds that the conquest of Mount Everest in 1953 was not the end but rather the end of a beginning. What does this tell us about the goals of mountain climbing?

One thing it might suggest is that it is the difficulty of the task and the fact that it has not been done that are the benchmarks of achievement in climbing. If so, then à propos our definition of the courageous act, the good of the goal seems to be swallowed up by the difficulty of the action required to achieve it. Being on the summit, by this interpretation, is of little or no significance in itself. The worthwhileness of the undertaking is calculable entirely by the difficulty and danger of the actions required to get there. But is this all one can say about the goals of mountain climbing? If so, the avocation seems a curiously empty, almost Zen-like activity. It seems hard to say how such an activity could be called courageous, by our definition. One might even be tempted to try to argue that mountain climbing borders on the foolish or sensational as a rationally grounded or goal-oriented form of activity.

However, it could be that a clue is to be found in Unsworth's suggestion that climbing is a form of challenge or struggle. Indeed, this very theme seems to be suggested by Hillary's own reflections. Once, when visiting Alaska, Hillary had no time for climbing but flew with a bush pilot in a small plane up the side of Mount McKinley. Observing the large glaciers and ridges from the air, Hillary (1975:256) was led to make the following remark: "I felt the old urge, half excitement, half fear, to pitch my tent on the snow and join battle with the great peak." The metaphor of battle against an opponent is suggestive. Could it be the struggle itself, against mighty forces, that motivates the climb? Is his goal to be sought in the element of competition or struggle as worthwhile pursuit in itself, so often cited as the rationale of competitive sports? But struggle is not worthwhile in itself, unless there is some benefit in it, even if that benefit is hard to articulate. Moreover, mountain climbing is much more dangerous than typical competitive sports. What could be the benefit of a freely chosen struggle against harsh and dangerous conditions which could justify it as a morally commendable activity?

I have heard one famous climber, who is married and has a large family, remark that climbing is a selfish activity. His wife was clearly not overjoyed by his having this risky avocation, but said nothing to stop him. His remark made me curious about his purposes in climbing mountains when, as a successful lawyer and family man who had lost close friends in previous climbs, he stood to lose a lot by keeping up his climbing activities. Could his remark mean that the benefits of climbing were primarily for himself, somehow related to his own internal needs or personal aspirations? We have already remarked that feats of endurance like climbing—or the Terry Fox marathon— seem to somehow represent a struggle of the person against himself. But this idea is difficult to grasp.

Somehow, by struggling against a monumental force or objective, one can, by this idea, achieve a personal victory against oneself. But why is the contest against oneself? The idea seems paradoxical. Could it be a metaphor for the idea that by testing one's ability against difficult tasks, a person can better begin to understand the extent of his own abilities and limitations? And is this not a kind of self-knowledge worth attaining, and perhaps obtainable in no other way except through such arduous experiences? If that is the suggestion, it is not paradoxical, but makes a good deal of sense.

The questions we should be asking are not what motivates a particular climber or what generally tend to be the goals of climbers as a cultural subgroup. These questions are relevant if we are attempting to evaluate a particular act of climbing as courageous or the cultural attitudes or beliefs of climbers as a group. But we want to know what the goal of a climber should be in order to qualify his actions as courageous. In particular, if a climber pursues his risky avocation though commitment to the principle that dangerous challenges on the peaks are character building and provide important self-knowledge that cannot be gained any other way, is that a good enough goal for us to say that his dangerous and difficult activity is courageous?

It is important to reiterate here that we are not trying to settle the empirical question of whether in fact mountain climbing is character building. Given that a good enough case can be made that it might be, we need to ask whether pursuing this goal of developing one's character by means of climbing is noble enough or worthwhile enough to represent a good objective to greatly outweigh the risk and danger involved. I think this question is a hard one, but some comments may help to clarify it.

First, self-knowledge and—especially in youth—the quest of understanding one's abilities and limitations are important goals. And I believe that it is insightful to realize that these goals may be achieved as much through action as by purely reflective contemplation. Moreover, learning self-discipline through attempting difficult and even dangerous tasks is a worthwhile objective, whether it succeeds or not. One reason to support this claim is that trial and error is an important aspect of learning. Another is that self-knowledge is an important goal.

There remains a good deal to say about the extent of risk it is reasonable to undertake in order to promote self-knowledge. As in any instance of evaluating actions, an action that is very dangerous may be foolish rather than courageous unless its objective is sufficiently worthwhile. But, for the sake of the important goal of self-knowledge, some risk may be justifiable, without the act necessarily being selfish or foolish. Needless to add, particular cases invite an evaluation of their particular circumstances. Generally speaking, I believe that in some instances a case could be made that taking risk to achieve a summit could not only be justified as reasonable but could also be accorded special merit as an act of courage.

Because of the ineffability of goals in projects of self-improvement in particular cases, mountain climbing still remains an elusive form of activity for the nonclimber to appreciate or morally evaluate. It seems the best an empathetic nonclimber can say is that the goal of self-knowledge may be important for some individuals, especially those who are in some moral perplexity about their goals and place in the scheme of things. And if they freely choose to take spectacular risks in the inner quest to seek out self-understanding, and nobody else is coerced into the risk as well, or suffers unduly from it, then there may be nobility and even courage in their actions.

In the end, the question of the courageousness of mountain climbing remains as elusive as it started out to be. No doubt this elusiveness is largely due to the private and internal nature of the goals of the individual climber in setting out to conquer a mountain.

MacIntyre (1981:176) makes a useful distinction between goods internal to a practice versus goods external to the practice. A "practice" is a coherent and complex form of social activity through which internal or external goods may be realized. Chess is one example of a practice given by MacIntyre. Money or prestige might be an external good of the playing of chess. But there are goods internal to the playing of chess which can only be achieved by playing chess, for example, learning analytical skills. MacIntyre adds: "[internal goods] can only be identified and recognized by the experience of participating in the practice in question" (ibid.). He also notes that those who lack the relevant experience cannot judge internal goods.

Since mountain climbing as an organized sport would seem to be a practice in MacIntyre's sense, it may not be too surprising that the good inherent in it as a practice is elusive to nonclimbers. Hence we should not be too quick to fallaciously conclude that, as a practice, it cannot have internal goods for those who participate in it.

We have seen that there is good reason to accept the presumption that the internal goals of mountaineering may often be linked to the building of character. Since character building is a worthwhile goal—if an elusive one to clearly define—there is reason to accept the idea in principle that a feat of mountaineering might, in some cases at least, be considered a truly courageous act. This judgment could possibly be made even in a case where the courageous climber did not save anyone's life during the climb or accomplish any external goal of contributing to social good or something of the sort. The act might be courageous for its own internal biographical reasons, as it were.

If my argument here is correct, then we have another justification for the thesis that not all courageous acts need be directly or explicitly altruistic in intent.

But another notable conclusion of our line of argument in this section is that we do need to bring in character-related notions to fully understand some acts of courage that would not otherwise be comprehensible as courageous acts. By these lights, the goal of character building should best be understood as a private quest for self-knowledge through self-discipline, and the need to explore, even in the face of danger and difficulty.

Perhaps further enlightenment on this difficult question can be sought in MacIntyre's notion (1981:203) that the unity of a human life is a narrative quest. A quest is a seeking of self-knowledge through looking for the conception of the good.

10.4 *Character and Commitment*

The old question of whether traits of character are something an individual has any choice in forming will continue to be disputed, as different models of "character analysis" prevail. For example, Freudians believe that character traits are related to unconscious motives too deeply buried in the unconscious wellsprings of motivation to be much affected by rational choices. However, the framework of the criminal law, and much traditional moral thinking, is based on the idea that very often there is a mental element of intention or volition in human action. The presumption is that moral decision making is at least rational or "competent" enough to make punishments and sanctions justifiably enforceable as methods of maintaining social order. I do not hope to influence this sort of disputed question very decisively here, however. One question is whether the term "courageous" as a trait of character can, even perhaps in some cases, refer to a quality subject enough to self-control by an agent in responsible actions that it makes sense to talk of courage as a character-related moral quality. Are there even some cases where we could argue that an act is courageous because of the underlying character of the agent? That is a second question relevant to the topic of courage as a trait of character.

I would like to suggest that even if one's character is not under one's control at the time of some action, still a person could be held responsible for acting in character if that kind of character could be based on some prior commitment to accepting it.

It can be argued that some acts of courage require a certain type of character in order to execute them. Practical reasoning in a dangerous situation may require delicate judgment and calm, unruffled actions. But these requirements cannot be acquired in a moment. They are matters of character, background, and perhaps training. If this line of argument is right, courage is essentially connected to character.

Hence courage can be defined as a property of particular actions rather than as a property of character, but even so defined it will be connected to general traits of character in some instances.

A good example of the requirements of character in a courageous action is the case of a hijacking that took place on Air Canada Flight 812 on November 12, 1971 (McGarry 1977). After the flight took off from Calgary that afternoon, a man wearing a trench coat, a black hooded mask, and a wig appeared in the lounge. He was carrying a sawed-off double-barrel shotgun and a bomb made up of sixty dynamite sticks. The hijacker demanded $1.5 million from the captain, then pointed the shotgun at the stewardess, Mary Dohey, telling them to follow instructions "or she's dead!"[17] He ordered the stewardess to hold apart the fuse wires that would explode the dynamite if contacted to each other. Subsequently, his shotgun accidentally discharged toward the cockpit, showering debris over the area. The hijacker apologized, saying "I'm sorry, I didn't mean to do that." Dohey responded, "I know you didn't dear. Would you like me to hold your hand?" She then asked the hijacker his name, and began to inquire into his interests.[18]

After the hijacker collected some of the money when he forced the plane to land in Great Falls, Montana, Dohey was instrumental in persuading him to release some of the passengers and crew. He said that she could leave as well, but she asked if that was what he really wanted. She stayed on. Once the flight was airborne again, the hijacker attempted to bail out with the money but the captain of the aircraft managed to kick the shotgun away and the hijacker was overpowered by four men.

Mary Dohey was awarded the Cross of Valor for her imperturbable courage, and the captain was awarded the Medal of Bravery.[19]

The actions of this woman in this particular situation are especially remarkable. Somehow she managed to be calm and engage in thoughtful dialogue with another person under circumstances where almost anyone would be terrified and demoralized. She was able to behave naturally, in a kindly and caring personal interchange, during a prolonged period when many lives were at stake and someone was pointing a loaded shotgun at her. With the best will in the world, not many of us could even come close to carrying off a feat like that. Clearly, it required a very special kind of character—an almost reflexive altruism that puts concern for others before oneself.

Commitment could be an element of character because commitment may be a long-term aspect of practical reasoning rather than something expressed only in one single action. If an individual has a moral commitment to helping others, as expressed in an altruistic action, then it may be likely that in other situations where somebody is in need of help, that person who has helped before is likely to help again, depending on the circumstances. This record of altruistic action, even at personal risk, may suggest a moral commitment to carrying out the objective of helping others where circumstances make such actions reasonable.

Commitment is not simply a disposition to act, automatically or habitually, in a certain type of situation. Rather it is a commitment to freely carry out certain goals thoughtfully adopted as morally tenable in general, where such goals can practically and realistically be carried out according to the judgment of the agent in a particular set of circumstances.

10.5 Courage as a Virtue

Having conceded to some extent that courage can be a quality of character, it may be in order to come back to the problematic issue of whether courage can also be viewed as a virtue. The problem here is to determine what should be meant by the term 'virtue'. Perhaps it could be that courage as a virtue has to do with commitment to what one holds to be good.

Courage as a virtue of caring and commitment is brought out clearly by MacIntyre (1981:179). According to him, the person who genuinely cares but cannot risk harm or danger to show it by his actions in effect defines himself as a coward.

> We hold courage to be a virtue because the care and concern for individuals, communities and causes which is so crucial to so much in practices requires the existence of such a virtue. . . . Courage, the capacity to risk harm or danger to oneself, has its role in human life because of this connection with care and concern.

Just as care and concern about certain things are expressed by actions, the depth of those commitments can be brought into question by a failure to act in the face of risk or difficulty.

However, I do not see courage as a "capacity" to risk harm or danger. For a failure to act courageously need not imply that one lacks a certain capacity, ability, or disposition. If courage is a virtue, it is both a way of bringing about a certain end by practical wisdom and the commitment to that end as expressed in the act of bringing it about.

That something be a virtue implies that it be good. Hence we are brought back to the question raised above (chap. 9): If courage is a means of bringing something good about, how can the means itself be a good or a virtue?

How can instrumental goods be justified as good? If A and B are equally good outcomes, why is bringing about B more of a creditable accomplishment where B was more difficult to bring about than A? Why is it a greater achievement, for example, to have solved the more difficult problem? Why can it be the greater valor to keep fighting in the more difficult situation?

The immediate answer may seem to lie in maximization of total good. Perhaps solving the most difficult problem could lead to the greatest payoff. Or winning the hardest battle might avert the greatest disaster with the least resources. But such factors can, at best, be part of the story. For even if the payoffs are equally great, and the risks averted equally disastrous, still, the more difficult struggle is the most meritorious act to have accomplished. Moreover, even when the attempt ends in failure and disaster, the merit in the act could still be supremely good.

A better answer lies in the depth of commitment of the courageous person to persist in the face of danger and difficulty to carry out an end held to be good by a deep moral conviction. The one comes forward to help in the face of personal risk (where others stand back) because of a more deeply held commitment to helping, and thereby demonstrates that deeper commitment through action. Actions can speak louder than words[20] when acts are an expression of depth of commitment to values.

We have found that courage is connected to character. Hence, even if courage as a quality of character is secondary to its role as a property of actions, we should still raise the question of whether courage can be a virtue. This question, as mentioned before, depends on what sense can generally be made from the traditional concepts of virtues and vices. But let us start from the definition of virtue given by MacIntyre (1981:178): "A virtue is an acquired human quality the possession and exercise of which tends to enable us to achieve those goods which are internal to practices and the lack of which effectively prevents us from achieving any such goods." By my definition of courage, it seems best to conclude that there is no virtue of courage in MacIntyre's sense. For courage is not an acquired quality that enables one to achieve goods. Rather, an act of courage is the achieving of any goods, or the attempting to achieve them, in a certain manner. The manner is that of practical reasoning in a difficult or dangerous situation. Hence there is no quality called "courage" which we need to enable us to achieve the goods in question. Or is there?

We have seen that there are certain qualities of a person that are, generally speaking, enablements to achieve good ends in difficult or dangerous situations. These include moral commitment (the ethical matrix) and practical reasoning (the base of courageous action). They also include the overtones of courage: altruism, determination, and so forth. Could these properties be identified with the quality or virtue of the courageous person? Possibly a case could be made for such an identification.

I remain somewhat skeptical about the extent to which we put too much evidential weight on claims like "Smith is a courageous person," apart from particular actions of Smith that can be seen to be courageous. I remain inclined to think that the evaluation of the action should be evidentially prior to the evaluation of the agent. Judgments of character should be derived from specific intentions and acts of the agent in particular circumstances. If Smith has ever done anything courageous, then it may be fair enough to say that Smith is a courageous person, on balance, even if Smith may have acted in a less than courageous manner in other situations. As one goes from the evaluation of particular actions to general judgments of character, there can be more room for error. However, it may be that, in the context of a well-filled-in narrative biography of Smith, broad historical judgments of courage or cowardice as a general property of Smith as a person can be reasonably weighed and adjudicated.

In the context of the biographical information we have, it is possible to claim on the basis of good evidence that Socrates, Stephen Hawking, or Frank Serpico is a courageous person. And each possesses certain qualities that have biographically been made evident, whether it be a commitment to being reasonable and intellectually honest, a solid personal integrity preserved against strong pressures, or a remarkable determination to carry on with difficult work in even more difficult conditions. Clearly, we have here cases of qualities preserved in a record of lifetime actions preserved over a whole biographical stretch of narrative. Hence, I suppose, we can call these men virtuous persons.

However, I would resist the idea that there is some quality of "courage" that enabled these men to attain what they did, apart from the actions they actually carried out. Rather, it should be said that they are courageous persons by virtue of what they did do, by virtue of their actions that have shown their commitment to worthwhile goals in many tough situations. This may seem a subtle distinction, but I think it important to stay away from the idea that there is some elusive property of "courage" that some of us have and some of us do not, and if you do not have it you cannot act courageously. That idea seems to me to be very dangerous.

According to our analysis of practical reasoning, the agent's intentions are part of the framework that enables us to understand actions as courageous or cowardly. If the agent's intentions are involved, then there could be a basis for saying that the agent, as well as his specified action, is courageous. Of course, it is one thing to claim that an agent's intentions, in a specific action, represent a courageous act. It is quite another sort of judgment to say that the agent's character is that of a courageous person.

10.6 *Persons and Virtues*

Sometimes the study of virtues is separated from the other parts of ethics by saying that virtue has to do with the moral qualities of persons, whereas the other parts of ethics have to do with the moral properties of actions. For example, Beauchamp (1982:149) suggests that deontological and utilitarian theories of ethics offer accounts of what we ought to do, whereas virtue ethics is about the kind of persons we ought to be. This way of characterizing virtue ethics has some justification in the case of courage. For our evaluation of whether an act is courageous may relate essentially to the personal aspirations and convictions of the person who performed the act.

However, if courage is studied as a virtue, there may be a danger in thinking of courage as too exclusively a quality of persons rather than of their actions. Indeed, my thesis has generally been that courage is best seen primarily as a property of actions as opposed to persons. If this thesis is justifiable, then the case of courage would seem to suggest that the study of virtues has very much to do with the moral properties of actions.

Clearly, action evaluations and agent evaluations can be conceptually connected, as Stocker (1973) points out. So we should not be too exclusive in making the decision that courage or other virtues are properties of actions or persons. Indeed, Beauchamp (1982:150) cautions that since character is made manifest in action, the distinction between action-based and character-based ethical theories may not be as substantial as might at first be supposed. This suggestion is revealing. But when Beauchamp goes on to define virtue as a disposition, habit, or trait, I think he drives more of a wedge between particular actions and virtues than he needs to. I have already argued against the thesis that courage, the virtue, should be defined as a psychological disposition.

It is my thesis that courage is best considered fundamentally as a property of individual actions rather than as a long-term property of character. However, several qualifications to this thesis have been drawn. If character is analyzed in terms of an agent's position, and his moral commitments as expressed in actions, then we can see courage as a property of character. Moreover, the overtones of courage, such as resolution and determination, do involve long-term qualities of character. These are qualifications we have already made.

One further qualification involves the distinction between agent and act evaluations. Some philosophers have drawn a sharp distinction between these two types of evaluations in moral philosophy. Agent evaluations are said to involve consideration of goodness or badness of intentions, motives, character traits, and people themselves. An example of an act evaluation would be to say that an action was morally obligatory.

This distinction may not be as sharp as philosophers were once inclined to think, however. For Stocker (1973) has shown that there are conceptual connections between agent evaluations and act evaluations. To show this kind of connection, Stocker (ibid., p. 55) takes the example of a surgeon who follows an outdated procedure of heart surgery, a procedure now recognized as too risky. According to Stocker, what is sufficient for acting wrongly in these circumstances is that the agent should reasonably believe that his act involves unjustifiable harm or risk of harm for others. In making such a judgment, both an act evaluation (harm and risk of harm for others) and an agent evaluation (the agent's reasonable belief) are involved.

According to my analysis of courageous action, you could equally well say that both kinds of evaluation are involved. To act courageously, an agent has to carry out his good intentions by acting in accord with his practical assessment of the situation. Agent evaluation is involved, because intentions and reasonable beliefs are classified as factors of agent evaluation.

Quite generally, one can see that agent evaluations are involved in moral evaluations of acts of courage. At least, according to our theory, the practical reasoning that is involved in courageous actions characteristically means that some reference to the agent's intention should be, at some point, part of the fuller sequence of actions at issue. Our analysis of courageous acts would therefore serve as additional proof of Stocker's thesis that there should be conceptual connections between agent and act evaluations.

In this light, it may be helpful to make a clarification. While it is correct to say that my analysis of courage implies that courage is best considered a property of individual actions, there remains generous room to concede that courage can also be a property of the agent. For the best understanding of actions and practical reasoning does very much involve the agent's intentions and practical reasoning in acting. Hence, to some extent, it is fair to say that courage is also a property of the agent. However, when talk of persons is stretched into talk of long-term character traits, evaluations of courage become more chancy and also require much more documentation and evidence.

Perhaps the best way to sum up these relationships, as I see them, is to say that in acting courageously the agent implements or displays his commitment to moral values in specific circumstances. In his perception of these circumstances, and in his commitments, the agent is being courageous in carrying out the action we evaluate as courageous. In other words, there is a certain legitimate transferability of 'courageous action' to 'courageous agent'. However, this transferability must be recognized to have certain limits, and a certain thinning out of plausibility.

These limits are suggested by various remarks we have already made. For example, we should not necessarily infer from the fact that someone has acted courageously in a certain instance, that this same person will act courageously in another instance. In short, to say that someone is a "courageous person," when the speaker means to generalize to long-term dispositions or character habits, may be a very shaky conjecture indeed on the basis of a single action. And such generalizations should be based on actions.

No doubt there will be many future controversies in the field of ethics on whether courage is primarily a property of excellence of conduct or a quality of personal merit. There is still room for argument on this question. For reasons given, my own approach accords a strong priority to actions.

Aristotle required of a virtuous act that it be done from a good character, based on his notion that practical wisdom is acquired over time and through the exercise of choice. Thus, through experience, the practically wise person has learned to understand the goals that make up the life of the virtuous person. This conception sets a high standard in the case of courage. For it requires that an act be chosen in light of its contribution to the good life—and in relation to all the virtues as they are grasped by the practical reasoner—in order to be fully courageous.

I think this standard is too high to certify many evaluations of acts as courageous as we normally make them, acts that I would defend as courageous. Although there is wisdom in Aristotle's thesis that the virtues are connected, and that no virtue stands alone, we have already noted the problem here. The Greek assumption that the virtues are well understood and accepted by everyone is no longer appropriate in this century. We are hard pressed to say, in a modern context, even what the virtues are. No doubt temperance is a virtue, for example. But what 'temperance' really means as a coherent notion of ethics is less clear and even more open to suspicion of antiquation than the case of courage. I think our analysis of courage as a virtue is a good place to start in the study of virtue generally, but clearly it is only a beginning.

When we have a better analysis of the different virtues other than courage, we may begin to see how each of them fits into a whole structure of virtuous conduct. Then Aristotle's thesis—that an act is only *fully* courageous if carried out through the experience and practical wisdom of the person who grasps the goals of the life of the virtuous person—may be vindicated. But, for the present, I think we need to concede that an act can be courageous, and can be reasonably certified as courageous on the basis of good evidence, even if it has not shown to be fully courageous in Aristotle's very demanding sense. It is not necessary to be the equivalent of Socrates in practical wisdom to perform a courageous action.

Notes

1. Courage as a Topic of Inquiry

1. The acronym COVA stands for U.S. Senate Committee on Veterans Affairs, which documents recipients of the Congressional Medal of Honor (see bibliography).

2. *Concise Oxford Dictionary of Current English.* 4th ed. (Oxford: Clarendon Press, 1951), p. 276.

3. *Merriam-Webster Dictionary* (New York: Pocket Books, 1974), p. 173.

4. Kant was particularly sensitive to this danger. In the *Critique of Practical Reason* he warns of the moral fanaticism and self-conceit caused by exhortations to actions portrayed as noble or sublime. See Heyd (1982:66 ff.) for discussion of this aspect of Kant's moral philosophy.

5. Even Heyd (1982), who provides a comprehensive treatment of supererogatory acts and thereby breaks new ground in ethics, has surprisingly little to say about acts of courage and moral heroism. His treatment of the class of supererogatory acts helps greatly, nevertheless, to bring some order to this previously obscure area of ethics.

6. Urmson (1958:206) criticizes utilitarianism for its classification of saintly and heroic acts as no different in principle from duties like truth telling and promise keeping.

7. Heyd (1983) notes that his theory supplies only general considerations for the necessity of distinguishing between supererogation and duty. He admits that he has not tried to offer a criterion for applying the distinction in a particular case.

8. Terrorist acts portrayed as "courageous" by the exponents of some group that feels it has been wronged often seem simply bizarre to the rest of us.

9. Of course, as we saw above, personal autonomy, if carried too far, results in a rejection of courage as a moral quality of serious value. The problem for ethical theory is to balance the needs and values of the community against individual autonomy of action.

10. Actually, Heyd stresses these everyday supererogatory virtues and says very little, by comparison, about acts of heroic courage.

11. See Eric J. Cassell, *The Healer's Art: A New Approach to the Doctor-Patient Relationship* (Philadelphia: Lippincott, 1976).

12. See Douglas N. Walton, *Ethics of Withdrawal of Life-Support Systems: Case Studies on Decision Making in Intensive Care* (Westport, Conn.: Greenwood Press, 1983).

13. Ibid., pp. 222–228.

14. In discussion during a talk on courage and cowardice given by the author at the University of Auckland in June 1983.

15. See Richard Taylor, *Action and Purpose* (Englewood Cliffs, N.J.: Prentice-Hall, 1966).

16. See William S. Cobb, "The Argument of the *Protagoras*," *Dialogue* 21 (1982):713–731.

2. Popular Images of Courage

1. I shall not try to offer a general analysis of what "virtue" should consist in. Rather, by analyzing the concept of courageous action as a species of practical excellence of action, I want to concentrate on courage as a quality worthy of analysis in itself. Since courage is an important member of the so-called virtues, however, perhaps our analysis will throw some light on virtuousness generally and thereby function, in small part, as a vindication of the virtues as worthy objects of study. See Wallace (1978), Geach (1977), and MacIntyre (1981) on virtues as a class.

2. See remarks of Hare (1963) in this regard.

3. See, for example, Geach (1977) and MacIntyre (1981).

4. See Rachman (1978).

5. Audi (1979) gives a very useful discussion of volitions.

6. A fuller acount of Aristotle's doctrine of courage, given mainly in the *Nicomachean Ethics*, is presented in the next chapter.

7. See Rachman (1978).

8. As was mentioned earlier, MacIntyre (1981) thinks of altruism as an essential characteristic of courage.

9. Plato's views are outlined in chapter 3.

10. Fascism has been characterized as a "rushing of the blood."

11. See Jaques Ellul, *Propaganda* (New York: Knopf, 1972).

12. Later, we will make a useful distinction between courage and bravery.

13. Wallace (1978) also makes this point.

14. I am thinking here of the fictional hero of popular entertainment.

15. Quoted in *Maclean's* (January 12, 1981, p. 34).

16. See Douglas N. Walton, "Why is the *Ad Populum* a Fallacy?," *Philosophy and Rhetoric* 13 (1980):264–278.

17. In chapter 5, the precise sense in which courage and cowardice are opposites is given detailed treatment.

18. This problem foreshadows my subsequent analysis of practical reasoning.

3. Existing Accounts of Courage

1. *Laches* (193b), quoted from Hamilton and Cairns (1961).

2. See Douglas N. Walton, "The Fallacy of Many Questions," *Logique et Analyse* 95–96 (1981):291–313.

3. Questions of how to deal with descriptions of actions are taken up more generally in the last chapter. The particular problem posed at this point relates to the fact that different (nonequivalent) descriptions can be given of the "same" action.

4. MacIntyre (1981) makes a good case for rescue.

5. However, see the interesting discussion of Føllesdal (1980) on lawlike explanations of actions as compared to the explanations in physics.

6. *Laches* (192a).

7. Von Wright does not devote much space to courage. But his views on practical reasoning, expressed in several important works on the logic of actions, are so important that what little he has to say on courage is worth special attention. See his recent paper "On the Logic of Norms and Actions," in Hilpinen (1981:3–35).

8. R. B. Brandt, "Traits of Character: A Conceptual Analysis," *American Philosophical Quarterly* 7 (1970):23–37.

9. Moral courage is more fully analyzed in chapter 5.

10. Originally published in *Mind* XXI (1912):487–499. The page references given are to the more easily accessible reprinting of 1966 listed in the bibliography.

11. See Walton (1983).

4. Basic Structure of the Courageous Act

1. A basic outline of what the fallacy of begging the question consists in may be found in John Woods and Douglas Walton, "*Petitio Principii*," *Synthese* 31 (1975):107–127. The theme that disputation is an essential part of reasonably evaluating the claims of practical reasoning is a theme of chap. 6. A general introduction to the logic of games of dialogue and disputation is given by John Woods and Douglas Walton in *Argument: The Logic of the Fallacies* (New York and Toronto: McGraw-Hill Ryerson), 1982.

2. A full treatment of this example is given in Walton (1983).

3. See Douglas N. Walton, *On Defining Death* (Montreal and Kingston: McGill-Queen's University Press), 1980.

4. See G. H. von Wright, *Norm and Action* (London: Routledge and Kegan Paul), 1963.

5. See the discussion of Mowrer (1961).

6. See Robert Audi, "Wants and Intentions in the Explanations of Action," *Journal of the Theory of Social Behavior* 9 (1979):227–249.

7. On the notion of an obstacle to action, see Douglas N. Walton, "Obstacles and Opportunities," *Philosophical Papers* 6 (1977):11–20. The notion of

an obstacle will also be implicit in the theory of practical reasoning advanced in chap. 6.

8. States of affairs are propositions that can be made true or false (in principle) by human actions. For example, the state of affairs 'My pen is on the desk this morning' can be made true (or false) by me this morning.

9. As the definition of courage stands, a counterexample can be formulated which turns on the way (P1) is formulated. Suppose that my regiment is being advanced on by an attacking force. If attacked by this force, my regiment will be destroyed. Between the attackers and my regiment are two bridges. The only way the attackers can attack is over one bridge or the other. Thus to prevent the destruction of my regiment, it is necessary to destroy the first bridge, and necessary also to destroy the second bridge. But if only one bridge is destroyed, my regiment will be wiped out anyway. Suppose I can destroy one bridge, at the likely cost of my life and some others' lives, but I cannot destroy the other bridge.

This situation is a counterexample, because my destroying the one bridge—given that I can't destroy the other and that it is certain that the other will remain intact and passable—is not a courageous act. All else in abeyance, it would be a foolish and pointless act. But it fits the proposed definition of courage. Preventing the destruction of the regiment is worth bringing about, and in order to do it, it is necessary to destroy the first bridge. Suppose I destroy the first bridge even though I could have refrained. Then all five clauses of the definition of courageous action are met. Yet I have not acted courageously.

Thus the definition, as it stands, needs another clause. Perhaps this clause is the required one: there is some state of affairs C such that C can happen or be brought about, and A and C are jointly sufficient to bring about B. This addition reflects the role of sufficient condition relationships in practical reasoning. What is required is that A be a contributing factor in bringing about B.

10. Lorraine Pecarsky, "Incurable Patient Fights Fear with Fun," *Winnipeg Free Press*, January 13, 1981, p. 17.

5. *The Outer Edges*

1. Sheldon Kelly, "Hero in the Fire," *Reader's Digest*, July 1982, pp. 42–46.
2. Ibid., p. 46.
3. Ibid., p. 44.
4. Terry Collins, "Roy Revels Despite Life of Tragedy," *Hamilton Spectator*, October 7, 1978, p. 23.
5. Robert Graves, *Good-Bye to All That* (London: J. Cope, 1929).
6. COVA 1973:541.

6. Moral Deliberation and Conduct

1. For a fuller account of the subject of explanation in history, see Dray (1957).

2. We will argue in chap. 7, however, that practical disputations can be rationally evaluated. The reader should not give up on the project just yet.

3. A fuller account of the matter is given in John Woods and Douglas Walton, *Argument: The Logic of the Fallacies* (New York and Toronto: McGraw-Hill Ryerson), 1982.

4. This account differs just enough from the other accounts of the practical syllogism given above and below that the reader can appreciate some of the differences of interpretation in the literature. Audi (1982) gives a much fuller outline of the different varieties of this form of reasoning favored by philosophers.

5. Act-sequences are explicated by Alvin Goldman, *A Theory of Human Action* (Englewood Cliffs, N.J.: Prentice-Hall), 1970.

6. Desmond Young, *Rommel* (London and Glasgow: Collins, 1950), p. 36.

7. COVA 1973:705f.

8. Ibid., p. 706.

7. Deliberation in Particular Circumstances

1. I do not require that altruism always be necessary for an act to be courageous. There may be some conflict with the view of Heyd (1982), who requires that all supererogatory acts be altruistic.

2. COVA 1973:509.

3. In the next chapter, we will see how this problem can be resolved by a theory of practical reasoning that is applied to actions in retrospect. The theory applies whether or not it was known by the agent or anyone else that he went through some psychological process or mental inference in his actual thinking.

4. See chap. 3.

5. In discussion at the University of Auckland, May 1983.

6. See the beginning of chap. 1.

7. A quite sophisticated and helpful account of this type of explanation is given by Christopher Peacocke, *Holistic Explanations* (Oxford: Oxford University Press, 1979).

8. Mackesy 1979:13.

9. See Walton (1985).

10. See Kenneth L. Woodward, "Politics and Abortion," *Newsweek,* August 20, 1984, pp. 66–67. Bishop James W. Malone, president of the National Conference of Catholic Bishops, is quoted as rejecting as "not logically tenable" the argument of candidates who say "their personal views should not

influence their policy decisions." That position, he is quoted as saying would be as unacceptable as "that of any office seeker who puts forth his personal views but no practical proposals to implement them."

8. Practical Reasoning

1. Remembering what H. A. Simon (1977) called the method of satisficing, outlined in chap. 7, we can see how a chain of possible actions can form a search procedure in Simon's method of decision making. Simon suggests that such a sequence has a branching structure he calls a search-tree.

2. What we call a procedure here is called a routine by Segerberg (1982). See also Krister Segerberg, "Routines," *Synthese*, to appear.

3. Audi (1983) gives a comprehensive survey of the different views of the nature of practical reasoning.

4. To say that an inference is deductively valid is to say that it is not logically possible for the premises to be true while the conclusion is false.

5. See Audi (1983) for some representative views.

6. Entail by deductively valid argument is meant here.

7. This issue is a very controversial and difficult one in moral philosophy. A helpful related discussion is Alan Donagan, "Philosophical Progress and the Theory of Action," *Proceedings and Addresses of the American Philosophical Association* 55 (1981):25–52. See also Donagan (1977).

8. Readers might like to see the discussion of this sort of example given in Germain Grisez and Joseph M. Boyle, Jr., *Life and Death with Liberty and Justice* (Notre Dame: University of Notre Dame Press, 1979).

9. See Andres Woodfield, *Teleology* (New York and London: Cambridge University Press, 1976).

10. The historical illustrations of explanation of human actions given by von Wright (1971) bring out this circumstantial relativity very clearly.

11. See John Woods and Douglas Walton, *"Ad Hominem," The Philosophical Forum* 8 (1977):1–20.

12. Richard Whately, *Elements of Logic* (New York: William Jackson, 1836), p. 196.

13. The reader who wishes to explore the analysis of ad hominem argumentation further is directed to Walton (1985).

14. See Woods and Walton (1982).

15. A logical structure that gives theoretical backing to these ideas is given by Segerberg (1982).

16. Gadamer is noteworthy among recent exponents.

17. The notion of the burden of proof in plausible reasoning appealed to here is analyzed by Nicholas Rescher, *Plausible Reasoning* (Assen-Amsterdam: Van Gorcum, 1976).

18. C. L. Hamblin, *Fallacies* (London: Methuen, 1970).

19. Jaakko Hintikka, "Information-Seeking Dialogues: A Model," *Erkenntnis* 14 (1979):355–368. Reprinted in *Konzepte der Dialectike*, ed. Werner Becker and Wilhelm K. Essler (Frankfurt am Main: Vittorio Klostermann, 1981).

20. Nicholas Rescher, *Dialectics* (Albany: State University of New York Press, 1977).

21. Lauri Carlson, *Dialogue Games: An Approach to Discourse Analysis*, Ph.D. diss., Massachusetts Institute of Technology, 1982.

22. E. M. Barth and E. C. W. Krabbe, *From Axiom to Dialogue* (Berlin: Walter de Gruyter, 1982).

23. A number of these action-games are outlined in Walton (1985). See also Segerberg (1982).

24. First defined in Walton (1985).

9. Ethical Theory and Justification of Courageous Acts

1. P. F. Strawson, "Social Morality and Individual Ideal," *Philosophy* 36 (1961):1–17.

2. See chap. 1.

3. Because of the dialectical nature of the reconstructive evaluation of an agent's intentions, the danger is always present of the specious argument that picks out particular heroic acts for reasons of ideology or propaganda. Though wishing to accentuate the positive, I could have devoted more space to the analysis of case studies of the utilization of so-called heroic acts to make fallacious appeals and arguments.

4. This is not to deny that courage is a good quality of character.

5. See H. L. A. Hart, *The Concept of Law* (Oxford: Clarendon Press, 1961).

6. *New Zealand Honours and Awards* (Army Headquarters 1969), p. 11.

7. Recall the discussion of side effects of action in chap. 8.

8. See Kant ([1785] 1964), chap. 1.

9. That is perhaps why the quotation from Meister Eckhart in the epigraph seems paradoxical to some.

10. See Kant ([1785] 1964), p. 30.

10. Courage as a Quality of Character

1. Several excellent examples are given in Kennedy (1956).

2. The account here is taken from the biography of Maas (1973). See also the remarks of Glazer (1983) on the moral aspects of this account.

3. See Maas (1973), p. 313.

4. Maas (1973), p. 304f.

5. Glazer (1983).

6. Gates and Stille (1984).

7. Ibid.

8. Ibid.

9. See von Wright (1971).

10. Toney was awarded the Star of Courage for this act.

11. See 7.4.

12. Dr. Bethune is also known for his pioneering use of a mobile clinic and portable blood transfusion units on the battlefield. He also made contributions to the fields of surgery and public health.

13. See Ted Allan and Sydney Gordon, *Scalpel, the Sword: The Story of Doctor Normal Bethune* (New York: Monthly Review Press, 1974).

14. See 2.4.

15. Unsworth (1981), p. 335.

16. Hillary (1975).

17. McGarry (1977).

18. Ibid.

19. Honors Secretariat (1983).

20. See 8.5.

Bibliography

ANSCOMBE, G. E. M. *Intention.* Oxford: Blackwell, 1957.

AQUINAS, SAINT THOMAS. *Summa Theologica.* Literally translated by the Fathers of the English Dominican Province. London: Burns & Oates Ltd., 1922.

―――― . *Treatise on the Virtues.* John A. Oesterle, trans. Englewood Cliffs: Prentice-Hall, 1966.

ÅQVIST, LENNART. "An Analysis of Action Sentences Based on a "Tree" System of Modal Tense Logic." *In Papers on Tense, Aspect and Verb Classification.* C. Rohrer, ed. Tübingen: TBL Verlag Gunter Narr, 1977. Pp. 111–161.

Army Headquarters. *New Zealand Honours and Awards.* 2nd ed. Wellington, New Zealand, 1969.

ARISTOTLE. *The Works of Aristotle.* W. D. Ross, ed. London: Oxford University Press, 1915.

AUDI, ROBERT. "Weakness of Will and Practical Judgment," *Noûs* 13 (1979): 173–196.

―――― . "A Theory of Practical Reasoning," *American Philosophical Quarterly* 19 (1982): 25–39.

BEAUCHAMP, TOM L. *Philosophical Ethics.* New York: McGraw-Hill, 1982.

BEAUCHAMP, TOM L., and JAMES F. CHILDRESS. *Principles of Biomedical Ethics.* 2d ed. New York: Oxford University Press, 1983.

BENTLEY, ERIC. *The Cult of the Superman: A Study of the Idea of Heroism in Carlyle and Nietzsche.* Gloucester, Mass.: Peter Smith, 1969.

BOSLAUGH, JOHN. "Inside the Mind of a Genius," *Reader's Digest* 124 (Feb. 1984): 74–78.

CARLYLE, THOMAS. *The Complete Works of Thomas Carlyle.* New York: Cromwell, 1902.

Carnegie Hero Fund Commission: Seventy-five Years, 1904–1979. Pittsburgh: Carnegie Hero Fund Commission, 1979.

Carnegie Hero Fund Commission Annual Report. Pittsburgh, 1982.

CHAMBERLAIN, W. M. *Victoria Cross Winners of New Zealand.* Australia: Military Historical Society of Australia, 1967.

COLLINGWOOD, R. G. *The Idea of History.* New York: Oxford University Press, 1946.

Committee on Veterans Affairs (COVA): U.S. Senate, *Medal of Honor Recipients: 1863–1973* (Committee Print No. 15). Washington, D.C.: U.S. Government Printing Office, 1973.

Concise Oxford Dictionary of Current English. 4th ed. Oxford: Clarendon Press, 1951.

CUNNINGHAM, STANLEY B. "Review of Foot and Wallace," *Dialogue* 31 (1982): 133–137.

DAVIS, STEPHEN. "Act Utilitarianism and Supererogation." Unpublished paper.

DENT, N. J. H. "Supererogation," *Philosophical Books* 24 (1983): 65–70.

DONAGAN, ALAN. *The Theory of Morality.* Chicago: University of Chicago Press, 1977.

DRAY, WILLIAM. *Laws and Explanation in History.* Oxford: Clarendon Press, 1957.

DWORKIN, RONALD. "Lord Devlin and the Enforcement of Morals," *Yale Law Journal* 75 (1966): 994–999. Republished as "Liberty and Morality," in *Taking Rights Seriously.* Cambridge: Harvard University Press, 1978.

Editorial. "Physicists Win Six Medals from Franklin Institute," *Physics Today* 35 (March 1982): 71.

FØLLESDAL, DAGFINN. "Explanation of Action." In *Rationality in Science.* R. Hilpinen, ed. Dordrecht: Reidel, 1980. Pp. 231–247.

FOOT, PHILLIPA. *Virtues and Vices and Other Essays in Moral Philosophy.* Berkeley, Los Angeles, London: University of California Press, 1978.

FORESTER, C. S. *The Ship.* Toronto: S. J. Reginald Saunders, 1943.

GATES, DAVID, and ALEXANDER STILLE. "Update: The Lonely Odyssey of an Honest Cop," *Newsweek,* Feb. 6, 1984. P. 9.

GAUTHIER, DAVID P. *Practical Reasoning.* Oxford: Oxford University Press, 1963.

GEACH, PETER. *The Virtues.* Cambridge: Cambridge University Press, 1977.

GLAZER, MYRON. "Ten Whistle Blowers and How They Fared," *Hastings Center Report* 13 (1983): 33–41.

GRAVES, ROBERT. *Good-bye to All That.* New York: Blue Ribbon Books, 1930.

GRAY, J. GLENN. *The Warriors: Reflections on Men in Battle.* New York: Harper & Row, 1967.

HAMILTON, EDITH, and HUNTINGTON CAIRNS, eds. *The Collected Dialogues of Plato.* New York: Bollingen Foundation, 1961.

HARE, R. M. *Freedom and Reason.* Oxford: Clarendon Press, 1963.

HANDS, A. R. *Charities and Social Aid in Greece and Rome.* London: Thames and Hudson, 1968.

HEYD, DAVID. *Supererogation.* Cambridge: Cambridge University Press, 1982.

———— . "Reply to Dr. Dent," *Philosophical Books* 24 (1983): 70–74.

HILLARY, EDMUND. *Nothing Venture, Nothing Win.* London: Hodder and Stoughton, 1975.

HILPINEN, RISTO. *New Studies in Deontic Logic: Norms, Actions, and the Foundations of Ethics.* Dordrecht: Reidel, 1981.

Honors Secretariat. *Decorations for Bravery.* Government House, Ottawa, 1983 [including Xerox collection of citations sent to the author from the Honors Secretariat].

HOOK, SIDNEY. *The Hero in History*. Boston: Beacon Press, 1943.

IMMANUEL KANT. *Critique of Practical Reason*. Lewis White Beck, trans. Indianapolis: Bobbs-Merrill, 1956 (first published 1788).

————. *Groundwork of the Metaphysic of Morals*. H. J. Paton, trans. New York: Harper & Row, 1964 (first published 1785).

————. *The Metaphysical Principles of Virtue*. James Ellington, trans. Indianapolis: Bobbs-Merrill, 1964 (first published 1797).

Investiture Bravery Decorations. Rideau Hall, Ottawa, September 9, 1983.

KENNEDY, JOHN F. *Profiles in Courage*. New York: Harper & Row, 1956.

LOWRANCE, WILLIAM W. *Of Acceptable Risk: Science and the Determination of Safety*. Los Altos, Calif.: William Kaufman, 1976.

MACINTYRE, ALASDAIR. *After Virtue*. London: Duckworth, 1981.

MACKENZIE, COMPTON. *Certain Aspects of Moral Courage*. New York: Doubleday, 1962.

MAAS, PETER. *Serpico*. New York: The Viking Press, 1973.

MACKESY, PIERS. *The Coward of Minden*. London: Penguin, 1979.

McGARRY, MICHAEL. "These Brave Canadians," *Reader's Digest* (January 1977).

MAYO, BERNARD. *Ethics and the Moral Life*. London: Macmillan, 1958.

Merriam-Webster Dictionary. New York: Pocket Books, 1974.

MITTON, SIMON. "Stephen W. Hawking," *Astronomy* 7 (Nov. 1979): 28–30.

MOORE, G. E. *Principia Ethica*. Cambridge: Cambridge University Press, 1903.

MOWRER, O. HOBART. *Learning Theory and Behavior*. New York: John Wiley & Sons, 1961.

NIETZSCHE, FRIEDRICH W. *Basic Writings of Nietzsche*. Walter Kaufmann, trans. and ed. New York: Random House, 1968.

O'SHEA, PHILLIP. *An Unknown Few*. Wellington, New Zealand: P. D. Hasselberg, Government Printer, 1981.

PEARS, DAVID. "Courage as a Mean." In *Essays on Aristotle's Ethics*. Amelie Oksenberg Rorty, ed. Berkeley, Los Angeles, London: University of California Press, 1980. Pp. 171–187.

PRICHARD, H. A. "Does Moral Philosophy Rest on a Mistake?" *Mind* 21 (1912): 487–499. Reprinted in *Contemporary Ethical Theory*. Joseph Margolis, ed. New York: Random House, 1966. Pp. 47–66.

RACHMAN, S. J. *Fear and Courage*. San Francisco: W. H. Freeman, 1978.

RAWLS, JOHN. *A Theory of Justice*. Cambridge: Harvard University Press, 1971.

ROBINS, MICHAEL H. "Practical Reasoning, Commitment and Rational Action," *American Philosophical Quarterly* 21 (1984): 55–68.

Royal Humane Society. *Annual Report*. London, 1982.

RUFF, G., and S. KORCHIN. "Psychological Responses of the Mercury Astronauts to Stress." In *The Threat of Impending Disaster*. G. Grosser, H. Wechsler, and M. Greenblatt, eds. Cambridge: M.I.T. Press, 1964.

SCHACHT, RICHARD. *Nietzsche*. London: Routledge & Kegan Paul, 1983.

SEGERBERG, KRISTER. "Action-Games," *Acta Philosophica Fennica* 32 (1981): 220–331.

————. "The Logic of Deliberate Action," *Journal of Philosophical Logic* 11 (1982): 233–254.

SHORTEN, SARAH. "Aristotle on Courage." Unpublished paper.

SIMON, H. A. *Models of Discovery*. Dordrecht: Reidel, 1977.

SLOTE, MICHAEL. *Goods and Virtues*. Oxford: Oxford University Press, 1983.

STOCKER, MICHAEL. "Act and Agent Evaluations," *Review of Metaphysics* 27 (1973): 42–61.

SULLIVAN, WILLIAM M. *Reconstructing Public Philosophy*. Berkeley, Los Angeles, London: University of California Press, 1982.

SWETTENHAM, JOHN. *Valiant Men: Canada's Victoria Cross and George Cross Winners*. Toronto: Hakkert, 1973.

THOMASON, RICHARD. "Indeterminist Time and Truth-Value Gaps," *Theoria* 3 (1970): 264–281.

UNSWORTH, WALT. *Everest: A Mountaineering History*. Boston: Houghton Mifflin Co., 1981.

URMSON, J. O. "Saints and Heroes." In *Essays in Moral Philosophy*. A. I. Melden, ed. Seattle: University of Washington Press, 1958. Pp. 198–216.

VON WRIGHT, G. H. *The Varieties of Goodness*. London: Routledge & Kegan Paul, 1963.

————. *Explanation and Understanding*. Ithaca: Cornell University Press, 1971.

————. "On So-Called Practical Inference," *Acta Sociologica* 15 (1972): 39–53. Reprinted in *Practical Reasoning*, J. Raz, ed. Oxford: Oxford University Press, 1978. Pp. 46–62.

————. "Replies to Commentators: Second Thoughts on Explanation and Understanding." In *Essays on Explanation and Understanding*. Juha Manninen and Raimo Tuomela, eds. Dordrecht: Reidel, 1976. Pp. 371–435.

WALLACE, JAMES D. *Virtues and Vices*. Ithaca and London: Cornell University Press, 1978.

WALTON, DOUGLAS N. "Relatedness in Intensional Action Chains," *Philosophical Studies* 36 (1979): 175–223.

————. *Ethics of Withdrawal of Life-Support Systems*. Westport, Conn.: Greenwood Press, 1983.

————. *Arguer's Position: A Pragmatic Study of Ad Hominem Attack, Criticism, Refutation and Fallacy*. Westport, Conn.: Greenwood Press, 1985.

WITTGENSTEIN, L. *Philosophical Investigations*. New York: Macmillan, 1953.

Index

Actions
  express beliefs, 167
  as sequences of steps, 158–159, 165–166.
  See also Practical inference
ad hominem, circumstantial, 167–168, 169–170, 175–176, 189
Aggressiveness, 4, 6–9, 33, 34–35, 36–37, 136
Altruism, 3, 34, 53, 85, 111–113, 114, 184–185
Ambury, Arthur Hamilton, 138–139
Anscombe, G. E. M., 119, 160
Aquinas, St. Thomas, 52, 62–64, 94
  Summa Theologica, 62, 63, 64, 94
Aristotle, 10, 50, 55, 56, 63, 71, 76, 92, 221
  criticized by G. E. Moore, 74
  definition of courage: as balanced deliberation, 6; begs normative question, 74–75; compared with von Wright's, 66; formulation, 61–62; as good, 40
  conception of courage, 83
  fearlessness distinguished from courageousness, 81, 136
  means and ends distinction, 58–59
  noble purpose or good ends of courageous acts, 52, 78, 79
  Metaphysics, 158
  Nicomachean Ethics, 59, 60–61; practical reasoning, theory of, 59–60, 167; sufficient condition schema of practical inference, 160–161
Aspeslet, 1
Audi, Robert, 118

Barth, E. M., 173
Bastian, Gordon L., 84–85, 90
Beauchamp, Tom L., 13, 28, 45–46, 195, 196, 218
Belief, justified, 131, 132
Benefits, unpredictability of, 54
Bentham, Jeremy, 76
Bethune, Dr. Norman, 205–206, 230 n. 12
Bishop, John, 68
Bishop's square, 135–136, 147
Bishop, Ken, 7
Brandt, R. B., 66
Bravery, 98–99. *See also* Courage; Courageous Acts; Fearlessness; Heroes
  distinguished from courage, 99
Breault, Henry, 112
Burr, Private Herbert H., 136
Burt, Captain James M., 16

Carlson, Lauri, 173
Carlyle, Thomas, 34–35, 37, 38, 39, 40, 45, 99, 102
Character traits, 213
Childress, James, F., 195, 196
Christian, Private Herbert F., 107–108
Collingwood, R. G., 172
Commitment (belief), 173–174
Commitment, moral, 121–122, 191, 192, 215, 216
Commitment, unknown, 175–177, 216
Commitment to group position, 112–113
Concise Oxford Dictionary, 4
Consequences. *See* Benefits; Goals; Intention

Cosens, Sergeant Aubrey, 38
Courage. *See also* Bravery;
    Courageous acts; Heroes
allegations of proving, 149, 151
animals, attributing to, 108–110
bravery distinguished from, 99
character, relation to, 213–214
as character trait, 50, 64, 197–199,
    213–214, 216–221 passim
cowardice as opposite of, 66, 92,
    135, 178
cowardice as not opposite of, 14,
    85, 89, 92, 136, 177, 179
creative response to disaster, 129
definition of courage (aspects of):
    importance of, 54; non-
    normative, 90–91; normative
    element of, 6, 40, 75, 78–80, 85,
    86; practical element of, 75, 85,
    86; psychological element of,
    80; secondary meanings of, 97
disposition or power, 45, 66, 152,
    182, 197, 202–207
heroism, compared with, 44
ideals, 180
judgments of, based on agent's
    position, 28–29
military, denigration of
    concept, 19
moral, 107, 108, 117, 127–128
as moral quality, 73
as negative quality, 20, 180–181
opposite, has no, 134
physical, 106–107
as practical reasoning, 58
principles, based on, 199
propaganda, as instrument of,
    5–6
as property of persons, 197–198,
    218–219, 220–221
rationality must be different from,
    142
value of, 11–12, 54–55 (*see also*
    Courageous acts, value of)
villainy, compatibility with, 52–53
as virtue, 10, 11, 31, 32, 59, 152,
    215–216, 217, 224 n. 1

virtue, cynicism about, 18–19
virtue, not always, 52
Courageous acts. *See also* Heroic acts
amoral, 97
characteristics of: aggressiveness
    4, 6–9, 33, 34–35, 36–37, 136;
    altruism, 3, 34, 53, 85, 111,
    112–113, 184–185; commitment,
    121–122, 191, 192; danger, 3, 6,
    14, 24, 69–70, 71, 72, 83, 85,
    87, 89, 91–92, 93, 138, 184;
    danger, awareness of,
    138–140; deliberation (practical),
    34, 36–37, 43, 61, 102;
    determination, 1, 35, 93,
    99–100, 102, 184; difficulty, 3,
    12–13, 14, 93–94, 142–143, 184,
    189–190, 216–217; disregard for
    self, 36, 100; fear, absence of, 1,
    32–33, 60, 92, 98, 109–110, 137;
    control of, 64, 82; feeling of
    65–66, 82, 94; overcoming of, 4,
    6; intention, appropriate, 39;
    intention, good, 14, 15,
    182–184, 189–190, 192; noble
    purpose or good ends, 25, 33,
    34, 45, 52, 53–54, 59, 61–62, 78,
    79; obstacles, overcoming of,
    85; practical reasoning, 25, 33,
    86, 99, 127; presence of mind,
    3, 99, 101, 102, 184, risk, 70–71,
    83–85, 91–92, 93, 191; will to
    power, 98
commitment to ideals, 182
as compromise, 126–127
definition of (Walton), 86–87,
    226 n. 9
disposition, resulting from,
    202–203, 204–205, 206–207
duty, beyond call of (*see*
    Supererogatory acts,
    courageous acts as)
duty, required by, 12, 15, 16,
    17–18, 41–42, 75
evaluating, 119, 148–149, 190–191
    (*see also* Evaluation, of historical
    acts)

Designer: Robert S. Tinnon
Compositor: Publisher's Typography
Printer: Edwards Bros.
Binder: Edwards Bros.
Text: 10/13 Palatino
Display: Salto